The Ritual Bath

Douglas Saylor

This is a work of fiction: any resemblance to actual persons or events is coincidental. The Jewish community center in this novel is imaginary, and in no way portrays these worthy institutions.

The Ritual Bath; Lulu 2011   Douglas B. Saylor. All rights reserved.
ISBN 978-1-105-28649-0

Table of Contents

Chapter 1

Terry was standing at the front door. My heart began to pound. It had been a month since I'd seen Terry, and we hadn't parted on good terms. It was four weeks, too, since I'd heard his voice, and listened to his slow, sweet Southern twang. I looked into Terry's pale blue eyes, and wanted to touch his curly mop of blonde hair. He was shivering; his face was red, and his nose was runny. Terry sniffed, and wiped his nose. He just stood there, and so did I. Neither of us moved, frozen in place by the icy temperature, and the chill that had come between us.

"Can I come in, Rico?" he asked plaintively. "I'm freezing."

Why was Terry here? It was cold outside, so different from winter in Georgia. Terry looked at me sadly, and then came in, gently nudging me aside. My heart beat still faster as I stood close to him. For a moment, I lost the ability to move or even respond.

"Have you been standing out there all afternoon?" I asked, finally speaking. I turned to him, closing the door behind me. It had begun to snow lightly, and the temperature dropped. I'd seen a man I didn't know across the street, not thinking for a moment it was Terry. One of the reasons I hadn't recognized him was that I'd never seen him bundled up in a parka before, and he was driving a new truck. It wasn't cold where Terry was from, not like it was here in Colorado. I didn't think it snowed much in Georgia, either. Terry had done some shopping. New car, new coat, but the same sweet, lost look in his eyes.

"What happened to your truck?" I asked. It was a trivial question; there were far more important ones, like why he was here at all. I still stood close to him. I couldn't move; I didn't want to. I didn't think I'd ever see him again. I'd never seen him as angry and hurt as when I'd left him. It had been at a funeral for a murdered civil rights worker in Liberty, Georgia, and seemed like a lifetime ago. He stood outside the cemetery fence, not approaching me. The only reason I'd seen him there at all was because of Sister Eveline, the mysterious blind woman who claimed to have known my father. She seemed to be staring at Terry outside the cemetery gate, and I'd turned my head and seen him.

"I sold it, and got this one. You like it?" He smiled at me like a boy with a new toy. I looked out the window at the red truck. It had a hard top, at least. I couldn't imagine driving an open-roof car through the snow. I'd loved his old blue pick-up, and this new one would take getting used to. I wondered why he'd come all the way across the country; was it just to see me? Had he forgiven me for my coldness to him? Why hadn't he called?

I didn't have groceries in the house, and hadn't cooked lately. It was Christmas Day, and the stores were closed. If only I'd known--- but I'd assumed it was over between us. Standing close to him, so close I could smell his soft, sweaty scent, I knew I could not say goodbye again. Terry was part of me. The same fate that had sent me to look for my father had brought Terry and me together. It was *beshert*, destiny, for us to be together.

"You don't want me here," he said, gazing down. "You walked right past me this afternoon. But I'm half-frozen, Rico, at least let me warm up a minute," he said, dejectedly. "I swear I'll turn around and drive back to Georgia. You'll never have to see me again. But Ric, I had to talk to you one last time. I couldn't leave things like they were between us."

I thought about our last conversation. Terry had sworn at me, and I deserved it. I'd sent him a "Dear John" letter, and he didn't think I ever planned on seeing him again. I changed my mind, and intended to say goodbye in person, but he didn't know that. In the month we'd been apart, I'd had time to think. Maybe I'd grown a little; at least, I hope I had. Terry wasn't responsible for what his father, a retired sheriff, had done. I was sure the sheriff had some role in my father's murder. My father, a rabbi, had been a civil rights volunteer, and disappeared in the mid- 1960's. We never knew what happened to him; we probably never will. At least his remains were found, as well as those of his travelling companion.

"I didn't know it was you out there, Terry. I saw this hulky figure driving a SUV, and I was scared. I wondered why you were staring at my house," I said. It sounded lame, but it was the truth. "I didn't know it was you," I repeated for emphasis.

"You couldn't walk across the street and find out, maybe say hello? Maybe 'Merry Christmas' or something?" He paused in his harangue. "Hulky? Is that good or bad? Are you saying I'm fat?"

I squirmed, and avoided his gaze. I felt stupid. But Terry knows I'm paranoid. I'd lost my job, and hadn't made any friends because of what had happened down South. My house had been egged, and my own grandmother hardly spoke to me anymore. Some said I was a traitor because I loved Terry, because of what Terry's father might have done. But Terry had saved my life.

"If you say it's completely over between us, that you feel nothing for me, that you haven't missed me, then I'll go. I have to hear that from your lips, Rico. Tell me to my face that you don't love me, that you never did. I'll believe you, and I'll leave." He stared me down, daring me to answer.

I looked away. We were still standing just inside the front door, and hadn't moved into the living room. Our faces were so close I could feel his breath on my cheek. His words taunted me, and I didn't trust myself to speak. I felt like laughing and crying at the same time. I looked at him, and Terry had to know I loved him. He softened, reading my emotion. Why would I try to hide my love? I couldn't if I wanted to.

"Merry Christmas, Rico," Terry said, his voice gentle now. He looked around the living room. "Where's your Christmas tree? Most of the houses on your street have lights. Why don't you? I like the blue and white candles in your window. They're pretty."

I just kept looking at him, and smiled. Terry is sweet, and smart, in his way. He isn't worldly, and though he knows I'm Jewish, he doesn't understand what that means. He said I was the first person he'd ever met who didn't believe in Jesus. What Terry lacks in formal education he makes up for with a gentle disposition. Terry is good-natured, not as moody and temperamental as I am.

I'd known Terry for less than six months, and a lot had happened in that time. Seeing him there, it all came back to me. All the good and the bad, the intensity; the love we shared. Terry didn't always talk about his feelings; still waters run deep. I'd often wondered what lay below the surface. I'd even wondered if he had the same violent temper his father had, but I've seen no evidence of that. His dad had beaten both Terry and his mother, and she'd finally left. I can't imagine what Terry's childhood had been like, with a rotten father and a mom who abandoned him. How had Terry turned out so normal, so loving?

I didn't offer any explanation for my lack of decorations, but studied Terry as he took off his jacket. He had lost some weight, and I noticed that his right shoulder was slightly slumped. His father had tried to shoot me, but Terry jumped in the way, saving my life, injuring himself. His right shoulder had been hit by a bullet, and he'd been in the hospital. I took a deep breath, and couldn't stand it anymore. I hugged him gently. I didn't want to hurt Terry, but I had to touch him. How I'd missed him, how I needed him. I kissed his ruddy cheeks, his lips. His whiskers tickled.

I love Terry. I've been lucky enough to be loved before, but no one had ever loved me as much as Terry. He had taught me a lot; I was still learning about forgiveness. That isn't my strong suit. The past was over and done with, and I couldn't keep holding on to my pain and anger. Terry was as much of a victim as my family.

He looked down at me, and I saw his look of sadness change to genuine affection.

"I've missed you," he said. He bent down and kissed me back. "You've put on a little weight," he said, with a smile. "It suits you." The confident way he looked at me, he knew I was hopelessly in love. I knew he loved me, too. He's shown it by driving across the country in winter time to see me.

"You've lost a little, and I've never seen your hair this short," I answered, running my hand over his scalp. "When did you get here? Why didn't you tell me you were coming?"

"I got here last night, late. I checked into a motel. I wasn't sure you wanted to see me. Why would I call you, you haven't called me once." His tone wasn't accusative, but his words stung.

"You haven't called me either," I challenged. "I sent you an e-mail."

"An e-mail. Man, that meant a lot. That was real personal. You really put yourself out." Terry grimaced. "I love you. I had to see you one last time. Like I said, if you don't want me to be with you, I'll go. Just tell me." But the fight had gone from him, I could tell. I hugged him, pressing close, but he backed away from me. My reaction to him was unmistakable. I took a breath, and regained self-control. Terry wanted me at a distance.

His pale blue eyes bored into mine, and I held his gaze. I wasn't about to argue. I was glad to see him, and I couldn't help but smile. I don't celebrate Christmas, and I'd explain that; still, this was the best Christmas present ever. I almost laughed, I was so happy. But Terry was serious.

"What about Sid?" I asked, clearing my throat. Sid is Terry's cat, and I love that black cat of his almost as much as I love Terry.

"He's in the car," Terry said. "I gave him a tranquillizer so he'd travel easier."

"Terry, go get him," I fussed. "It's cold out there. No, you stay and warm up, and I'll go get him. Give me the keys." I went to the thermostat, and turned up the heat. I got the knit afghan from off the sofa, and covered Terry with it. "Terry, put your feet up," I said, ushering him to the living room, and to my favorite chair. "I'll get you something to nosh on in a minute."

"I don't know if I can trust you with my new wheels," Terry said, finally smiling, as he tossed me his keys. I put on my coat, and walked outside. It was bitterly cold, and the late afternoon sun was fading. The snow had stopped, at least for the moment. We had a white Christmas, with drifts of over a foot on the curb. I walked across the street, and, fumbling, I finally figured out how to open the truck's keyless entry. His car was packed to the hilt, boxes and clothes filling the back. I wondered why Terry had brought so much stuff with him. How long had he been on the road? I heard a soft meow.

"Sid," I exclaimed, "it's me, boy. Come inside, little guy." I lifted out the cat crate, and closed and locked the door. I walked back to my house, and went inside. Terry was looking in the fridge. I set the carrier down, and went to him.

"You don't have much food in here, Rico," he said. He looked on the counter, and saw some bagels. "Can I have a doughnut?"

"Sure," I said, "but it's not a doughnut. It's a bagel. Sit, I'll fix it for you. I can make some supper." There had to be something in my freezer. Terry is bigger than me, and what fills me up leaves him still hungry. He's over seven inches taller than me, and a good 50 pounds heavier. I took a bagel, sliced it, and put it in the toaster. I got some cream cheese and lox out of the refrigerator. There was no place to buy bagels in Paris, Georgia, and I wondered if Terry had ever eaten one. "Do you like lox?" I asked.

"What's that?"

"Fish. Try some. You like fish. It tastes kind of like anchovies." The bagel was ready, and I spread cream cheese on it, topping it with lox. I put it on a plate and set it in front of him. "How about a glass of milk?" I asked, pouring him one.

"Thanks, Rico," Terry said, and began eating eagerly.

I looked in the freezer, trying to figure out if I had enough in there to put a meal together. I had pasta, but did I have any meat? If only I'd known he was coming. My cabinets were as empty as Mother Hubbard's. I needed to go food shopping. I thought about Terry's kitchen, and how well-stocked it had always been. Of course, Terry works in a grocery store, and is a butcher as well as store manager.

"I don't like these sardine thingies," he announced. He pulled the lox off, and set them on a napkin. I'd opened the door to Sid's crate, and the black cat wandered out unsteadily. Terry set the napkin down on the floor, and Sid ate the lox greedily. I didn't say a word, though lox are expensive. I didn't want to seem like some *schnorer*, cheapskate.

I found some frozen chicken in the freezer, and put it in the microwave to thaw.

"Chicken and spaghetti?" I asked Terry. He said nothing, and I turned to the table. His eyes were closed, and he was drifting off to sleep sitting in the chair. I wondered how long he'd been on the road, and I thought about him standing out in the cold all day. I looked at his right shoulder, still slightly hunched. Terry was recovering from the bullet wound, as well as from the death of his father. As much as I hadn't liked the sheriff--- and that had been mutual--- I had a lot of questions. Now I'd never know what role the sheriff played in my father's disappearance.

"Terry?" I asked softly. His eyelids fluttered.

"Yeah?" he said sleepily.

"Go stretch out on the bed till supper is ready." We had a lot to talk about, but it could wait. Terry was worn out. I wanted to hold and kiss him, but he looked too tired for that.

"OK," he said sleepily, and I pointed down the hall to the bedroom.

"The door at the end. Just stretch out, rest a little, and I'll get you when supper is ready."

"Thanks," he said, with a smile. I turned back to the microwave, wanting to see if the chicken was thawed. Chicken and spaghetti is always good. I felt a hand on my shoulder, and jumped. It was Terry--- he was still there.

"Rico," he said, smiling. "I may not have all your fancy college learning, but I can find a bedroom without directions. I've been in houses before, you know, and it's not just you Yankees that have bedrooms. We even have beds."

"Don't make me hit you, smart-ass," I said, "because I will. I don't care if you're tired and wounded."

He snickered, and went down the hall to the bedroom. Sid the cat went scampering after his master.

I turned back to the stove. I was glad to have a task, and I began chopping an onion. There is something soothing about cooking. It's creative, good for the body as well as the mind. I chopped some garlic, and the phone rang. I grabbed it quickly, not wanting the sound to wake Terry.

"Hi Mom," I said, when I picked it up.

"How's your day going?" she asked, in her rich, alto voice. My mother had been a music teacher, and spoke with a sing-song quality. She'd lived in Colorado 40 years, but I still heard a hint of New York in her accent. "Look, Harry and I are going for Chinese. Are you hungry?"

Harry is my mother's husband. I've known Harry almost my whole life; I know him better than I knew my real father. After many years together, Harry and my mother had finally gotten married. I considered her invitation. Should I bring Terry along? They'd met Terry, once, when they were on their honeymoon. For some reason, Harry hadn't liked Terry. I wasn't sure what my mother thought of him; she knew that Terry had saved my life.

"I'm not real hungry, Mom," I lied. I didn't know how long Terry planned on staying. He might leave in the morning. He would have to get back to work, and I wanted to be fair. He had driven a long way, and we had a lot to talk about. I said goodbye to my mom, and returned to my cooking.

I thought about the night when Terry's father, armed with a shotgun, had confronted me. Terry had jumped in front of me as his dad fired the weapon, and he'd fallen on top of me. Terry hadn't moved, and was bleeding profusely. I was sure he was dead. I felt crushed under him, and couldn't move from fear as well as Terry's motionless weight. Terry's father, the sheriff, collapsed from a heart-attack and died. Fortunately, some friends, Erica and John, happened to stop by Terry's lonely house and found us in time to call an ambulance.

Terry and I were both covered with his blood. It purified us, like a *mikveh,* a ritual bath. He and I were cleansed of the past, and became blood brothers. I don't know what the future holds, but I know Terry will be part of it. We have gone through too much together to ever stay apart. I couldn't say goodbye to Terry again.

My tomato sauce was simmering. I cut the chicken into bite size pieces, and mixed it in. I brought some salted water to a boil for the pasta. I wasn't sure how long to let Terry sleep. He had driven through a couple of time zones. I thought about all the boxes and clothes in the car. It had been a month since Terry and I talked. Our relationship had been on hold. I couldn't live in Georgia, not professionally, not emotionally, but Georgia is Terry's home. I'd lost my job, but Terry still had his. I didn't know how we would stay together. We both have to work.

Sid the cat wandered back into the kitchen. "Hi fella," I said, stroking his ears. I thought about the feline. Why had Terry subjected the poor kitty to such a long road trip? Surely one of his friends in Georgia could have taken care of Sid while Terry traveled.

My thoughts went back in time to when I had met Terry. I remembered his hometown in the South. I had gone there to take a teaching job, and when word of my relationship with Terry had gotten out, I'd been fired. Small- town Georgia isn't like progressive Colorado. There are still places in this country where you can lose your job just for being gay, but I never thought it would happen to me.

Maybe, I speculated, I had gone down South for reasons besides a job. I am a man of the 21st century, but also a rabbi's son, steeped in that religion's tradition. I believe certain things are *beshert*, destined. I wonder if fate had directed me down South, just as it led me to meet Terry.

I thought about my teaching career. Worries about the future kept me up at night. I'd moved back to Colorado when I'd lost my job in Georgia. I wondered what I would do next. I had some savings, but not enough to last indefinitely. A friend of mine, Rabbi Braun, suggested I do some volunteer teaching for a while. It was good advice, and I taught a Spanish class to seniors at the Jewish community center. It was rewarding, but didn't pay the bills. I wasn't sure how I would get a job. I couldn't use the college in Georgia as a reference. I was over 40 years old, and the economy wasn't good. There isn't a shortage of Spanish teachers. Fear and anxiety plagued me.

My thoughts became happier, thinking about Terry. Maybe he thought I would stay with him in Georgia. But how could I? I'd only known Terry a few months, and we had never talked about living together. Yes, we'd been dating, but we hadn't been ready to settle in together, had we? I knew I loved him, and he said he loved me. But we hadn't discussed any permanent arrangement. The circumstances were wrong. It wasn't just his father, that wasn't the only reason I had to leave. I don't fit in down South.

"It smells good."

I started. I expected Terry to sleep for a while, but he was back in the kitchen looking refreshed. The nap had done him good. His face was still reddish, chapped from the cold wind outside. If I was as brave as Terry, I would have gone over to see who was standing there, and Terry and I could have had the whole day together. I'm not always brave.

"I hope you like this," I said. I know Terry well enough to know he is habitually famished. I worried I hadn't made enough. I got a bag of salad out, and put it in a bowl. There were still some bagels, and I toasted another one for him, and spread some pesto on it. Maybe he'd like that better than lox.

We sat at the table, and ate in silence. I had things to say, and I was sure he did, too. It would take us a while to get back in our stride. I was glad to see him, and I wanted to just enjoy him, there in my warm kitchen, sitting across from me. I felt happier than I had in weeks. It was like we were an old married couple, calm and domestic. I took a deep breath, and savored the moment. Words could wait. I wanted to hold and kiss Terry, but that could wait, too. Sid the cat scurried under the table, hoping, perhaps, there would be more lox. I pretended not to notice Terry slip him a little piece of chicken.

"It's good, Rico," Terry said finally, when he was done. "Thanks."

"Did you get enough?"

"Yes. I was hungrier than I realized." Terry stood up, and took his plate to the sink. He came back to the table, and sat down again.

"I don't have anything for dessert," I said, feeling bad. I reached over and took his hand.

"Don't worry," Terry said. "You didn't know I was coming. And I have something in mind that might make up for it." He paused, then asked, softly, "Are you glad to see me? I'm happy to see you." He squeezed my hand.

"You know I am," I assured him. "It's a surprise, a really nice one." There was a moment of awkward silence, and I wondered what to say. Should I tell him I loved him? Would that sound corny, especially after not speaking to him for a month? A million thoughts and questions swirled around my mind. I wanted to hold him and not let go, not ever. But I couldn't tell him that, either. It wasn't the right time. In love, you sometimes have to hold your cards close to the vest.

"How's work?" I asked, finally. "How's Miss Lillian?" Miss Lillian is the cashier at Terry's grocery store, a lovely African American woman who was always kind to me. My mind drifted back to the afternoon I'd first met Terry and Miss Lillian. I've always had a smart mouth, and it gets me into trouble. I had words with a redneck outside the grocery store where Terry worked. Miss Lillian and Terry looked out for me. If it wasn't for my smart mouth, I might not have met Terry. Maybe it's not so bad to be a *pisk,* a big mouth.

"Miss Lillian sends her greeting," he said. "How... are things for you?"

He'd caught himself before asking about my job. He knew I'd been fired, and how much that hurt. It was a humiliation. I hoped Terry didn't blame himself for what had happened to me.

"Things are OK," I lied. "I'm teaching Spanish at the Jewish community center."

"The community center? Is that like your church, where Jews worship?" he asked, curious. "It sounds like a good thing for you. You're Jewish, and you're a Spanish teacher."

"Terry," I said, smiling at his optimism. "Jews worship in a synagogue. A community center is just that, a place where we go to hang out, and take classes; there's a gym, activities, that kind of thing."

"Sounds nice. Does it pay OK? I mean, I'm not trying to be nosy or anything. Is it full-time?" he asked.

"It's volunteer," I answered. "Just to keep me busy. It keeps me off the streets."

He looked at me and smiled. "Well, that's a good thing. Boulder wouldn't be safe if you were out on the streets." He paused. "It's so beautiful here. The mountains are amazing. And all this snow. It's cold, but it's lovely. I'm glad to see you in your hometown. I know how much you love it here, and I can see why."

"The Rockies are amazing," I agreed. "I'm glad you came. I hope you can stay for a while, that you don't have to return to work right away. How are you feeling? How's that shoulder?"

"I'm OK," he said, not meeting my gaze. "I'm right- handed, so it's been hard to work. I can't use the knife too well with my left hand. I have some time off."

"I wasn't sure I'd see you again," I said, tentatively. I stood up, and went behind him, rubbing his shoulder gently.

"You're the one who left, Rico, not me," he said, so softly I almost didn't hear.

Chapter 2

That night, lying next to Terry, it was like we had never been apart. We were up late getting re-acquainted. My bed is small, and the mattress is soft. Since Terry is heavier, I kept rolling towards him. I didn't want to hurt his shoulder, so I rolled back to my side. Finally, very late, I gave up, and nestled close to him. I fell asleep; my worries about the future didn't keep me up. Questions for Terry could wait.

I had barely dreamed since I'd returned home. That night, though, my dreams were back. I dreamed I was sitting on a bench in a green field, full of colorful wildflowers. The scene was pretty, and I felt peaceful. The light shifted, and I began to feel unsettled, afraid. It was odd; there was no explanation for my fear. I had the sense I was not alone. In the distance, I saw three children. They approached; three little boys, dressed in rompers. The clothes looked old-fashioned, but the boys were clean and seemed happy. I wondered if they were brothers. They all had blonde hair and blue eyes. I had to fight a growing sense of dread. They were just children; why was I frightened?

I woke up to muted sunlight. The bed was empty, and I wondered if I'd overslept. Where was Terry? I was disappointed not to find him next to me. I slipped on my sweat pants, and went to the window. It had snowed several inches overnight, and the sidewalks were covered. There was white powder on top of the cars on the street. I went out to the kitchen, but Terry wasn't there. I called the cat, but Sid didn't come. I wondered how he was adapting to my home, and I hoped Terry had remembered to bring a litter box. I didn't want to have the carpet ruined. Sid is house- trained, but the trip must have been hard on him.

I thought about my dream. It worried me. I hadn't had any nightmares since leaving Georgia. Had seeing Terry again jarred something in my subconscious? Surely that was the explanation. I felt fear nagging at the back of my mind. In the past, when I had nightmares, something was about to happen. I dismissed the thought. I'm no psychic. Dreams mean nothing. I was emotional seeing Terry, that was all.

15

Terry had made coffee. He is nothing if not thoughtful. Today we would have to go food shopping, I thought. I stopped myself. I had already made the leap from "I would have to go shopping" to "we." If I didn't stop myself, I'd have Terry moved in, and we'd settle in to domestic bliss. I couldn't go back to Georgia, I wouldn't. And I wasn't sure how I could stay in Boulder, especially since I had no job. I owned the house I lived in: the down payment was a gift from my mom and Harry. If I had to, I could rent it out again. I'd have to move wherever I found a job.

I heard laughter coming from the backyard, and I went to the patio door. Terry was in the backyard, playing in the snow like a little boy. He saw me, and motioned for me to come. I stuck my head out the door.

"Are you *meshugah*?" I teased. "It's cold. Haven't you ever seen snow before? Come back to bed." Before I could close the door, a snowball came hurling at me, and Terry laughed. I grabbed my jacket, and went storming out. "This means war," I called. Terry had disappeared. The yard is small, and there were few places he could hide.

When I was half-way out, though, another snow ball came at me. It hit me on the arm, though it wasn't thrown hard. "You'll regret that, Terry!" I cried. I heard more laughter. Before I could get my own snowball made, Terry came running at me. He hugged me tight, and picked me up, holding me off the ground for a second. I was so startled I didn't even yell. So much for feeling sorry about Terry's injury. Terry began spinning around with me hanging on.

"Terry, you are *meshugah*, that's for sure," I said, laughing, dizzy.

He set me down, and kissed me hard. "That's so sweet. You're my sugar, too."

"That's not what I said."

"Oh really?" he said, pulling away. "Is that one of your Jewish words or something? Like calling me a *putz*?"

"Terry, I've never called you that. Where did you even hear that word?" I asked, pretending to be scandalized.

Terry hugged me hard, and was about to lift me up off the ground again. "I'm bigger than you," Terry taunted, like a teenage bully.

"Yes, you are," I said, trying to sound patronizing, trying not to laugh. "You are so immature."

He hooted, and tackled me down on the ground. Then he was on top of me, in the snow. "Score!" he called out, "you're down!" Terry is built like a former football player; I think he played sports for the small- town high school where he's from. I wriggled one arm free, and grabbed some snow. I managed to get a clump of the cold stuff down the back of his pants. Terry howled, and stood up.

"Geez, Ric, that was mean. You don't fight fair," he complained.

I smiled. "But I got you off of me."

"You don't like me on top of you?" he asked. "You did last night."

Although he was referring to something happy, the memory of when he was shot came unbidden into my mind. I remembered his weight on me, the smell and feel of his blood. I'll never forget it, I can't shake it from my mind. I shivered in spite of myself. Terry saw the look on my face, and said, "I'm sorry, baby. I didn't mean to hurt you." The tenderness in his eyes brought me back to the present.

"You didn't," I said. "I'm cold, that's all." We went inside. Sid was waiting for us, and curled around my legs. "Did you bring a litter box?" I asked.

"Don't worry, he's house-trained," Terry assured me. "Hey, Rico, do you have any more of those bagels? They were pretty good." They were "everything" bagels, my favorite brand, and they were good.

"I'm out, Terry, but if you don't mind a little walk, we can go get some." He smiled, and I kissed him. He smelled like coffee. Afterwards, we took a shower together. I put on a pair of jeans; Terry did the same. I combed my hair, and grabbed some mittens and a stocking cap. Neither of us bothered to shave.

I live in an interesting part of Boulder. It's near the college, where some of the faculty are, and not far from the synagogue. Boulder is a liberal town; the synagogue is Reform. My father was an assistant rabbi in the synagogue, and I am just a couple of blocks from my mom's house.

The streets were mostly devoid of people and traffic. It was the day after Christmas, and a lot of people had time off from work, sleeping late after celebrating. I held Terry's hand as we walked; Terry looked surprised and uncomfortable. We couldn't have done that in Georgia, but in Boulder no one cares. We walked over to my folk's house.

Harry was out in the driveway with a broom and shovel. I called out to him.

"Harry, you should let someone else do that. Isn't there some kid in the neighborhood who can shovel snow for you?"

Harry waved me away. "I'm not helpless," he said. He noticed Terry, and I wondered if he recognized him. They had met just once.

"Harry, you remember Terry," I said. The two men shook hands. If Harry felt anything other than friendliness towards Terry, it didn't register on his face.

"Hi, Terry," Harry said. "Nice to see you again. Are you in town for the holidays?"

Terry cast his eyes down. "Kind of," he finally answered.

There was a moment of awkward silence, and I asked, "Harry, Terry and I are going for bagels. Do you and Mom want us to bring you anything?"

"I don't think so," Harry said. "But your mom's inside. Go ask her. She's practicing."

Since my mom retired, she practices the piano for an hour before breakfast each morning. She's talented. I wish I had her musical ability. I left Terry there in the driveway with Harry, and went inside. I heard the piano playing. I walked into the den, closing the door softly.

"Hi, Rico," she said, not turning from the piano. I was startled. How had she known it was me without turning her head? But that's like Mom. Her family is from Romania, and she always says she has gypsy blood, and gypsy intuition. I doubt her story; still, she has some uncanny insights. When she's emotional, which is fairly often, her green eyes flash silver. I wish I inherited her eyes, instead of my father's brown ones. I have her thick, steel- gray hair.

"Mom, I'm going to Eisenger's Bagels. Do you want me to bring you back anything?"

She stopped playing, and turned to face me. "No, I don't think so. Besides, you want some time with your friend."

18

"How'd you know I had a visitor?" I asked, surprised. She couldn't see out front from where she was.

"My gypsy powers," she said, mysteriously.

"Oh, cut it out," I cried, exasperated. "How did you know? Do you have an invisible camera, or have you hired a private detective to watch my house?" I teased.

She just smiled. "Rico, you are so transparent. There's only one reason why you wouldn't want to get Chinese last night. You have a friend over. It is elementary, my dear Watson."

I kissed her on the cheek. "You're too much," I said. "See you later." I left, closing the door behind me. She returned to her music.

Back on the driveway, Harry was talking to Terry intently. I wondered what they were discussing. Terry looked up when he saw me.

"Man, Rico," he said. "You're dad sure knows a lot about cars." I thought about correcting Terry: Harry isn't my father. I call Harry by his first name, and that hasn't changed even after he and my mom got married. I decided to hold my tongue. It would seem peevish to correct him.

"That he does," I agreed. "Harry, I hope you haven't been filling Terry's head full of automotive *schmegegge*."

"Ric," Harry said with a smile. "I'm disappointed in you. You always underestimate my priceless opinions."

Terry looked puzzled. I doubt he ever talked sarcastically to his parents; for my family, sarcasm is the *lingua franca*. I gave Harry a hug, Terry shook his hand, and we continued our walk.

When we were out of earshot, Terry looked at me. "What does spaghetti have to do with cars?" he asked.

"Not spaghetti, Terry, *schmegegge*. It means nonsense," I explained. Terry doesn't know all my little Yiddish-isms, and since I've been back home, my language has returned to the ghetto.

"I like your dad," Terry said. "He's a smart guy."

"He's not my dad," I said, sounding more irritated than I intended. "He's my stepdad. You know that."

Terry was my guest, the man I love, and here I was being a jerk.

"He got married to your mom," Terry said, not missing a beat. "That makes him your dad. Stepdad sounds ugly and distant, like one of those old fairy tales."

I held my tongue. Terry had a point, and I couldn't explain my strong feelings on the subject. Harry is Harry; he's a great guy. He's been like a father to me. But he isn't my father, that's the thing. It feels like a dishonor to my dad to give Harry his title. I said nothing. I am lucky to have Harry, but I feel bad that I don't have more memories of my father. He died when I was so young.

Terry had neither a kind father nor a stepfather. I reminded myself that I had to be Terry's father, and nurture him the way Harry nurtured and cared for me. Those of us with kind parents owe something to people who weren't also blessed with them. I turned to Terry, and kissed him. A car drove by, and Terry drew back.

"Geez, Ric," Terry said, "are you trying to get us beat up?"

"Terry, this is Boulder. They don't beat up gays here." After I said the words, I wondered if they were true. Do I look at my hometown through rose-colored glasses? I remembered reading about an exchange student from Africa who was beaten up late one night near campus. We live in mean-spirited times. Sometimes it seems like the country is going backwards instead of forward. Still, Boulder has strong hate-crime legislation. I pulled back from Terry, and we walked the next block in silence.

We passed the house of my friend, Linda. Linda was recently divorced, and she came back to Boulder about the same time I did, earlier that fall. We'd been spending time together, commiserating. She was out on the driveway, scraping the ice off her windshield.

"Hi Linda," I called. She stopped scraping and turned.

"Hi, Rico," she said, looking glad to see me. She looked at Terry, and I saw a glint in her eye. Terry is a good-looking man, and he has an effect on women. Back in his hometown of Paris, Georgia, my neighbor, Erica, confided that many of the ladies in town had a crush on Terry, finding reasons to go to the store just to see him.

"Who's your friend?" Linda asked.

"I'm Terry Boone," Terry said, extending his hand. Linda clasped it eagerly, and I tried not to roll my eyes. Linda was almost drooling.

"You're not from around here," Linda gushed. "What a lovely Southern accent you have."

Terry blushed, but that only increases his charm. I wanted to smack him and tell him to save his magnetism for me. I should be proud to have a friend that people desire, instead I'm jealous. I'm a small, petty man.

"Linda," I said, finally, "we're going to get bagels. You want to come?" Linda looked like Cinderella being asked to the ball.

"Sure," she said. "I'd love to. Let me get my purse." She hurried inside, and came back a little while later. I noticed she'd put lipstick and some makeup on. Terry is the Pied-Piper; if we happened to see any more people out, we'd have all the women and some of the men of Boulder going for bagels with us.

We continued walking, with Linda walking close to Terry, hanging on his every word. I felt invisible, and sighed. That is life with Terry. Ted, my first love, hadn't been much better looking than me. I'm sometimes envious of the attention Terry gets. It makes me feel ugly. I'm short, thin, my face is long, and my nose is prominent. I'm no magazine model.

Pearl Street, where we were going, is one of my favorite places in town. It is usually busy, a big pedestrian mall. People say Boulder is the most livable place in America. We have a lot of joggers and cyclists; there are biking and walking trails. The climate isn't bad. It's chilly in winter, with some snow, but you can usually go outside.

Eisenger Bagels was packed. There was only one empty table. "Terry," I said, why don't you grab the table, and I'll order for you." Linda looked forlorn, so I added, "you wait here with him, Linda, and I'll order for all of us." Linda looked relieved.

"Be sure to ask for the light cream cheese for me," she said. "I'm on a diet."

As I walked to the counter, someone called my name. I turned, and recognized Petie, a guy I'd gone to college with. He lives in Denver, and must have been back in Boulder for the holidays. It isn't very far.

"Hi Pete," I said, as he made his way towards us. All the way through college we called him Petie, but now we are in our forties. Surely he wasn't still going by the diminutive.

"Hi, Petie," Linda called over, recognizing him the same time I did. She motioned for Terry to follow, and we all stood in line together. Naturally, someone grabbed our table. Now we'd have to wait.

"Linda," Petie said, turning to her, giving her a hug.

I introduced him to Terry, and Petie turned to me and said. "Oh, this must be the…" he let his words drop, and there was a moment of awkward silence. What had he stopped himself from saying? Had he been about to say, "this must be the son of the man who tried to kill you?" Terry blushed, too, probably thinking the same thing. I wondered if that would plague Terry and me wherever we go. Would Terry always be thought of as the son of the murderous sheriff?

Linda came to the rescue. "Petie," she said, "are you in town for Hanukah?" This was one of the years that Christmas and Hanukah were celebrated about the same time. Usually Hanukah comes in early December. Linda and Petie are both Jewish. We'd all been friends together in college, those many years ago. Linda was my neighbor, and I met Petie at Hillel, the Jewish center on campus.

Before Petie could answer, our party grew larger by one.

"Linda," someone else called. I turned, and saw another old friend, Josh. It was like a college reunion. Josh came over with a grin on his face. "You'd think we planned this!" Josh exclaimed, greeting Linda, Petie, and me. Josh, too, had gone to college with Linda and me, and I had met him in a Spanish class. Josh is a psychologist, and like Petie, lives in Denver.

It was my time for embarrassing and painful moments.

"I got an e-mail from Ted," Josh said to me, referring to my first love. Ted and I had been together for years, but went our separate ways before I moved to Georgia. Josh and Ted were close friends.

"I was sorry to hear you guys broke up," Josh said, in a low voice, that was still loud enough for everyone to hear. Josh must have thought Terry was with Linda; the way she was hanging on to him, it was understandable.

Terry looked away, discretely. I'd told Terry about Ted. Terry was married after a year in college, and he has a daughter. Neither Terry nor I talk much about the past; what does it matter? We met each other, and that's when our life together began.

"Josh," I said, "I'd like you to meet Terry." Josh was my height, on the short side, and he eyed the man who stood so much taller than him. Josh clamped his mouth shut, aware, maybe, that he'd been indiscrete. Then his face resumed a neutral expression that was no doubt his psychologist's mask. The five of us grabbed an empty table, and took turns going up to the counter to order.

Although the morning started out awkwardly, it ended up all right. It was good to catch up with old friends, and Terry seemed to have a good time. I am blessed to know a lot of great people. Terry tried hard to be a part of the group, and I was proud of him. It could not have been easy; he didn't know anyone but me. Terry is good- natured and likable, and my friends saw that immediately.

Josh and Petie had both driven to the bagel place, and Josh offered to give us a ride home. Petie said goodbye, and went to see his family there in Boulder. I sat in the front, deciding to let Linda sit next to Terry in the back seat. Why not? She is a friend, and Terry is a good-looking man. When Josh dropped us off, we all promised to keep in touch. Maybe we will.

I was glad to see Josh for another reason as well--- he's a psychologist. I'd wanted to get him apart and ask about my dreams. Would he think I was crazy? It might be a good thing to talk with him. I didn't like the idea of asking a stranger about my psyche; Josh knows me, and he'd shoot from the hip.

Terry and I got back to the house just before lunch time, and I still needed to go to the store. We'd eaten bagels, so I didn't think Terry would be hungry right away. Sid came to greet us. He had been lazily sleeping on a chair in the window, warming himself in a little spot of sunlight.

"Terry," I said, after taking my coat and boots off, "I need to do some food shopping." I wondered how long he could stay, and I wasn't sure how to ask. I would have to make a list, and I needed to know how many meals to plan for.

"I'll go with you," Terry said. "Let me drive--- you can have your first ride in my new truck." After letting our brunch digest, we got up and put our coats and boots back on.

"Let's go," Terry said. "You are a little low on supplies."

We got in his truck, which was piled with Terry's things, and I wondered where we were going to put groceries. As we drove, I remembered my strange dream. If only I'd been able to ask Josh about it. Who were the three little kids, and why had they scared me?

The streets still had some snow on them; the plows hadn't completely cleared them. We hit a pothole, and I snapped back to the present.

"Do you have chains on your tires?" I asked. He couldn't have made his way to Boulder without them; I wasn't sure they sold them in Georgia.

"No," he said. "I had to buy snow tires. They wouldn't let me through the pass without them. We don't have this much snow in Georgia. Sometimes we have flurries, but it doesn't make the roads impassable, not like here."

We drove the short way to the grocery store. I noticed again how packed his car was, and I didn't know how we could haul food, too. I looked at him, questioning. "There's still a lot of room in back," he said.

In the store, I pushed the shopping cart while Terry loaded it with meat, vegetables, and potatoes. At the checkout, he surprised me by paying.

"Terry," I protested, "you don't need to do that." Terry knew I wasn't working, and maybe he thought I was hard up financially. I felt bad, like a mooch or a charity case. I needed to assure him things were OK. By the quantity of food we bought, I wondered if he was going to feed the whole neighborhood. My kitchen would be well-stocked for a long while. I handed him the things from the cart, and let him find the space in the back of the truck he'd assured me of.

Back at the house, we unloaded groceries, and Terry brought some of his boxes and suitcases inside. I didn't ask questions, or comment on the number of things he'd brought with him. Ted had taken some of the furniture with him when he'd moved, and the third bedroom was almost empty. Terry put his suitcases and a couple of boxes in there.

Terry cooked supper, making a hearty beef stew. It was delicious; he's a good cook. When we were finished, I did the dishes. We went to the living room, and I flipped on the TV. Terry sat on the sofa, and motioned for me to come over. He put his arm around me, and I was full, warm, and happy. He lay on his side, and I lay on mine, like spoons. It's a good thing I have a big sofa.

"Terry," I said, sleepily. "Tell me about your shoulder. Does it hurt a lot? Are you still on medicine, antibiotics or anything?"

"It's a little tender sometimes," he answered.

"Terry," I said, summoning up my courage, "do we need to talk about it, I mean, everything that happened?" I didn't want to bring up the past if it was painful for him. Still, there were things that needed to be said. I wondered if I should apologize for not going to his father's funeral. Funerals are more for the living than the dead.

In the past months, I attended the funeral for my father's friend, Mr. Johnson, whose remains were also found in the sheriff's backyard. Sadie, my friend since childhood, and Mr. Johnson's fiancée, had died; I'd been to a graveside service for my father. I lost my job, and I was mourning that loss, too. No wonder I had a nightmare. Surely the future was going to be brighter.

"Rico," Terry said, sitting up to face me, "as far as I'm concerned, we don't need to talk about anything that happened. The past is over, and I want to look ahead. If you need to talk, I'll listen. But none of it matters anymore. It happened, it can't be changed. We're together now, let's enjoy it."

I thought about his words. He didn't sound defensive. Maybe he was right; maybe the past didn't need to be discussed. Part of me worried that if we started talking, it would all come back to the surface. As painful as it had been for me, I was sure events had wounded Terry emotionally as well as physically.

The previous night's dream kept intruding in my thoughts. I had a sense of déjà-vu. A moment earlier, I'd been certain the future would be better. But my nightmares had returned. Why? Who were those three little boys, and why did they make me so uneasy? I put it out of mind, and focused on Terry.

I faced Terry, wriggling out of his comforting arms. I turned the TV off. "Terry," I said, looking into his pale blue eyes, "I have to thank you again for what you did. You saved my life. There's no way I can repay you." I'd done it, I'd brought up the past. But I couldn't let it go forever without saying my piece.

Terry held my gaze, and sighed. "You don't need to say that, Rico. I couldn't lose you then, and I don't want to lose you now. I'm sorry---" his voice choked, "about what happened. I'm sorry about everything." His face grew red, and his raw emotion pained me.

I'd been wrong to run from Terry. Whenever things get rough or uncomfortable, I run away. It is what I've always done. I'm not proud of that, but it's what I do. Maybe I can change, but I'm not sure. I love Terry; still, I'm not always the person I'd like to be.

I saw the troubled look on Terry's face, and I thought about what he had been through. I'd run away, but Terry couldn't. What had it been like for him? Were his childhood friends accepting, or were they shocked? What is worse: having a father who murdered civil rights workers, or being gay? For rednecks and Southern bigots, I suspect being gay is the greater offense. I thought about everything Terry had brought with him, including his cat. Was Terry running away, now? It seemed like he was prepared to move in with me. Was I ready for that? I thought so.

"Terry," I began, "have people back there been unkind to you? Have they treated you bad?"

Terry turned his head, but not before I saw a tear form in the corner of his eye.

"Oh, Terry, I'm sorry," I said, holding him close to me. It was hard to see Terry cry, it broke my heart.

"What do you think, Ric?" Terry asked, finally. I heard the pain when he spoke. "People in the South, they want to pretend those things never happened."

"What things?" I asked gently. I wasn't sure what he meant--- did he mean murder or being gay?

Terry looked at me with exasperation, like I was a slow student. "Folks back there, they want to act like nothing bad ever happened. They want to forget people like your dad. They want to forget prejudice, what black people went through." He sniffed. I got up, and went to the bathroom for some tissue. When I got back, his face was dry. He took a tissue, though, and blew his nose.

"Every time they see me, they have to remember that over 40 years ago, someone killed your father and his friend. No one wants to be reminded of those ugly things.

It's OK to play dress-up at a plantation, or re-enact some Civil War battle. But racism? People want to forget. Nobody wants to remember discrimination."

"Oh, Terry, I'm so sorry," I said again.

"Rico," Terry said, "you have nothing to be sorry for. Your dad was a hero."

I tried to see things from Terry's perspective. My father was the victim, Terry's father the perpetrator. It's awful to have lost my father, but my father died doing good. Terry's father killed himself after getting caught doing something evil, and after shooting his son.

"I'm sorry if people hurt you," I said. "You're a good man." I didn't add what I was thinking: unlike your father.

Terry turned away, but I saw another tear in his eye. I dabbed at it, and he pushed my arm away. Poor Terry, he is embarrassed by his feelings.

"And then there's the gay thing," Terry said, still looking away from me. "It makes people uncomfortable. Everyone knows about you and me. In a small town, people know everyone's business."

I put my hands around his face, and turned his gaze back to me. Terry looked miserable.

"Terry," I said, after a moment, holding his gaze. "Don't go back. Stay here with me." I was sincere, and meant the words I said.

Terry looked at me with his sad, pale blue eyes. "Rico," he said, "you're just saying that because you feel sorry for me. I know how I feel about you, but you aren't sure how you feel about me. I love you, but you pity me. That's no basis for a relationship. I won't stay here just because you feel bad for me."

"Terry, I love you," I said. "How can I make you believe that? I know I was wrong… the way I left, it was all *farkakta*. But I didn't leave you, Terry, I left that town. Boulder is my home. I want you here with me." I had never been more sincere: I would be heart-broken if Terry left.

"I talked about things with Erica and John," Terry said, finally.

"Did you?" I wasn't sure what our friends Erica and John had to do with anything.

"They might be moving," Terry said.

27

"Erica will want to go, John won't," I said. Erica felt like I did about life in small- town Georgia. John was from the area, and they were living in his family home.

"John and me talked," Terry said. "He's a really nice guy. But you know that."

I certainly did. John and Erica are wonderful. If they hadn't arrived in time to help, Terry would be dead, and his father might still be alive. John and Erica saved us both. Erica and John are loving and accepting; Erica has a gay brother. John is a clergyman, and he has no problem with gays.

"You knew John and Erica saved us?" I asked. "You were unconscious by then, so you may not remember any of that."

Terry looked past me, deep in thought. I hadn't been there for him when he was in the hospital. I'd been too caught up in my own grief. I wondered who had told him what happened, if anyone did.

"I talked to John about you and me," Terry said, finally. "I told him I loved you, that I didn't want to lose you. I never felt that way about anyone before. I didn't feel that way about Donna." Donna was Terry's wife. They got married right after high school.

His words touched me. I'd talked to my rabbi friend, March Braun, and I'm glad Terry has a friend who he could talk with. I was closer to Erica than John, but they are both great.

"John told me about Ruth, and that I should be like her," Terry said, after a moment.

"Ruth who?" I asked.

Terry looked exasperated. "Ruth from the Bible, you know."

My mind went back to Torah study. I read some of the Bible when I was studying for my *bar Mitzvah*. I tried to remember Ruth. It's the story of a widow, but I couldn't remember the details. I hadn't read the Bible in a long time.

Terry looked at me. "John said since I loved you, then I shouldn't let you go without telling you how I feel. Rico, I drove all the way across the country to see you, to be like Ruth."

He concentrated, closing his eyes. Then he opened them, and held my gaze. "Wherever you go, I will go. Wherever you live, I will live. Your people will be my people, your God will be my God. Where you die, I will die, and I will be buried next to you." Terry's eyes were dry, but I felt like crying.

Chapter 3

Terry kept his clothes in the empty guest bedroom, till I could clear out space in the closet. In time, he would go back to his dad's house and bring some of the furniture he wanted, things that have sentimental meaning. I didn't want anything of his father's in my house, but it is going to be *our* house. Of course, we will have to get a bigger bed. I keep rolling to his side at night. He bought a litter box for Sid, and the cat seems happy.

Although Terry and I never lived together in Georgia, I was surprised how easily we settled into a comfortable routine. We cooked and ate; we spent time with Linda, Josh, and Petie. We spent time with my mother and Harry. If Harry didn't like Terry, he hid it well. In fact, the two have a lot in common, and share an interest in sports and cars. Harry invites Terry to come and watch football and hockey, and Terry always goes. He loves the Broncos, and so does Harry.

New Year's came, and Terry and I spent the holiday at home. It was enough just being together. The last year had been a rough one for both of us. Surely the New Year would be brighter. In spite of what we'd each lost, we have each other. Terry made black-eyed peas and cabbage, typical Southern New Year's food; it is supposed to bring luck and money. We needed that. I prayed for a bright new year for both of us. It would have to be better; it couldn't be worse.   In the months that followed, I would remember that New Year's prayer, and my simple, if naïve hope.

Our lives weren't worry free. Terry had some savings, and I had some savings, but we couldn't live for too long without working. I sent out resumes, and kept on teaching Spanish at the community center. I heard nothing back from my letters of inquiry. Terry was out on extended sick leave, and wouldn't return to work till his shoulder was fully healed. He found a doctor in Boulder, and the doc recommended some physical therapy, which Terry did. Terry kept in touch with Miss Lillian from the store, and we both kept in touch with Erica and John. They decided to move to Atlanta. Erica will be happy living in a city.

In addition to worries about work, nightmares kept troubling me. There were no ghosts, no supernatural entities in them. They worried me, they were so vivid. Every few nights I dreamed of the three little blondc- haired boys. I had a sense of dread every time I saw the children. I don't know what was so terrifying about them, but I woke up with a sense of foreboding. I had the uneasy feeling that my life was going to change yet again. Life is a series of changes.

One night, I drifted into a troubled dream world. I was in my backyard, and I was trimming a rosebush. As I pruned the leaves, I noticed two new blossoms. The buds were bright red. They were so bright and beautiful, I decided to cut them and take them in the house. I cut the first one off, and set it gently on the ground. It was lovely. But as I cut the second one, I pricked my finger, and began to bleed. The cut was painful, and I was surprised by the profuse loss of blood. I cried out. The blossom tumbled to the ground, and as it did, it crumbled in to dust. I woke up abruptly, and tried to shake the sinking feeling in the pit of my stomach. I sat up in bed.

"What's wrong?" a groggy Terry asked. Darn, I'd woken him.

I looked at my fingers intently, wondering if I was indeed bleeding. The dream had been so real. I went to the bathroom and turned on the light. I examined my hand carefully, but there was no blood.

"What is it?" Terry said, coming in to the bathroom. "Are you sick?"

"It's nothing, Terry," I said. "Go back to sleep."

Terry hugged me, and I kissed his neck. "Your whiskers tickle, Rico," he said, pushing me away.

"As long as we're both up," I said, kissing him again.

"You're too much. I don't think you have nightmares at all. You just do this to wake me up," he said, holding my hand, leading me back to bed.

I attributed the strange dreams to anxiety about my career, and the adjustment of life with Terry. I was happy that Terry moved in, but it was still a change. Maybe I was worried Terry would leave. I've seen enough of life to know that the best things never last.

The next night, I dreamed of the children again. I was standing in a field, and the wind blew fiercely. I had the feeling someone was hurt. The wind blew so hard I could barely move, but I forced myself to walk, putting one foot in front of another. The wind abruptly stopped, and I was in front of two of the little boys. They were both covered in blood, and I cried out. I was afraid they were dead. What happened to the third? Was he hurt, too? Where was he?

I moved slowly through the field. The wind picked up again. There was no rain, no snow, just the terrible wind. Suddenly I heard laughter. It sounded diabolical. Maybe what I'd heard was thunder. But I listened carefully, and I heard it again. It was unmistakable. The wind stopped. In front of me I saw the third boy. He smiled at me, and I shivered. It wasn't a happy smile, not the smile of an innocent child. It was an evil sneer.

"What did you do?" I called to him. "Did you hurt them? Come here!"

Although I spoke to him, I didn't want him to come near me. He was terrifying, even though he was just half my size. He held out his hands to me. They were red, covered in blood, dripping with gore.

"Monster!" I yelled at him. "What did you do? Why did you kill them?"

The child looked at me, and then put one dripping finger in his mouth, licking the blood.

"Stop that!" I screamed. "What is wrong with you?"

The boy just laughed and laughed. The wind picked up. I was too scared to run.

"Geez, Ric, what's wrong?" I heard Terry's voice, but at first it didn't register. I finally woke up, and Terry was looking at me with concern. "Another bad dream?" he asked.

"Yeah, just another bad dream," I said, waking up. "Sorry if I bothered you."

"Oh well," he said tiredly. "I'm getting used to sleeping with a guy who screams when I touch him."

"I screamed when you touched me?"

"Yeah," he said. "I kissed you. It must have startled you. I couldn't sleep, and I hoped that maybe you were awake."

"Sorry," I apologized.

"Rico, you don't think maybe you should see a doctor about these nightmares?"

I didn't answer. I kissed Terry, wanting to distract him. How could I tell him that I hadn't had these dreams for a month, that they'd only just come back? The nightmares returned when Terry had come back in my life. I really needed to talk to Josh. He might have some insight for me, a way to stop the nightmares. They had nothing to do with Terry. Terry made me happy, not scared.

Terry didn't mention my dreams again, and I didn't either. They worried me. But what if Josh thought I was crazy? Josh, I'd heard, was a little controversial. Some thought he embraced too many New Age principles. Still, this is Boulder, what did people expect?

When Terry was at a doctor's appointment, I finally called Josh. I left a message, and within an hour, Josh called me back.

"Nice to hear from you," Josh said. "It was great running in to you and everyone at the bagel place. What are the chances of that happening? It almost makes you believe in coincidence."

"It was *beshert*. Josh," I said, "could I talk to you, kibitz a little?"

"That's what you're doing now, isn't it?"

"I mean, could I talk to you, see you in a professional way?" I was nervous, and felt myself blush.

Josh's tone changed. "Sure, Rico. When can you come by?"

I glanced at the calendar, and looked for the date of Terry's next physical therapy session. He had one the next day, and I scheduled an appointment with my old college friend.

I was still teaching at the community center, but that was easy for me, and didn't require much work. I loved having Terry with me; still, I worried about the future as well as my reoccurring nightmares. Was anxiety about the future causing me to have frightening dreams? In the past, when I'd had nightmares, change was in the air. It had been that way as long as I could remember.

Terry was feeling better; the physical therapy helped his sore shoulder. He had quite a scar where the bullet hit him, but he walked with less of a hunch. Terry was getting bored. This was the longest he had ever gone without working.

Terry loved Boulder, and I had fun showing him the sights. I was eager for him to see all my favorite places. I love the mountains most. They always make me feel safe. In ancient times, my people believed God lived on a mountain; it is easy for me to understand why people thought mountains were sacred. I wanted Terry to get to know the mountains near Boulder before he or I went back to the grind. He was intrigued by the Rockies, and though it was winter, there were still trails we could explore.

Boulder is situated just south of the spectacular Front Range; the mountains closest to town are known as the Indian Peaks. Surrounding Boulder proper are the Flatirons, flat rock formations that look like--- flat irons. When people think of Boulder, they most often think of the Flatirons. I'm not much of skier, unlike most Coloradans, but I love hiking in the mountains.

We were having a wet winter; there was a lot of snow. The only way to hike in winter is either on snowshoes or cross-country skis. I have snowshoes in my garage, but I didn't have any extra for Terry. Luckily, Terry's truck had four-wheel drive, and he had snow tires. We planned on driving up to the Indian Peaks in Terry's new wheels, and then go snowshoeing on the trails that were still open in winter. Harry has a pair of snowshoes, so one morning I called my mom and asked if I could borrow his.

"Harry isn't here right now," Mom told me. "I'm sure he won't mind if you borrowed them. He doesn't use them much anymore. They're somewhere in the garage, and if you can find them, you can take them. Come by and look any time, Rico."

Terry was excited by the prospect of snowshoeing. He wanted to buy some thicker gloves for his hands, and a wool scarf for his neck and face; he didn't have the right clothes for Boulder's harsh winters. Terry went to Pearl Street, and I walked over to my mom's to borrow Harry's snowshoes.

Mom turned on the garage light, and said, "Have at it, Rico. Good luck finding anything. I keep telling Harry to tidy things up, but he's always too busy."

The garage was disorganized. Harry loves cars, like Terry, and he has a lot of automotive tools. In the messy garage, car parts are interspersed with unlabeled boxes. Maybe Harry knew where things are, but I had no idea. I felt a little guilty snooping around in his domain. Still, my mother said, and I concurred, Harry wouldn't mind if Terry borrowed the snowshoes.

On the workbench, I got distracted from my search when I came across a shoebox filled with photographs. Some of them looked old; a few were in color but most were in black and white. There were even some in sepia. I hadn't given my mother and Harry a real wedding present, and I wondered if I might find photos that I could copy or make a collage with. Some of the photographs were in envelopes, and some were loose. I forgot about the snowshoes and looked at the pictures instead.

Some of the oldest photos were from Harry's childhood. Harry had grown up on a farm in Nebraska. He sold most of the farmland, but still owns his family farmhouse near the Blue River. I'd been there once as a kid. Some of the pictures, especially the older ones, showed a teenage Harry casting a fishing rod. Others showed a young Harry riding a tractor. Harry is Swedish; his last name is Carlson. He looks Swedish: he's big, blonde, blue- eyed. His face is reddish. Terry's big and blonde, too, but he doesn't look Swedish. Terry's coloring is tanned, darker than Harry, but not as olive-toned as me.

I came across a snapshot that was just what I wanted. It was a picture of a black-haired beauty with a 1960's beehive, arm in arm with a young Harry. The exotic looking woman was my mother. I turned the picture over to find the date, but the writing was small, and the garage dark. I pocketed the snapshot, and remembered why I'd come to the garage in the first place: the snowshoes.

I began to put the photographs back in the box, when I saw something that that almost made my heart stop. There was a sepia photo of three little blonde-haired boys, in old-fashioned rompers. They were the boys I'd been dreaming about. My mouth went dry. How could it be? Maybe I'd seen the photograph a long time ago, and it had stayed in my mind, tucked in some dark corner of my unconscious. I turned the photo over, but there were no names written on the back. I stared at the picture, and felt afraid. My dreams, I now knew, meant something. I didn't know what. I put the snapshots back in the box. I couldn't bring myself to ask Harry about the picture: I was too puzzled and upset.

My hands still shaking, I looked in a cupboard, and found the snowshoes. I was anxious to get out of the garage. I patted my pocket, making sure I had the picture of my mother and Harry. I took the snowshoes, and dusted them off in the yard. I said a quick goodbye to my mom, and went home, puzzling over the picture of the three little boys, trying to understand it. I was glad to have an appointment with Josh. If I was crazy, then, at least, he'd tell me. Maybe there was medicine he could give me. A million worried thoughts raced through my mind. The rest of the day was a blur.

Luckily, my appointment with Josh was the following morning, during Terry's physical therapy. Nervously, I drove into Denver. It is just about a half- hour drive south of Boulder. In rush hour, it can take longer, but my appointment was mid-morning, and the worst of the traffic was over.

I parked my car outside a Victorian house, not far from downtown. I was able to find a spot on the street, something that isn't always easy. The day was cold, and I was bundled up in a knee-length wool trench coat and leather gloves. The sun was bright, and with snow on the ground, I was glad I'd worn sunglasses. You need them year round in Colorado.

I walked in the front door, and into a large room. "Joshua Greenberg," a plaque on the inner door discretely read. If you didn't know you were going to see a psychologist, you'd think Josh was an architect or interior decorator. I sat down on a dark blue sofa. The waiting room was soothing; the walls were painted light blue. Josh had instructed me not to knock on his door, that he would come out. I didn't wait long.

"Rico," Josh said, emerging from behind the wooden door. "Come in."

I followed my college friend into a softly-lit room. Josh sat on an easy chair, and motioned me to a love seat across from him. "Make yourself comfortable. Tell me why you're here. What's going on? How can I help?"

I took a deep breath, and tried to calm myself. My heart was pounding. But this was Josh, I reminded myself, and he isn't scary. I'd known him half my life.

"I'm having nightmares," I said, finally. "I don't know why."

Josh looked at me, then shifted his gaze slightly. He didn't answer me, not right away, but asked, "What brought you back to Boulder, Ric? Last I heard, you moved to Atlanta."

"Near Atlanta," I said. I began talking about my experiences down South. One thing led to another, and I ended up telling Josh everything that happened: finding my father's remains, and the sheriff's attempt to kill me. I told him about being fired from my job because I loved Terry. If Josh had heard the gossip about me, he didn't let on. His expression was sympathetic.

When I was through, I stopped to take a breath. I hadn't realized how fast I'd been talking. Josh looked at me, curiously. "You've been through all that, and you wonder why you're having nightmares?" He smiled wryly. "It sounds like your life has been a nightmare. I'm glad you're back home. The South wasn't good to you."

"I've been through some tense times. But the funny thing is, I only have these kinds of dreams when something bad is about to happen. I know that sounds crazy. I'm not psychic, I don't believe that. Terry's back in my life, I should be happy. I shouldn't be having bad dreams."

Josh was silent, and I began to feel nervous. "Do you think I'm … crazy?" I asked, worried by my friend's silence.

"No," he said, "do you think you're crazy?"

"I'm not sure," I confessed. "I need you to tell me I'm not."

"Rico," Josh said, "you used to have nightmares in college. Remember?"

I thought back. It took me a moment to recall. Josh was right--- but how had he remembered? As best I could recall, I'd met Ted, my first love, and a long series of nightmares ended. I didn't think I'd told anyone about them. I'd liked Josh, and we studied together, but we weren't best buddies or anything. I felt closer to Linda and Petie than I had to Josh. Josh had been close to Ted, my first love. Had Ted said something to him? Had I mentioned my nightmares to Linda, and she said something Josh?

"You're right, I had bad dreams back then, too," I finally admitted. "I used to dream about a house, this cute little cottage. I don't know why I dreamed about it. I can still see it in my mind." I took a deep breath, and pictured it. "The house was lovely, but then it started falling apart, with me trapped inside. The dreams stopped, or at least got a lot less vivid, when I met Ted."

"Tell me more about the house," Josh said.

"It was white, with yellow trim. There were flowers, and it was a happy place. It was clean and bright, at first. Then it got dirty and dilapidated. The beams and walls began to fall down, and I was afraid I'd be crushed."

"You dreamed about a cozy cottage, and then you met Ted. The dreams stopped. Maybe the house no longer fell apart when you found love. Without love, a house isn't much."

"Yeah, could be," I said. "It's funny, huh?"

"If the house represented your life, then everything came together, or stopped falling apart, when you were no longer lonely. Rico," Josh said, carefully. "Not all of my peers agree with my theories. They think I'm controversial."

"People think I'm controversial, too, Josh. I trust you, and your opinion. I've known you for 20 years. You've never judged me, even when Ted and I broke up."

"No one understands the origin of dreams, not really," he said, ignoring my comment about Ted. "We think they come from the unconscious, some call it the subconscious, mind." Josh paused, and sighed. "And we believe that time is linear. There is the past, the present, the future. I don't think it's that simple. Things don't always happen in a straight line. Some people, and you might be one of them, seem to be able to catch glimpses of things that are about to happen. You dreamt of a cute little house right before you found domestic happiness. In Georgia, you had nightmares about a stream, about violence, and then you found your father's remains. Now you're dreaming about children, frightening ones."

"Are you saying that I'm psychic?" I asked.

"That isn't the right word. We don't have a good term for it. What if you are, shall we say, sensitive? Maybe some people can tell when something important is going to happen, and they don't know what to do with that information. It gets filtered through the mind, and comes out as a dream."

Time not always linear? Some people sense things? Josh is smart, someone I've known half my life. Still, I wasn't sure that I believed him.

"What I'd like you to do, Rico, is to pay attention. Listen to your dreams. Trust your hunches. If you sense something, if you have an intuition, don't disparage it. Be open to possibilities. Can you do that, Rico?"

"Yes," I said, thoughtful.

"Listen to your dreams. Don't be afraid. Learn from your nightmares, they might be warning and guiding you. Maybe part of your mind is picking up on subtle information you're gathering."

I remembered something my grandmother once told me. She had said similar words. She told me my father had struggled with vivid dreams and nightmares, and had come to terms with them. She urged me to do the same. Did my father have an ability, a gift that he learned how to use? Did he have nightmares before he was murdered? If so, why hadn't he listened to them? I had a lot of questions, but Josh was looking at his watch. I hadn't had a chance to tell Josh that I found an old picture of the children I'd dreamed about.

"Come back and see me any time you want, Rico," Josh said. "If the dreams disturb your sleep too much, we can try hypnosis." He smiled at me, and in that second I saw the teenager, the college kid, I'd once known. "Now, do you think *I'm* crazy?"

As I drove home, Josh's words echoed through my mind. If my nightmares were telling me something was about to happen, could part of my unconscious mind see the future? If certain things are destined, *beshert,* was it possible to sense that? I sometimes wonder what Terry believes; religion is something we don't discuss much. It's a private matter, and Terry's not too interested in that kind of thing. That's a difference between us: I tend to ruminate.

Back at the house, Terry was waiting for me. He was walking straighter and straighter. I'd ceased asking him about his shoulder; he didn't like it when I did. He wanted to forget what had happened, and I couldn't blame him. Terry always sees himself as healthy, manly, in control. For him, the past is over, and it's time to move on.

We'd decided to go snowshoeing up at Indian Peaks, on the way to Estes Park, that afternoon. We got dressed in warm walking clothes and hiking boots. Terry had made sandwiches, and filled a thermos with coffee. He drove us into the mountains behind Boulder, a broad smile on his face. The roads weren't too bad. We passed the Flatirons, and the car climbed higher.

"It's a great truck, isn't it?" he asked. I told him for the hundredth time what a fantastic vehicle it was, and how there wasn't another one like it in the whole world.

"No need to be sarcastic, Rico," he said, looking hurt. Once again, I'd gone too far. In addition to our differences of religion, we have a different sense of humor. Terry's humor tends to be physical and a little rough; I prefer sarcasm. We try to be understanding of each other's differences, but it isn't always easy. Life with another isn't smooth. I said nothing as we drove on, and let my mind wonder. I tried to keep from worrying about my nightmares, and my concern about the future. Soon, one of us would have to go back to work. Things were going to change: they always do. The past few weeks had been almost perfect.

"It's beautiful up here," Terry said, trying to draw me out, signaling he didn't harbor a grudge. That's Terry, always forgiving. Terry doesn't rehash things, he moves on. I'm glad he isn't as neurotic and anxious as me. That's not to say he's perfect or better than me.

I directed Terry to a peak with some beautiful, well-marked trails. You can't go too far off the beaten path without a wilderness permit. In the winter, you wouldn't want to, it can be dangerous. Colorado has many "Fourteeners," mountains above 14,000 feet. It is way too cold to climb those in the winter unless you're a pro, but we were well under that altitude. He parked the truck, and we got out. It was cold, and I was glad Terry bought some better cold-weather clothes. He was wearing the navy parka that covered the lower part of his face, the parka that he'd been wearing when I'd thought he was a stalker outside of my house. He wore a new red scarf, matching gloves, and a hat underneath the parka's hood.

The sun felt warm, but we would be walking on some forest trails which were shady. I worried we had started too late in the day; in the winter it gets dark early. I put the lunch Terry had made in my backpack, and we put on our snowshoes. They kept our feet from falling down in the snow, which was several feet deep. Snowshoes are bulky, and it takes effort to walk in them. You can walk snowy trails and see beautiful places you can't go to without them.

I couldn't see Terry's face underneath his crimson scarf, and I had a little trouble hearing him. There were other hikers on the trail; some were on cross-country skis. We greeted our fellow mountaineers as we passed. Our path wasn't crowded. The mountains are vast, and you can go a long ways without seeing anyone. The trail I took us on was flat, and skis wouldn't have helped us much.

Terry and I walked in silence. My thoughts began to clear; maybe it is the high altitude, but I think better in the mountains. I mulled over the possible meaning of my dreams, and Josh's advice to me. What did he mean when he said time isn't linear?

We came out into a clearing, a place that would be a meadow filled with wildflowers in spring. There was an abandoned miner's cabin, and we walked towards it. It was the perfect spot for a winter picnic. The top rail of an old fence was a good place to sit, and we did. It was probably five feet high, but with all the snow, the top was just visible. I was hungry, and I was sure Terry was, too. I hoped he'd eaten some before we left. He's bigger, and needs more food than I do.

"Do you want to eat now?" I asked Terry.

"I can always eat," he said. Then, turning his head to make sure we were alone, he pulled down his scarf and kissed me. The mountains aren't teaming with hordes in the winter, especially on a weekday. His lips tasted like lip balm. "I've said this a hundred times, and you're going to say something snarky, but it really is beautiful up here," he said.

"Terry," I said, "you make me out to be a vile-tongued monster. Am I such a smart mouth, such a *pisk*?"

"Yes, you are," he answered earnestly.

"Terry!" I cried out.

Terry laughed, and said, "See what it feels like? You can dish it out but you can't take it." He leaned over to kiss me again. I discretely scooped up some snow in my hand, and put it down his back. "Rico!" he yelled, smiling in spite of himself, "you're a *schmuck*!"

"Terry," I reprimanded, shaking my head, "you don't speak Yiddish."

Terry smiled broadly, "Oh, I said it right. Your mother's been giving me lessons. She told me to call you that."

I laughed. "I don't believe you... well, maybe she did." We ate our lunch in companionable silence. It was getting late in the day, and I didn't want us to be up in

41

the mountains when it got dark. It was just after 3:00, and the shadows were lengthening. We reluctantly headed back the trail to Terry's pick-up.

Terry was happy and relaxed, and he began to sing on the walk back. He hadn't played guitar or sung since he'd been in Boulder, and I thought it was a good sign. I retreated into my own thoughts as we walked.

My mind returned to the photograph of the three little boys I'd found in the garage. The only possible explanation was that I'd seen the photo a long time back, and for whatever reason, it made an impact on me. Why did I dream about the children, and why did they frighten me? Why didn't I tell Josh that important detail? I thought it was because I had been so afraid he'd tell me I was insane. Why was I dreaming again? Hadn't Sister Eveline said the dreams would stop?

I thought about the blind woman, and my conversation with her back in Georgia. I was sure she saw Terry at the funeral. It was impossible; she's blind. I tried to recall her exact words to me.   She'd said I wouldn't have any more nightmares about my father. I remembered how she'd lightly touched my face, and told me I looked like him.

I stopped walking suddenly. Terry was ahead, and didn't notice. If Sister Eveline had seen my father, there must have been time between his car breaking down, and when he'd been murdered. I'd always assumed that he had been murdered shortly after his arrival in Georgia.   But if Sister Eveline had met my father…. I needed to contact her and talk with her. Why hadn't I realized the implication of her words before? I would have to ask her when and where she'd met my dad. I didn't have her telephone number or address, but I could call the African American pastor at whose church I'd met her. If there was anything more I could find out about my father's time in Georgia, maybe I could find out who murdered him. Maybe it would exonerate Terry's father, the sheriff.

Terry must have noticed that I wasn't following; I heard him call my name.

"I'm back here, Terry," I said. Suddenly I was tired, and the snowshoes seemed heavy and bulky. I was too weary to walk fast; Terry, that good man, hurried back to me.

"Are you OK, Rico?" he asked, concern on his face.

"Yeah, I'm fine," I said. I didn't confide in Terry about what I'd been thinking. For him, the past is over. My mother, too, had chosen to move on. But I won't rest until I follow every lead. My father was finally buried, but his death has not been avenged. Justice was not done. If the truth is out there, I have to find it.

Chapter 4

Driving home from the mountains, Terry continued to sing, giving a little concert for me. I was glad; I wanted him to be happy. He deserves contentment and peace; we all do. I was pensive, though; my thoughts were elsewhere. I was eager to contact Sister Eveline. If she had information about my father, I had to learn it. I'd been struck by her uncanny ability to know my thoughts. There were questions I should have asked. She knew things no one else did.

It was dark by the time we reached home. Terry went to take a shower, and I started supper. I wasn't hungry; I was preoccupied and tired from the walk. I went into the guest bedroom I use as an office. It was full of Terry's boxes, overflow from the previously empty third bedroom. I looked through my papers. I found the telephone number for Rev. Walker in Liberty, Georgia, the small town where I'd met Sister Eveline. It was 6:30 p.m. in Colorado, and two hours later in the southeast. I decided to take a chance and call Rev. Walker. I had to talk to Sister Eveline.

Luckily for me, Rev. Walker picked up the phone. I greeted him, and we chatted.

"Mr. Wise," he said. "Good to hear from you. How are things? I heard you left our state, and went back West."

"Yes," I said. "I lost my job, and there wasn't much point in staying on."

"I'm sorry to hear that," he said. "I'm afraid Georgia wasn't good to you. It must be a place of sad memories. But we are grateful for men like your father. I'll keep you in my prayers, if that's all right."

"Thanks," I said. "Rev. Walker, I'm sorry to bother you, but I was wondering if you could tell me about a member of your church, Sister Eveline."

There was a long pause, and then he said, "I didn't realize that you had met Sister Eveline."

"I did. She told me she saw my father. That made me wonder if she had information I should know."

"I see," Rev. Walker said. "Mr. Wise, I remember that you are Jewish, and I don't know if you are familiar with our faith tradition."

"A little," I said, tentatively.

"Mr. Wise, yours is a religion of prophets; our is, too."

"Yes," I said. "Prophets like Moses?"

"Some think that prophets didn't end in biblical time. Our church members believe that even today, some people have the gift of prophesy."

"You mean," I asked, confused, "that they are mind readers or healers, something like that?" It didn't sound bizarre to me; I'd just spoken with Josh, who told me to trust my dreams and nightmares. If time isn't linear, who am I to judge?

"Kind of," he said. "We think that God gives certain people insight. They are able to see things that others can't."

"Sister Eveline is a prophet?"

"You've met her," Rev. Walker said. "What do you think? Did her knowledge of things surprise you?"

I remembered her words. "She is uncanny," I said. "I was wondering if I might talk to her."

"Of course," Rev. Walker said. "Sister Eveline lives with her granddaughter. Her granddaughter is devoted to her. I hope she can tell you what you need to know. I am sorry for all you've been through." Rev. Walker gave me the telephone number for Sister Eveline and her granddaughter, and told me to keep in touch if there was any way he could help. I'd met many good people back in Georgia; they certainly weren't all monsters. I'd met Terry there.

Terry knocked on the door. "Ric," he said, "are you hungry? What should we do about supper?"

"I put soup on the stove. I'm not hungry," I called. "And I'm in the middle of something. Give me an hour, OK?"

Terry didn't even peek in the door, but left me alone. I heard him humming. He was a happy man. Absently, I looked at the old picture of my mother and Harry from their garage. I took it under the desk lamp, and read the date on the back. It had been too dark in the garage to see it clearly. I stared at the date. 1963. I turned the picture back over. Harry and my mother looked very much in love. 1963. My parents had been married in 1964, and I was born three years later. Had my mother known Harry before she married my father? Judging from the photo, they were more than casual

45

acquaintances. Harry had his arm around my mother's waist, and looked at her adoringly. My mother is from New York, Harry is from Nebraska. Where had they met? As far as I knew, my mother had never been to Nebraska. She hadn't been to Colorado till she married my father. There was nothing in the photo that indicated where the picture was taken. Someone must have written the wrong date.

Or, had Mom been in love with Harry before she met my father? Harry had been married, too, but his marriage fell apart after my father disappeared. At some point, he had moved in with my mom. They lived together for years, but hadn't married till recently, when Harry converted. Had Harry known my mother before either of them married someone else? Did it matter? I don't care if they whitewashed the situation for me, that is understandable. But had Harry been waiting in the wings all those years? Had my father's murder presented Harry with the opportunity to leave his wife and join his first love? I didn't want to think about it.

I returned to my original task. I dialed the number Rev. Walker gave me. A woman I assumed was the granddaughter answered, and I asked to speak with Sister Eveline.

"Rico Wise," a familiar voice said. Sister Eveline's voice was melodious and haunting.

"Hello," I said. I was caught off guard. How did she know it was me? I hadn't identified myself to her granddaughter.

"I knew you would be calling," she said, simply. "Your dreams have returned."

"Yes, but…." It wasn't why I'd called. How had she known about my nightmares? How had she known it was me?

"It's been rough for you, poor darlin.' You have been having a peaceful time, full of blessed rest. But it can't last, Rico, it never lasts. Life has a way of… of… well, there's always something, isn't there? You are at a crossroads, Rico, and that's what your dreams are telling you. That's why they're back. Your dreams are a gift. They are giving information. Pay attention."

Her words were strangely similar to those Josh had spoken to me.

I was silent for a moment. "You told me you saw my father, that I look like him."

"Yes, Rico, I saw him. I didn't know it was him, not till later. I saw two men in a car, one was a rabbi, one was black. There was a terrible storm, and their car was wrecked. The next week, someone told me two men had been murdered, one white, one black."

"How do you know it was my father?" I asked. I was skeptical. Just because she had seen two men didn't mean she'd seen my father. I didn't know if she had always been blind, if her eyesight could be trusted. I decided to ask her. "You weren't blind back then?"

"I was indeed," she answered.

"Then how did you see my father? I don't understand at all." Furthermore, his car hadn't been in a wreck, there was mechanical failure.

"It was him," she said, simply. "I'm sure of it." She sighed deeply. "Rico, when I was a young girl, just 16, I was in a car accident. They didn't think I'd live, but I did. The doctor told me I'd never be able to see again. But something happened, and I began to see. I thought my eyesight had returned. When I told the nurses, they called the doctor. He didn't believe me. The doctor said it was some kind of hallucination. He called it Anton's Blindness, a condition where blind people think their sight has returned. I could see, all right. The things, the people I saw--- they were significant. I saw a man in a white robe visit my grandmother, and the next day they told me she had died. That's when I knew I was having visions. God took my eyesight, but he gave me something else."

"The things you see, they aren't always negative?"

"The visions aren't always bad. They give me information, like your dreams tell you."

I wanted to believe her, I don't deny it. "Sister Eveline," I implored, "do you have any idea who killed my father and Mr. Johnson? If you know something, anything, please tell me."

"I don't know, honey, I wish I did," she said, sounding tired.

I had to back down. "Sister Eveline," I said, sounding less frantic, "Please forgive me. I'm not trying to bully you."

"Honey, I saw you being followed by a shadow," Sister Eveline continued, as if I hadn't spoken.

That didn't seem awful. Everyone has a shadow. "You saw my shadow?" I asked.

She didn't answer my question. "He's not who you think he is. He's hiding something," Sister Eveline said, adding ominously, "he's nothing good."

I felt a chill down my spine. "Who's not who I think he is?" I was confused.

"The dark thing following you is not *your* shadow," she said, slowly. "He may try to hurt you. Oh, I keep saying 'him' but I'm not sure it's even a man. All I see is a shape. It's a creature of darkness, something evil. This presence is getting close to you, and you are in danger."

I looked down at my desk, and saw the picture of my mother with Harry. Was Sister Eveline warning me about Harry? Oh, that was ridiculous. I've known Harry my whole life. Harry is exactly who he seems to be. I love Harry, I trust him. Maybe the dark shadow was Terry, the man who I'd invited to live with me? The problem with Sister Eveline's prophecy is that it would make me paranoid. It was vague enough to make me suspect everyone.

"And honey," Sister Eveline continued, "you will be moving. I saw you carrying a suitcase."

I didn't know what to think. I had no plans to move, and I didn't feel in any danger. "Thanks, Sister Eveline," I said. The things she saw were just neurons misfiring, a result of her injuries, Anton's blindness. It was what her doctor had diagnosed, I was foolish to put faith in the things she saw.

"Be careful, Rico. I don't want to worry you none, but promise me you'll be watchful. The evil may try to hurt you. The darkness is getting close."

I had been through a lot the last year. I didn't like thinking some new trial was awaiting me. "Why would it be after me?" I asked her. "I've been through enough."

"Sometimes," Sister Eveline said, as if she were musing, "sometimes when you've been close to darkness, it gets a taste for you. It comes back for more. The evil doesn't like losing, it wants to fight you again. It ain't fair, I'm not saying it is. But the evil has noticed you, and you must take care now. It's going to try and win this round."

I said goodbye, and rang off. A dark shadow? She made it sound like some madman was after me. Ridiculous. And I had no plans on moving. Everything she told me was wrong, and I'd do best to ignore her. I should disregard my own nightmares, too, in spite of what Josh told me. No one understands the mind, it can play tricks.

Before going to find Terry, I decided to check my e-mail. I'd written Ted, and asked him if he could take any more of his furniture. I told him I had a new roommate. If he wanted details, he could ask. There was no message from him, but there was one from Rabbi Braun. The rabbi was in Omaha. I smiled to myself as I read his invitation. Well, score one for Sister Eveline. I would be moving.

I left the office to tell Terry. All the lights were off, and I couldn't hear the TV. Had he gone out somewhere? It was late for that, and he would have told me.

"Terry?" I called. I went to the kitchen, found an apple, and ate it. I was tired after snowshoeing. I thought about going to bed, though it was only 9:00. "Terry?" I called again. I went to the bedroom. Terry was snoring softly on the bed. He was tired, too. I folded up my clothes, and joined him.

I found it hard to fall asleep. Terry had just come here from Georgia; it was a lot to ask him to move again. But one of us has to work. Rabbi Braun had offered me a teaching job, and I had no choice but to take it. I thought about waking Terry up to talk, but it could wait till morning. Finally, I fell asleep.

I had a nightmare that night, but its meaning was easy to understand. It was odd that I hadn't had such a dream before. I was sitting on the banks of a stream, Terry sitting next to me. I heard footsteps, and turned. Terry's father, the sheriff, was pointing a gun at us. I cried out, but it was too late. The sheriff shot Terry, and Terry began bleeding, falling into the stream below. The sheriff laughed, and reloaded his shotgun. He pointed it at me, and pulled the trigger. I was frozen in place, unable to move. I heard the gun fire, and I felt a sharp pain. "No," I shouted. I was slipping, falling off the steep banks of the stream. I was bleeding, dying. Suddenly, the sheriff put his arms on my shoulder to push me into the river. "No!" I called again, and hit him.

"Rico, wake up, you're having a bad dream," Terry said. "Ouch, quit hitting me."

It wasn't the sheriff touching me, but Terry. I was disoriented, and it took me a moment to realize where I was.

"It's OK, Ric," Terry said, gently.

"Terry," I said. "I'm sorry. You were so tired and I woke you up. Did I hit you?"

"It's all right," Terry said, sleepily. "Must have been some nightmare," he added, holding me.

I felt reassured by Terry's gentle presence. The dream had been so vivid. Its meaning wasn't hard to understand; I didn't need Josh to analyze it. "Terry," I said, softly, "don't ever leave, OK?"

"I'm not going anywhere," he mumbled, and then began kissing me. "As long as we're both awake…"

Afterwards, I couldn't fall asleep, remembering Rabbi Braun's job offer. We're moving to Omaha, I wanted to tell Terry. Rabbi Braun was working at the Jewish community center there, and they needed someone to teach English to immigrants and refugees. He knew I was a teacher, and wasn't working, and had asked me to come. It was a last minute offer; their regular teacher had become ill. The pay wasn't great, but he would help me find an apartment. It sounded good, especially since it was the only job offer I had. Terry wouldn't mind moving again, would he? He'd fallen back asleep, and it could wait till morning.

When I woke up, the sun was shining. I looked at the clock. It was just before seven, and Terry was out of bed. I slipped my sweat pants on, and made my way to the kitchen. Terry had showered, shaved, and put on dress clothes. He was finishing his coffee.

"You're up early," I said, groggily. "I'm sorry I woke you last night."

He smiled, and looked distracted. "Don't worry. I'm used to your dreams by now. Just don't hit me so hard, I'll get a bruise. Besides, you made up for it." He winked at me. "Look, I've got some errands to run today, and I've got to head out."

"Geez, Terry, already? What do you have going on?"

Terry looked like a man with a secret, and smiled mysteriously. "By the way," he added, getting ready to leave, "we have supper at your folks tonight. Your mom's making brisket."

"Why? What are we celebrating?" My mother doesn't like to cook, and if she was going to the trouble of making brisket, it had to be a special occasion. It wasn't Purim, and certainly not yet Passover.

"It's a surprise. See you later," he said, kissing me quickly, and leaving.

What was going on? Did Terry have more physical therapy for his shoulder? He seemed to be feeling better, and if his shoulder hurt, he didn't show it. I drank my coffee, feeling left out of the loop. It was strange to think of Terry planning something with my mother and Harry, without telling me.

My mind returned to the photograph of Mom and Harry, taken before they were supposed to have met. What did it matter? It wasn't any of my business, and had no bearing on the present. It was mildly interesting, that was all; I had caught Harry and my mother in a little white lie. The picture of the three boys I'd found disturbed me more. How was it possible I'd dreamed of them before finding the photo?

I thought about my conversation with Sister Eveline. She said she "saw" my father. I didn't believe in prophets or psychics. Had she been trying to frighten me, telling me some dark shadow was after me? I thought about Josh's advice, and then remembered my dream about being shot by the sheriff. Some dreams don't predict the future, they just bring up a recycled memory of the past.

I went into my office, and logged onto the computer. I thanked Rabbi Braun for the job offer, and told him I would gladly accept. Classes were starting the next week, so there was no time to waste. I looked over the books on my shelf. I had taught Spanish, not English. Many of my students would be native Spanish speakers. The Jewish center in Omaha was providing services for immigrant workers in the kosher slaughterhouse just outside of that city. In addition, there were refugees from Africa and the Middle East the agency was helping, and I would be teaching classes to these disparate groups. It was exciting.

I've never been to Omaha, but Harry is from Nebraska. He could give me information, and tell me about the place. I was glad Rabbi Braun or at least someone would be finding me an apartment. There wasn't time to move, find a place to live, and get my classes ready within the span of a few days.

I logged on to an online education site, and looked over textbooks. I picked out a couple that looked interesting, and ordered them with overnight shipping. I also picked up a few Spanish-English dictionaries, and three Arab-English dictionaries. The Jewish center would probably have some, but it would be good to have them on hand for myself.

I called my mother. "Terry said we're celebrating tonight," I said. "What exactly is it that has him so happy? How come he's told you, and not me?"

My mother just laughed. "Terry wants to surprise you. He has some good news, that's all."

Terry had left the house looking sharp, all dressed up. I was glad to see him happy, feeling better. And if he wanted to surprise me, well, that was sweet.

"So you won't tell me?" I asked. I didn't have time to think about it too much, I was worrying about my move. I was bored not teaching, and unemployment wasn't helping my financial situation. "Mom," I said. "I've got some news. I got a job offer in Omaha."

"Omaha?" she said, sounding distressed.

"Yeah. They need an English teacher at the Jewish community center there. Rabbi Braun invited me to move out."

"There's a Jewish community center here. If you're going to work for nothing, you might as well stay here." Her tone was sharp.

"Mom, this is an actual job, the kind where I get paid. You remember work, don't you? I know you're retired now, but try to think back."

"There's no need to be sarcastic," my mother sniffed. "I don't think you should move, that's all."

"I have to work. There's a correlation between working and eating, and I'd like to eat. Terry's not working, and we can't live on love alone." It was understandable she didn't want me to move; I had just returned to Colorado.

"Have you told Terry?" she asked, plaintively.

"I haven't had a chance. He had some errands to run. But I'm glad you're making brisket. We do have something to celebrate."

There was silence on the other end. My mother didn't sound happy. She knew I'd been looking for a job, and I didn't understand her lack of enthusiasm.

"I've got to go now," she said.

"You're not even going to congratulate me?"

"Congratulations. *Mazel tov*," she said, finally.

I didn't have time to analyze her odd behavior. "Is Harry there?" I asked. "He's from somewhere near Omaha. Could you put him on the line?"

"Sure, Rico, just a minute. But look, break it gently to Terry when you tell him, all right? He loves Boulder so much."

"OK" I said. "He won't mind coming along," I said, breezily, not at all sure it was true. Terry really liked Boulder, understandably. Boulder is beautiful, there is no place like it. I thought about the lovely day we'd spent in the mountains. There are no mountains in Nebraska. But Terry would adjust. So would I, wouldn't I? As long as Terry and I were together, that is what matters. Mom put Harry on the line, and we chatted. He still had friends in Nebraska, but he didn't have a house or land there anymore.

"I sold the farm house years ago," Harry said, sounding pensive. "I hated to do it; it was the home I grew up in. But it was on the market for a long time before I got an offer. Not many people are interested in moving to Buffalo Crossing. The house was torn down, and there's not much of anything there anymore."

"That's where you're from, Buffalo Crossing?" I stifled a giggle. "You're a country boy, Harry, I had no idea." I rang off, and Harry promised to answer any questions that evening when Terry and I came over.

Terry still hadn't returned by lunch time. I called his mobile phone, but there was no answer. I left a message. I was a little worried. What kind of errands took so long, I wondered. The truth was, in the month we'd been living together, I'd become dependent on him. I love Terry, and I can't imagine life without him. What if he wouldn't come with me to Omaha? My heart skipped a beat just thinking about it. But he would come; one of us has to work. Besides, in a few months or weeks he would be well enough to return to work himself. There are grocery stores in Omaha that need butchers. There was even that kosher slaughterhouse, whose worker I would be teaching. Terry would have no trouble finding a job there.

Terry came back home late in the afternoon. "Where have you been?" I asked, sounding more accusative than I'd intended. "What took you so long, and why didn't you check your phone?"

Terry looked tired but happy. He gave me a hug, and kissed me hard on the lips. "I'm a working man, Rico. I got a job. Congratulate me! This was my first day. I like it. I talked to the people at your local grocery store, Donaldson's; they needed a butcher, and I applied. The owner said it might lead to a management position. From now on, you're a kept man, Rico! I'm making money."

My heart sank. This was the surprise, and the reason my mother sounded so strange. "Congratulations," I said mildly. I tried to summon up enthusiasm, and added, "*Mazel tov.*"

"You don't seem happy," Terry said, sounding hurt. "I thought you'd be pleased. We need the money, Ric. I'm feeling good, my shoulder is better."

I wasn't sure how to break my news. We weren't the first couple to be separated by diverging careers. This was Terry's moment to shine, and I held my tongue. I tried to enter into the spirit of things by adding a sly comment: "I'm sure they'll like you, Terry. No one can handle meat like you."

Terry grinned, and winked at me. "I'm glad you appreciate my talent," he said, coming close, and holding me. But even as he hugged me, I felt my little world coming apart. I didn't have the heart to tell him, not just then.

We walked over to my mother's, and we celebrated Terry's new job. The meal was delicious. My mother knows how to make brisket. Terry had picked it out for her. We had some *latkes*, potato pancakes, and a salad. For dessert there was *kugel*. We were stuffed, eating till we almost *plotzed,* burst. My mom and Harry did their best to keep the mood light, but I felt sad. Terry and I would soon be separating. I tried to be hopeful, I tried to think the best. When we got home, I couldn't keep my secret any longer.

"Shit, Rico, shit!" Terry said, disconsolately. "Why didn't you tell me you had a job offer? Why didn't you discuss it with me? You'll have to tell your rabbi you can't move. You don't need that position now."

"I can't do that, Terry," I protested. "And why didn't you tell me? I didn't even know you felt well enough to go back to work. Did the doctor say it was OK?"

"I don't need the doctor telling me what to do," Terry said. "I guess we both messed up. It was such a great surprise. I thought you'd be happy, and proud of me. It's not easy to get a job. I can't quit after the first day, Ric, I can't do that. You'll have to tell your rabbi you can't go."

I didn't like Terry telling me what to do, and I told him so. "Look, Terry, you're not my boss, I know what I need. I can't turn down this job. I've been sending out resumes for two months now, and I haven't even had a response. You think it's easy for teachers to get a job? You think the economy's great for me?"

Terry turned his face away. "This was supposed to be a celebration. Now it's all turned to shit."

"Terry, we're both at fault," I said. "We're new at being a couple, and we don't know the rules, what to do, how to be with each other."

"Oh, cut it out," Terry said, impatiently. "Now you're trying to tell me how to feel, talking all that modern psychology."

I went over to him, and put my arms around him. "These are the challenges of the 21st century," I said.

Terry smiled, but I think he brushed away a tear. His hand moved so quickly I couldn't tell. "It's late. Let's go to bed," he said. "I've got an early day tomorrow. We'll work things out, huh? I love you, you love me, that's what matters. It will work out."

"That's right," I agreed, with more assurance than I felt. I love Terry, but I didn't see any solution. We went to bed. I was distracted; not every disagreement can be solved easily. Terry soon began snoring, but I just lay awake. Terry and I would be separated, and I wanted to remember what it felt like to be lying next to him. I concentrated on the moment, memorizing how it felt; the way Terry looked, his scent. I stored up memories for the lonely nights ahead.

Chapter 5

Harry drove with me to Nebraska. The weather was stormy, which was fitting, though there was snow on the ground. The winter gray of the sky mirrored the sadness I felt leaving Terry. It is around 600 miles from Boulder to Omaha. That is a long drive, but it isn't a long airplane flight. Since Terry and I were both working, we could afford to visit. Having a long distance relationship isn't ideal, but it wouldn't be forever. Terry's job was in a chain supermarket, and there was the possibility that he could transfer. I didn't know how long I would be in Omaha. Teaching English as a second language was a contract job, there was no tenure. It would depend on how much funding the program received, and the number of students I had.

Terry made me promise to call, and not use e-mail. He still hadn't forgiven me for the month when we hadn't talked at all. It would work out between us, surely. Our love was *beshert*, meant to be. We had just gotten back together, and now we were separating again. I relied on Terry, and I think he needed me, too, in a good way.

I was glad for Harry's company. He knew the road well. Sharing the driving, neither of us would get too tired. Harry told me stories about growing up in Nebraska as we traveled.

"Buffalo Crossing is on the Blue River," he explained. "That part of southeast Nebraska was never visited by European settlers till around 1860. A few years later there was the Homestead Act, and then there were conflicts with Indians."

"There aren't Indians there anymore?" I asked. "They all got moved to Oklahoma?"

"There are some reservations near Omaha, but most native people were forced to move either north to South Dakota or south to Oklahoma. One of the last Indian wars was in 1864, near Buffalo Crossing. When I was a kid, we sometimes found arrowheads. Of course, it's possible our parents planted them to give us something to do."

"I'm assuming there aren't any buffalo in Buffalo Crossing," I said.

Harry smiled. "No, they've been chased out, too. There's not much of anything there anymore. Just a few farmhouses, a grain elevator, a gas station. Most people have moved away."

"But you still have friends in the area?" I asked. The plan was for us to stop in the late afternoon or early evening at Harry's hometown. Harry might spend the night there, and I would drive the hour or two farther to Omaha. Harry would take the bus to me the next day. Our plans might change, depending on the weather. It was cloudy, and while we hadn't run into snow, it looked like it could start at any moment. It was bitterly cold.

Once we left the Rockies, the landscape was flat. I was surprised how dry and desolate western Nebraska is: it's a continuation of eastern Colorado. The highway follows the Platte River; calling the Platte a river is a stretch. It looks more like a wide stream. I couldn't tell if it was frozen solid or not.

"The twins still live in town," Harry said, apparently speaking of his childhood friends.

"The twins?" I repeated.

"They're fraternal, not identical, Darrel and Earl Johnson."

"They still live in Buffalo Crossing?" I asked. "Do they have families?"

"Darrel was married, but didn't have children. His wife died a few years back. Earl never married. I'm closer to Darrel," Harry said. "He's more outgoing than Earl."

"Is Earl gay?" I asked.

"There's other reasons people don't get married, Ric," Harry said. He looked thoughtful. "Earl's a little, well, he's quiet. You never quite know what's going on inside his head. Both of them are religious, and more conservative than I am. We probably won't discuss religion or politics."

"Do they know you've become Jewish?" I asked.

Harry smiled. "I'm not sure they even know I've gotten married."

"Will they freak out that you've married a Jewish woman?" I asked.

"I don't know," Harry said thoughtfully. I'd been teasing him, but he had a serious expression on his face. I wondered if his brief visit to Buffalo Crossing would be awkward.

Although we'd long ago left the high elevation of the Rockies and their foothills, there were snow drifts along the highway. The road was well- plowed; the only problem was occasional gusts of wind, spraying the car with white powder. There weren't many cars on the road, but there were a fair number of trucks.

As the day wore on, there was no change in the sky, which was steel gray. Once we reached central Nebraska, we passed a few more towns. There were other changes, as well; there were more trees, and gently rolling hills. A few farm houses dotted the landscape. The farms looked lonely, and I wondered what Harry's life had been like, growing up in such a solitary state. Nebraska didn't seem populous.

Around four in the afternoon, we had to stop for gas. The wind was blowing hard, and I was sure a blizzard was coming. It felt colder than Colorado.

"How much farther?" I asked Harry. We were both out of the car, stretching our legs.

"Not far to Buffalo Crossing, still a ways to Omaha," he answered. We almost had to shout to be heard above the wind; it was howling ferociously. We got back in the car after filling the tank and using the restroom. Harry looked tired. I hadn't noticed before that he was growing older. His blonde hair was mostly silver, and his face etched with fine lines. How was it that I hadn't realized that he is aging? And if Harry was growing old, so was my mother. So, no doubt, was I. My own hair is gray.

My thoughts drifted to Terry. I am lucky to have found him. He's a good man, a *mensch*, and those are in short supply. What will become of us, I wondered. Ted and I broke up; we became estranged in the same house. We weren't living miles from each other, like Terry and I would be. Sometimes distance is emotional, not spatial. I hadn't heard from Ted in several weeks. Maybe he didn't want to be in contact anymore, even as friends. Would the same thing happen to Terry and me?

"Slow down, Rico," Harry said.

The sound of his voice brought me back to my driving. I hadn't noticed any sign, but Harry told me to turn. I did, and we were on a two- lane highway. Some of the fields were planted with winter wheat. The snow banks weren't as high, but there were still several inches of the white stuff on the ground. I noticed a river. It couldn't be the Platte, which we had left. "The Blue River?" I asked.

"Yes," Harry said.

The river was wide, though not as wide as the Platte, and looked frozen. We drove across a bridge. The two- lane road wasn't well- plowed, and I hoped there weren't hidden icy patches. I slowed even more.

The road followed the Blue River. The banks of the river were lined with cottonwood trees. The bare branches looked eerie in the lengthening shadows of the late afternoon. I was filled with sadness. My thoughts drifted to the native people who used to live on this land, and had hunted the once- plentiful buffalo. Gone are the Indians, gone are the buffalo, and gone are most of the inhabitants of the land.

An old sign welcomed us to the town of Buffalo Crossing, where, it said, "a brighter day is on the way." The sign needed paint, and was peeling. I felt melancholy, looking around at the dying town. "Town" was an overstatement: it was a collection of about five forlorn houses and a gas station. Across the street from the gas station, there was a grain elevator. It was a tall structure, and in the wan afternoon light, it looked like some grotesque, science- fiction monster. The houses were fairly large; most needed repair. The town had seen better times. It was hard to believe the sign's slogan. If a brighter day was on the way, it needed to hurry before the place crumbled.

I drove slowly on the town's main street. "Stop," Harry said. I did, not knowing why. We parked in front of an old, rusting car in a field. Harry got out, excited. I joined him, and looked around. I wondered why an old car had his interest. I was wearing my overcoat, but the wind was blowing so ferociously, I wished I'd worn a hat and some mittens, too.

"This was where we lived," Harry said. "Look, you can see the sidewalk to the house." I followed his pointing finger, and saw a cracked sidewalk peeking out from the snow. The sidewalk led to nothing other than the rusted car. "Our house was here," Harry said, gesturing. "The barn was over there." He pointed to a fence. I could see no signs of a structure. Tall weeds poked through the snow of the empty lot.

Harry's expression changed from delight to sadness. Maybe he felt the same things I did, the loss and desolation. I looked at the gray, twilight sky. The rusted car was surrounded by a few old trees, and if I squinted my eyes, I thought I could see the outline of what had once been a yard. The foundations of the house and barn were gone, making it seem like nothing ever stood there. Behind the trees, the Blue River flowed. Maybe it was prettier in the summertime.

"It's cold," Harry said.

I said nothing, too tired even to make a sarcastic comment. Besides, it was wrong to mock this shell of Harry's hometown. We got back in the car, and slowly drove a few yards. Harry told me to stop in front of the largest house on the street. It had become almost completely dark now, and I had to strain to see. There was a single street light, and it barely illuminated our way.

The old house was two stories high, with an attic window. It was white and box-like, almost ramshackle. The home was wide, from the street side, and went back far. The porch light was on, but it lit the place only dimly. The town seemed to swallow all the artificial light. Harry knocked on the front door, which was painted gray. There was no answer. Harry smiled at me, but the smile seemed more for himself than for me. He knocked again. I thought I heard voices in the distance, but I couldn't tell if they were coming from the house or somewhere else. Maybe one of the neighbors had the TV on.

"I guess no one's home," he said.

"Do both of the twins live here?" I said softly. I don't know why I whispered. There was no one around to hear me. The little community seemed deserted. I felt uneasy.

Harry nodded. "Earl lives on the first floor, and Darrel lives upstairs. They share the kitchen." Harry seemed subdued, and I wondered if it was fatigue, or if he was affected by the decline of his hometown. The fading light, the cold wind, and the town's decay produced a feeling of depression in me.

"They knew you were coming?" I asked. Harry said nothing, but began to walk down the sidewalk.

"They'll know about the twins at the gas station," Harry said. "I told Darrel we would be here." I followed him, and we went to the self-service station. It sold ethanol. There is a lot of corn grown in Nebraska, and I remembered a horror movie about corn fields and creepy children. It didn't seem farfetched. I was tired from the drive; maybe

60

that's why I was nervous. Buffalo Crossing is a town time forgot, untouched by modernity. It belonged to a previous era.

The gas station reassured me by its mundane appearance. We walked in the door, which announced us with a loud ring. Behind the counter, a large woman with impossibly black hair piled high was reading a magazine.

"Yes?" she said, not shifting her gaze from her reading.

"Where's Darrel and Earl?" Harry asked.

The woman looked up, and her expression changed. "As I live and breathe, is that you, Harry Carlson?"

Harry smiled. "Sure is, Susie," Harry said.

The woman came from behind the counter and planted a kiss on Harry's cheek. Harry blushed. "You haven't changed at all," Susie said. "You look exactly the same."

"So do you," Harry said. I fought a giggle, picturing a chubby little girl with too much makeup and a black wig.

"Darrel had to run to Omaha, but he should be home by now," Susie said. "Earl's there, far as I know. Of course, he don't hear so well, so if you knocked on the front door, he might not have heard. Try the back."

"I'll do that," Harry said.

"How long are you in town?" Susie asked. "And who's your little friend?"

I'd stood quietly behind, letting the two old friends talk. I didn't like being called "little." It isn't so much that I am short, it's that Harry is tall, I thought, defensively.

"This is my son," Harry said. "Rico's moving to Omaha." Harry always introduces me as his son; I introduce him as my stepfather. It makes me happy to think Harry is proud enough to claim me as his own.

"Rico," Susie repeated. "That's an interesting name." She looked me over. "He must take after his mother," she added, tactlessly. "He don't look nothing like you."

"Nice to meet you," I said, though it wasn't. But it didn't cost me to be polite to the odd woman.

Harry said, "This is Susie… what's your last name now?" he asked her.

"I'm still Susie Hearn," she said. "Of course, I'm widowed now that Mel passed away." She looked at him. "Your wife still living?" It was impossible to miss the glint in her eye.

"Happily, she is," Harry said, and ushered me outside, back into the darkness and bitter cold.

"She's a vulture," I said, as we walked down the street. "What a dreadful woman."

"Oh, she's not so bad. She's lived here all her life, and doesn't know any better." The sidewalk was hard to see; we soon returned to the depressing house where the twins lived. I'd left my car there. Harry and I went behind the large old house to the back door, and I smelled cooking odors, onions, maybe. I didn't know about Harry, but I'd made up my mind not to spend the night in Buffalo Crossing. The place made me uneasy.

"It's creepy here," I whispered to Harry. "It's a ghost town."

"Nonsense," Harry protested. "You're being dramatic, just like your mother." I wasn't sure if he was angry or teasing me. We walked up three cement stairs to a little overhang. Harry knocked on the back door.

"Yeah?" a gruff voice said. Moments later, a tall man opened the door. He was stooped, with thinning gray hair and an angular face. He looked at Harry, then he looked at me.

"Who are you?" he asked, fixing his eyes on me. "I'm not buying anything."

"Earl," Harry said, stepping in front, "it's me, Harry."

The old man stared hard, then said, "wait here a minute." He closed the door, and came back a few moments later wearing glasses. He left us standing there in the cold.

"Harry Carlson?" he said. His expression changed. I can't say he looked happy, but he looked less angry.

"Yes, Earl, it's me," Harry said.

"Well, get your butt in here," the old man said. "Bring your friend, too. If he's with you, well, he's all right."

Harry and I went in to the kitchen. The room was huge. The linoleum floor and appliances looked old, but it was spotlessly clean. On the ancient stove, a pot of something simmered.

"I'm making chili," Earl said. "You guys want a beer?"

"Sure," Harry said; I declined. I had to use the bathroom; they surely had one. I hadn't seen an outhouse. It was too warm in the kitchen, and I began to feel drowsy in spite of my discomfort. I was hungry, and my stomach growled noisily. Harry laughed.

"Hold on, it won't be long," Earl said, stirring the pot.

"Earl, I don't think you've met my son Rico," Harry said.

"Don't believe I have," Earl said, not looking at me. "Didn't know you had kids. This the only one?"

"The one and only," Harry assured him.

"You sure about that?" Earl asked, slyly. Finally he looked at me. His eyes were bloodshot, and his lenses were thick. I wondered how good his vision was. "You're father is a rascal," Earl confided. "He had a way with the ladies."

"That was a long time ago," Harry said, sounding pleased.

"I didn't know you got married," Earl said. "Last I heard, you had a girlfriend. But you weren't married."

"Can I use your bathroom?" I asked, not sure how much longer I could hold it.

"Right there," Earl said, pointing at a door near where we were standing.

Harry sat at the kitchen table, and Earl returned to the stove. I went into the bathroom. When the bathroom is off the kitchen, it is a sign a house is old. In the past, plumbing was trickier and more expensive, and all the plumbing was in a small area of the house.

The bathroom was large, too, and there was a huge claw foot tub. The walls were covered with ancient- looking wallpaper, which was peeling away near the high ceiling.

I tried to pee quietly, and turned on the faucet. I washed my hands, and went back out to the kitchen. Earl was guffawing, and I assumed Harry had told one of his off-color jokes. Harry smiled wryly, and looked away. I was right. I know the old man.

I sat down at the wooden table next to Harry.

"You want a beer, son?" Earl asked.

"You have a diet cola?" I asked. I know real men don't drink diet soda, but it never hurts to ask.

"Don't think so, but help yourself to whatever you see in the icebox," Earl said.

I opened the door of the old fridge, half expecting to see its temperature regulated by a block of ice. The refrigerator door was covered with flag decals and a bumper sticker that said "I want my country back." So Earl was a right- winger. I found some juice, and poured it into a glass Earl had set out for me. Sitting back at the kitchen table, I gazed around the room. The wallpaper was peeling in the top corners of this room, too. In some places near the high ceiling, whole sheets were missing, and you could see the plaster. The cabinets were painted white. Besides the flag decals, the only decorations in the room were religious calendars with color pictures of an Aryan-looking Jesus. This Jesus looked as Swedish as Harry.

Earl set out some bowls and plates, and the three of us began to eat.

"Say the blessing," Earl told Harry.

Harry looked uncomfortable. He hadn't told his old friends about his conversion to Judaism. Earl looked at Harry, then said, "All right, I'll say it, then." He muttered a few words I could hardly hear, and then looked up at us. "Amen!" he said loudly. "Amen!" Harry and I echoed reflexively.

The three of us were silent, and began to eat. The chili was pretty good, nicely seasoned. I was hungry. It was a little meatier than I would have liked, and greasy. Suddenly the back door flew open. It was so sudden and unexpected I cried out. Buffalo Crossing made me nervous.

"Sorry," I said. Harry laughed at my skittishness.

Another large man entered the room. I assumed it was Darrel. He seemed much younger than Earl. Although they were twins, Darrel looked strong, full of life. Maybe he was in better health. Darrel recognized Harry immediately. He didn't know what to make of me, though.

"Harry," the man said, shaking Harry's hand vigorously. "It's been a long time."

"This is my son, Rico," Harry said, for the third time that evening. "He's moving to Omaha to teach." Darrel shook my hand. His handshake was firm. Like his brother, he was tall, but he wasn't as skinny, or stooped over like Earl. Darrel's full head of blonde hair was turning white, and looked distinguished. He wasn't a bad looking man.

Darrel got a bowl, and helped himself to chili. Earl was quiet during the meal. It was clear that Darrel was the more outgoing of the two.

I was curious about the rest of the house. A door that surely led to other rooms was closed. The kitchen was clean, that was certain, but it wasn't homey. The house was old and not particularly well- maintained. The furniture, at least in the kitchen, was dilapidated.

Most men, even bachelors, have nice homes, and take an interest in creating a warm, inviting space. Almost anyone can turn a house into a home, but the twins' place was the opposite. The brothers had turned a home into a house. It was old, certainly, but that wasn't what made the place so uncomfortable, almost menacing. The house matched the town. It looked like the set from a horror movie, and I expected to see Norman Bates or Freddie Krueger come in at any moment. The uber-patriotic flag decals on the fridge, and the religious calendars made it seem like an unfriendly church or cult.

We finished eating, and Darrel took the bowls to the sink.

"When was this house built?" I asked, curious. It looked Victorian to me, but I am neither an architect nor an historian.

"1910, I think," Earl said. "This here kitchen was built later, added on."

"And you two share the house?" I continued.

"Earl's got the arthritis, so he takes the downstairs, and I stay mainly in the upstairs," Darrel answered.

We fell silent. I heard creaking above me, and looked up at the ceiling. It sounded like someone was walking across a wooden floor upstairs. The brothers didn't seem to notice, but I wondered who else was there.

"You have a roommate?" I asked. It was none of my business. Darrel grinned at me, and said to Earl, "He heard the footsteps."

Harry smiled, too, and I felt excluded from some inside joke. Finally, Harry said, "They have a ghost." As if to punctuate his words, the lights dimmed, and then became bright again.

"Really?" I asked skeptically. "The ghost affects the power?"

"That was the wind," Darrel answered.

"The house is old," Earl said. "Lots of the family died here. Some of them don't want to leave."

If I were a phantom, I would want to get the hell out. I was more determined than ever to leave the place as soon as I could. I don't believe in ghosts, but the house, the town--- they were creepy. I didn't care that much for the twins, either. Darrel was OK, but I didn't want to know his politics.

"That your little car out there?" Darrel asked me.

"Yes," I answered. "It gets great gas mileage."

"Folks here drive trucks," Earl said, making it a jab at my masculinity.

"Harry, I got something to show you," Darrel said, standing, and walking across the old linoleum to the closed door. Harry followed, and so did I. I didn't feel like being alone with Earl. I felt even less comfortable with him. At least Darrel talked.

Darrel opened the door, and we walked into a spacious dining room. A large table in the middle of the room was piled high with books and magazines. Darrel flipped a light switch, and an old chandelier cast dim light around the room. It was clean, but not tidy; there was painted beadboard wainscoting half way up the walls; the plaster was painted a sickly beige. Darrel walked to the table, and picked up a photograph.

"Look what I found," he said, showing the picture to Harry.

Harry smiled, and motioned for me to come over. The light was so dim, I wasn't sure I'd be able to see. I looked at the photo and tried to keep from starting. It was the same picture I'd found on Harry's workbench--an old sepia photo of the three little boys I'd dreamed about. It was the same picture I'd seen in Harry's garage.

"That was the three of us when we were kids," Harry explained.

A shiver ran down my spine. Why, how, had I dreamed of the children before I'd seen the photo? The three little blonde haired boys all looked alike. I couldn't tell who was who, and I asked Harry to tell me.

"That's kind of hard to say," Harry admitted. "That's me," he said, pointing at the child in the middle. The young Harry looked serious, intense. The little boys didn't look happy and carefree, like most children do. They looked secretive, as if they were hiding something. For some reason, Sister Eveline's words came into my mind. "He's not who he seems to be," she said. I felt uneasy, and I wondered about Harry's friendship with the twins. How could he remain friends with such strange men? He knew their politics were objectionable. Maybe I was just fatigued, but I fought the urge to run.

I looked out the dining room window. The moon was just a tiny crescent, and the stars shone brightly. I tried to remember the last time I had seen so many stars. The tiny streetlight didn't block the bright winter starlight. I could see the Archer's belt.

"Harry," I said suddenly, "we should go. It's getting late. Shall I leave you here for the night? I can come get you after I get settled, day after tomorrow."

Harry was still looking at the photo, and seemed lost in another world. "What, Ric?" he asked. "Oh, yes, we should be on our way. It's been good to see you, Darrel."

"You're both welcome to spend the night," Darrel said. "There's plenty of room, we have a few empty beds here." Given the house's size, I didn't doubt it.

"That's kind," Harry said, wavering.

"I should go then," I said, insistently. I wanted to leave. I didn't like Buffalo Crossing. The twins and their creepy old house made me uncomfortable. Darrel and Earl had fed me, and they were Harry's friends. I wasn't being rational, but I had a visceral fear, something I couldn't explain. I had to leave-- I had to. I walked back to the kitchen, and Harry followed me reluctantly.

Back in the kitchen, Earl was listening to the radio as he did the dishes. "The wages of sin is death!" a radio preacher cried. "Death! Eternal hellfire!" The volume was loud, and seemed to echo all around the kitchen. "Your homosexuals are going to hell, so are your fornicators," the preacher went on. "So are your Muslims and Jews." The radio preacher pronounced "Jews" with two syllables. I looked at Harry, and he colored slightly. Would he really spend the night in the house? I wondered.

"Thanks for supper," I called to Earl loudly, as I left the house. "Nice to meet you, Darrel." I didn't shake either of their hands. I wondered if hospitality would have been offered if they knew Harry and I were Jews, and I was a gay one.

67

Harry and Darrel followed me outside. I wanted to run to my car. I walked quickly, and the two men rushed to keep up. "Harry, you'll need your overnight bag," I said. I hadn't locked my car; I didn't think Buffalo Crossing was a high- crime town. The inhabitants I'd met were all over 60. I wasn't sure there more than three people in Buffalo Crossing, anyway. The houses looked abandoned.

Harry looked ambivalent. "I hate to have you drive by yourself," he said.

"I'm a big boy," I teased. "It's not much farther to Omaha, is it?"

"A couple of hours," Darrel assured me. "Look, I've got business there day after tomorrow. I can give Harry a ride." Omaha had the state's largest airport, and Harry planned to fly back to Boulder. He was returning stand-by; he was retired and had no tight schedule.

"Great, thanks, nice to meet you," I said hurriedly. I almost thrust Harry's overnight backpack at him.

"Rico," Harry said, "call me with your new address. Maybe Darrel will take me to see your place before I go."

"OK," I said, giving Harry a quick hug. I was eager to get away. I didn't like night driving, but I liked Buffalo Crossing even less. I would get to Omaha too late to call Rabbi Braun, but I could check into a cheap motel and call him in the morning. "Thanks for supper," I said to Darrel, as I got in the car. I drove away from the strange house, and was relieved to leave the town of Buffalo Crossing. I wasn't anxious to see the twins again. If the rest of the state was like this, I didn't think I would be happy.

Chapter 6

I was pleasantly surprised: I liked Omaha from the first. I wasn't seeing it at the best time of year; there was snow on the ground, and along the curbs slush was turning black. The city itself was lovely, even in wintertime. It has an urban feel, with two colleges. Omaha isn't the state capital, but it is an important business center. A number of large companies are headquartered there. In addition, Omaha has theater and a Jewish community. It is the birthplace of Malcolm X, with a large African American population as well.

I stayed in a chain hotel that first night, and called Rabbi Braun the following morning. He gave me directions to the Jewish community center, where I met him. It was on a tree- lined boulevard in a newer part of town, and I tried to picture it in spring time.

"Welcome to Omaha," Rabbi Braun said. "I hope you'll be happy here. Maybe it will work out for you to stay on." My contract was for five months, the winter/spring semester. The meatpacking plant gave part of my salary, and the money for teaching refugees came from the government. There was no guarantee of future funding, and Rabbi Braun had been upfront about the temporary nature of the job.

The young, red-headed rabbi took me on a tour of the community center. It was large, and there were a number of classrooms. After I'd looked all around, he told me that I wouldn't be working in the building. I was confused.

"This building is mainly administration. You'll be teaching in a school near downtown. The center rents it, and we have you and some other classes there because it's close to the students, not too far from the meatpacking plant. We don't have great mass-transit in Omaha."

I signed my contract, and filled out all the necessary paperwork. "Thanks for thinking of me, Rabbi Braun," I said. "I hope you will be pleased with my work."

"Call me Marc," he said. "And you're helping us out. Our regular teacher has been sick. Did your friend come with you?"

"No," I said, but didn't offer any more information. There would be time for that later. Besides, our roles had changed. Marc was no longer my confidant and counselor; he was my employer. It was nice of him to ask about Terry.

Marc got in his car, and I followed him away from the suburbs to the downtown. I would teach all my classes in the same location, three sections of English, he'd explained. In the morning, I was to have Spanish speakers from the kosher meatpacking plant; mid-day, there were political refugees from Africa and the Middle East. In the afternoon, I would teach the late shift of Spanish- speaking factory workers. It was good of the meat plant to pay for its employees to learn English. I worried that the immigrant labor was paid too cheaply. If they were paying fairly, they would find local workers. I kept those thought to myself.

Driving away from the suburbs, I began to get a sense of the city. Marc explained the terrain for me. The suburbs, where the main community center is, are west of town; downtown is long and goes for many blocks. East of downtown, there is the Old Market area, consisting of old, red- brick buildings. There are restaurants and art galleries in the Old Market, and it borders the Missouri River. North Omaha is predominantly African American, and south of town is farmland.

The place where I was teaching, the school the Jewish community center rented, was near to north Omaha, which is economically challenged. Both the workers at the plant and the refugees live in that area. The community center made the wise choice to offer its classes near the students. There was no sign in front of the school; Jewish community centers are often discrete. I wondered what that said about Omaha.

Marc showed me around the school building; it was old, but well-maintained. There were other classes taught here; besides my English classes, there were parenting seminars, exercise, and Jewish genealogy. Marc had a small office in this building, too.

He gave me directions and the key to the apartment the center had found for me. No doubt it belonged to one of their donors. I was grateful not to have to look for housing. There was too little time. "If it works out for you to stay in Omaha, you can always find some place you like better," Marc had told me. "But in the meantime, you should be OK there."

I thanked him, and drove the short distance downtown to my new apartment. It was furnished, so all I'd had to bring with me were clothes, books, and my laptop. I would be living in a large old house that had been converted into three apartments. It was nothing like the big old farmhouse in Buffalo Crossing where the twins lived. One of the apartments was empty, but Marc told me the other one was inhabited by a police officer. It gave me a sense of security, not that I didn't feel safe in Omaha. I couldn't help contrast my positive feelings about this city compared to the unhappiness I had in Georgia. If only the weather in southeast Nebraska was as mild as it was down South.

My apartment was on the second floor; I went in from what had once been the entry hall of the house. I had the key to the front door; in the entry way there were mailboxes to all three apartments. The rest of the downstairs was sealed off, consisting of an empty apartment. The third floor apartment was accessed from an outside stairwell, and that was where the cop lived.

I unpacked my car, taking clothes and boxes up the flight of stairs that led to my apartment. There wasn't a carport, which was a definite disadvantage; I had to park on the street. It would be shady in the summer, though, since the street was lined with large old trees. In the winter, many of the branches were covered with ice. Omaha felt colder than Boulder, though the temperature wasn't much lower. Maybe it was the humidity. And in the two days I'd been in Nebraska, I hadn't seen the sun at all.

The floors of my apartment were hardwood, and there were gas space heaters in the living room, kitchen and bedroom. The kitchen was less than inspiring; it had a two burner stove, microwave and small refrigerator. It was the smallest room in the apartment, and looked like it had been an afterthought in 1945, not changed since. It had a tiny table that barely sat two.

It didn't take me long to unpack. I took the final box in, and turned on the gas heater in the living room. It didn't automatically light. Luckily, there was a box of matches in the bathroom. You're supposed to crack a window when you have a gas space heater on, which seems counterproductive, but otherwise there is the chance that fumes accumulate. It's an old-fashioned way to heat an apartment. The house was old, full of charm and idiosyncrasy. The conversion into an apartment was awkward; the second story had probably been all bedrooms originally.

I began to organize things, putting my books on an empty bookcase. The textbooks I'd ordered had come in time, as had the Spanish and Arab-English dictionaries. I hadn't brought a TV, and there wasn't one in the apartment. I could buy a small one, it wouldn't be expensive. There were dishes in the kitchen, but I wished I'd brought some of my own pans. There were some worn towels in the bathroom, and some drab looking sheets in the bedroom. Luckily, there were a lot of blankets. Terry hadn't brought household items with him when he'd come from Georgia, and if I'd taken my own stuff from Boulder, he would have to buy things. Thinking about Terry made me lonely. The month we'd had together in Boulder had been so happy.

I sat down in front of the heater, feeling tired from the newness. Someone knocked on the door. I must have left the front door to the house unlocked; there was a buzzer down at the entry, which hadn't buzzed. Harry and Darrel stood there. I'd called Harry to give him my new address. He came a day early.

"Come in, guys," I said, giving Harry a hug. Although the two men were about the same age, Darrel looked younger. Farming life agreed with him; he could have passed for late 40's instead of early 60's. I went to the kitchen to get ice water for them; I'd passed a small store, but hadn't picked up anything. I'd have to do some serious grocery shopping. Back in the living room, Darrel was looking at my books.

"You're quite a reader," he said, glancing at the titles. I wasn't sure how he intended that comment, so I said nothing.

"Did you have a good visit?" I asked. I wondered if they still had anything in common. I was curious if Harry had been able to navigate through the right-wing politics.

"It was fine," Harry said. "I do thank you, Darrel. And thanks for bringing me up here."

"Glad to do it," Darrel said. "Well, I'll head out, if your son can take you to the airport."

"Sure," I said. I glanced at Harry. I had the feeling he'd been eager to get away from Darrel. Harry sat on the sofa, looking relieved, and we heard Darrel walking down the stairs.

"Not a bad place," Harry said, looking around the apartment.

"It's fine," I said. "What time do you need to be at the airport? How was your visit?" I asked. "Did you get your fill of radio preaching? You told them you're Jewish?"

"My flight leaves at 2:30," Harry answered. I glanced at my watch. It was just after 11:00 a.m. He didn't seem eager to talk about the visit, or answer my questions.

"Should we grab a bite?" I asked.

"Sure," Harry said, "I know where I'd like to go."

We bundled up. A cold wind blew, and the chill went right through me. The skies were gray. Harry directed me to a restaurant south of downtown, just past the Old Market area. The façade of the building was brick, and a small sign said "Czech Corner." We parked, entered, and found ourselves in a homey, ethnic café.

"My favorite place to eat in Omaha," Harry said. "It's been here for years." The waiter directed us to a booth. "We'll have two lunch specials," Harry told the waiter.

"Shouldn't you find out what it is?" I asked Harry.

"You won't be disappointed with whatever they serve," Harry said.

"What if it's not kosher?" I asked, with mock disapproval.

"Like that's ever stopped you," Harry said, rolling his eyes.

"So tell me about your visit," I said.

"It was OK," Harry said vaguely. "They're nice enough. And Earl's a good cook. But I've changed a lot since I lived there. The twins haven't. They're so conservative. I wonder if I was ever like that. I hope not." He fell silent. "Back in the day, we all went to the Lutheran church in town. Now the church is gone, torn down."

"You can't go home again," I said.

"Thank you Tom Wolfe. But look, if you ever have a problem, need something, your car breaks down or something, you can call them. Darrel says they come up to Omaha a lot. I don't agree with their politics, but they have good hearts."

"If my car breaks down, I'll call the auto service," I said. It is just like Harry to think of my welfare. He's been a great stepdad. I'm lucky, and I know it.

Harry didn't talk any more about his visit with the twins. The waiter brought us two heaping plates filled with central European food. There was sausage, sauerkraut, and bread dumplings. It was delicious. Harry and I ate in silence, enjoying the meal.

"Next time I come, we'll have runzas," Harry said. "They're like knishes."

"I like this place. I'll come back here," I said. I approved of Harry's dining choice.

Harry smiled. It was time to take Harry to the airport; we had to hurry. The meal took longer than I'd thought. They served a lot of food, and there was some to take home with me.

Before he boarded, Harry took something from his pocket and handed it to me.

"What's this?" I asked, opening a package wrapped with tissue paper. It was a *Mogen David*, a silver star of David. I looked at Harry.

"You have something from your father," Harry said, referring to the cufflinks I wear around my neck. "I wanted you to have something from me, too."

I had trouble speaking for a moment. I hate getting all emotional, but I was touched. I cleared my throat, and thanked him. "You'll check on Terry?" I asked, as Harry boarded the plane.

"Of course," Harry said. "I like Terry. Good luck, Ric."

"He doesn't know many people in Boulder," I said. I felt anxious, *agitato*. I was in a new city, and I didn't have friends. I wished Harry could stay, and I wanted Terry and my mother, too. Is it wrong to want family around? Is it childish and immature? I didn't remember being this upset when I'd moved to Georgia.

"Take care," Harry said, giving me a quick hug. I watched as he boarded the plane. I drove back to my new apartment. It didn't feel like home, and I was disoriented, *verklempt*. I worried about my new job, and I missed Terry. I'd been lucky, living in a place I loved with the man I loved, with friends and family close by. Now, everything had changed.

I called Terry. I knew he was probably at work, and might not be able to talk. Hearing his voice on the answering machine reassured me, though.

"Just calling to say I love you," I said, "*Ich liebe dikh, bubele*." I unconsciously repeated the words my mother said to me; they mean "I love you, dear," in Yiddish. I hung up. I sat on the sofa. My arms were sore from lugging up the boxes, and I couldn't quite bring myself to unpack the last one, or put my clothes in the dresser.

I must have dozed for a while; I was woken up by a knocking on the door. I would definitely learn to close the downstairs front door harder. I wasn't expecting anyone, and I went to open it slowly. An old man in faded clothes was standing there. He didn't look or smell dirty, but he wasn't a salesman. He looked homeless and lost. The poor guy was probably mentally ill. I hoped evening visits from the homeless wouldn't be an everyday occasion. Surely there was a shelter nearby. I didn't like to think of a confused, older man out alone in the cold. It was sad.

"I'm sorry to bother you, but I wonder if you've seen Darrel."

"Hey, come in," I said, finally recognizing the unkempt man as Earl. "He was here earlier, with Harry."

Earl came in, his face red from the cold. His breathing was labored, and I wondered if the stairs had winded him. He looked old, much older than his brother or Harry, who was his same age. How did Earl know where I lived? Harry must have told him. Maybe he'd asked Earl to check on me.

"Darrel brought Harry just before noon," I said. It was sweet that the old guy was worried about his brother. They say twins have a special bond. I studied Earl. There was a softness about him I didn't expect in a farmer. Harry said he had never married, and I wondered for a moment if he was gay. It would have been difficult for a man of his generation, living in a small town.

"I'm sorry to trouble you, then," Earl said, gruffly, looking uncomfortable. "He didn't answer his cell phone, but sometimes he doesn't. The seed man came by, and I didn't know what Darrel wanted."

He smiled slightly, and then handed me a book. "I remember you saying you were a teacher, so I brought you something to read." He thrust a small, black book in my hand.

"Thanks," I said, confused. It was a Bible. I wondered if concern for his brother had been a pretext to evangelize. "It's nice of you, but I have one. Maybe you'd like to give it to someone else who doesn't."

Earl was insistent. I took it from him, and there was a moment of uncomfortable silence. I looked in his eyes. They were pale blue, and his coloring was similar to Terry's. Would Terry look like him when he was old, I wondered. Would Terry and I still be together when we were Earl's age? I believed our love was *beshert*, destined. But surely every divorced couple in the world once believed their love would last forever. Sometimes love isn't enough.

"I'll go now," Earl said softly.

"I'm sure Darrel's fine. Drive safely," I said, gently closing the door as he slowly walked down the stairs.

As I set the Bible on my desk, two leaflets fell out from between the covers. The first one read "Why Jews need to accept Jesus." Apparently Harry told the twins we are Jewish. The second tract alarmed me more; it was entitled "The coming race war." What race war was coming? Was Earl a racist? I looked on the back page; it had been printed in Omaha, the copyright simply said "RaceWars.com." That was interesting. I'd read Omaha was the birthplace of Malcolm X; it also seemed to be a hotbed of bigotry.

Curious, I glanced through the pamphlet, and read about the "danger" of urban blacks, and the "horror" of brown immigrants. Immigrants, the tract said, brought disease and disorder. I was hired to teach brown immigrants. Worse still, according to the leaflet, were Muslims. They are all terrorists, the tract's author claimed.

I sat back on the sofa, tired and sad. I had another box to unpack, but I just stared at it. I tried to put Earl's strange visit out of my mind, and then dozed off again.

It was very dark when I woke up, and I was cold. It took me a minute to remember where I was. The little gas heater had gone out, and I got up. I'd left a window cracked, so I didn't think I'd poisoned the air. Cautiously, I lit another match, but the flame didn't take. I'd have to call the landlord. I hated those old gas heaters. Couldn't the landlord spring for a furnace? Maybe I'd buy a couple of electric heaters. I heard footsteps above me, and figured the cop must be home. He wasn't too noisy, but I could hear him walking around. It was reassuring, and I felt less alone.

I wished I could watch the evening news, but without a TV that was impossible, and I didn't have local Internet service for my computer yet. There was a clock radio next to the bed, and I turned it on to hear the headlines.

"Once again," the news announcer said, "the chief of police has been murdered. His mutilated body was found in a field outside the city limits." I didn't want to hear any more. It was surprising to think of such a terrible crime happening in America's heartland, but there is violence everywhere.

I switched to a music station. I turned it up so I could hear it in the other rooms. I hoped it wouldn't disturb the upstairs neighbor. I didn't want to anger a cop. I went to the kitchen for something to eat. I had the leftovers from lunch to nosh on.   I nuked them in the microwave; they were still yummy. I wondered when Terry would call back.

I went back to the living room, and saw the final box. I decided to unpack it, then take the empty boxes back down to the car. I could fold them up and store them in the trunk.   I took out some books and pens. Then I came across something that I was sure didn't belong to me: a hunting knife.

I stared at the evil- looking thing. It was at the very bottom of the box, beneath some books. It was in a leather pouch, and I pulled it out. It was dagger-like; the blade was probably six inches long, and slightly curved, "c"- shaped. A scimitar, I think they call it. It was sharp on both sides. The knife must belong to Terry. It's the kind of thing a butcher would have. I smiled, remembering his Halloween costume, a bloody butcher's apron. He'd come to the door brandishing a knife, I couldn't remember if it was this one. Had Terry put it in my box as a joke?

I made myself a mental note to ask Terry about the knife. I wished he would call. It was just past 8 o'clock his time, and he was probably still at work.

I put the last book in the bookcase, and then went downstairs. I put the folded boxes in the trunk. I closed the front door of the building hard, but the latch didn't catch. That was why people could get up the stairs to my apartment. At least I had a deadbolt on my door. It was cold outside, and I thought about the inadequate gas space heater. I looked back at the house, and saw lights on the third floor, the apartment above me. Should I ask my neighbor, the cop about the heat? It would help to talk to someone who lived in the building. Maybe there was some trick to it.

I went to the outside stairwell, and climbed the steep stairs. Any cop that walked three flights of stairs to get home would be in good shape. I knocked on the outside door. I hoped he would answer; I knew he was home since I'd heard footsteps. I waited a few moments. When I was about to go back downstairs, the door opened. A woman in her mid 30's stood there. That was why he'd taken so long to answer: his girlfriend was visiting.

"Oh, I'm sorry. I didn't mean to bother you. Is your boyfriend around?" The woman stared at me. She was pretty: she had jet black hair and a dark complexion. Her eyes were red, and I wondered if she'd been crying. Maybe they'd had a quarrel.

"My boyfriend? What do you want?" she said, icily. "Who are you?"

"I live beneath you, on the second floor. I was wondering if your boyfriend could take a look at the heater. It doesn't stay lit, and I wondered if he knows some trick to it I don't. I'm Rico Wise; I just moved here from Boulder."

"My boyfriend?" she repeated, stonily. She looked ready to slam the door closed.

"Yeah, the cop. They said I lived below a policeman."

The woman slowly reached behind, and brought something off the counter. She thrust a police badge in my face. "I'm Officer Gans," she said. "You having fun with this little joke of yours? I'm not laughing."

I blushed. What had Rabbi Braun said, policeman or police officer? If he'd said police officer, I'd just assumed it was a man. Shame on me--- I was sexist. Still, it wasn't like I'd said something deliberately rude. Her anger was disproportionate.

"Oh, I'm sorry," I stammered. "You're the police officer, yes, I see. I don't want to disturb you." I cleared my throat, nervously. "Where do you grocery shop around here? I saw a Quick Mart, but not a grocery."

She gave me directions to a nearby store. "If you want organic, you have to drive across town." She wasn't friendly, but at least she didn't close the door in my face.

I decided to push my luck. "Do you know about these gas heaters?" I asked. "I can't get them to stay on. It's so cold. Think I should just go buy an electric heater?"

"Don't set the building on fire," she said, humorlessly. "Give me a minute, I'll be down." She closed the door firmly on me.

I went down the stairwell. I had to walk down the steep outside stairs, then into the house. The third floor mailbox was in the entry way, so I assumed she had a key to the entry way. I went to my living room, and waited. A half-hour later, she knocked on the front door.

She was pretty, I thought again, as she came in. She was taller than me; it might have been her shoes, maybe it was the fact that she wore her hair swept up. She was elegant, looking more like a model than a cop. She wasn't warm and cuddly, but then, I considered her profession. Besides, the police chief had just been murdered. Maybe she knew him. I know the world is a violent place; my own father was killed. I feel kinship with crime victims.

Officer Gans walked over to the wall heater, lit a match, and the flame came on instantly. I felt like a *schlimazel.*

"Thanks," I said. "I must have been doing something wrong."

"You must have been," she said.

I extended my hand, but she didn't shake it. Maybe she was afraid I was hitting on her. She didn't know how safe she was.

"I'm Lisa, by the way," she said, as if sharing her first name pained her. She glanced at the knife on the bookcase, and looked questioningly at me.

"That's not mine," I said. But why was I telling her that? It was none of her business. Knives aren't illegal. Officer Lisa turned, and made her way to the door. "I heard the news about the police chief," I said, before she left. "I'm very sorry to hear it. Did you know him? It must be a shock to the whole department. What a terrible loss." I almost told her about my own father, but I didn't think I'd be seeing much of Lisa Gans.

She turned and faced me. For a moment, just a moment, the hardness in her expression melted, and she looked human. I wondered if she was going to cry.

"I knew him," she said, softly. She turned to go, and then added, "welcome to Omaha, Mr. Wise. You'll like it here. I've lived here 15 years." Her words were kinder than her tone. It wasn't clear whether she meant she'd lived 15 years in Omaha, or 15 years in the apartment above me. She was beautiful, exotic-looking: it might be a liability in her line of work.

"Nice to meet you," I said, softly. "Thanks for lighting the heater. I feel a little lost right now, everything's so new."

She turned back to face me, nodded, and then left.

Before I went to bed, I reached in my pocket and found the *Mogen David* Harry gave me. I set it on the bookcase; I wasn't sure whether to get a chain for it, and wear it around my neck, or attach it to my key chain.

I wondered why I hadn't heard from Terry, and felt a little miffed. Surely he wasn't that busy. I checked my cell phone for messages, but there was nothing. I'd called him twice that day, and hadn't heard back. He was probably busy at work. I was hurt. I thought about calling him again, but decided against it. I wasn't in the right frame of mind. I wanted Terry to call me because he wanted to, not because he was in trouble for not calling.

I wondered, sadly, when I would see him next. With my job, I would have weekends off. Terry would probably work most weekends. Boulder doesn't have blue laws, and grocery stores are open on Sundays. His two days off might not even be consecutive. On those sad thoughts, I went to bed.

My nightmares returned that night. I dreamed of the three little blond haired boys. I stood at a distance, watching them. They played hide and seek, and one of them ran away. "Come back," I called to him. "You need to play where I can see you," I said sharply. The boy didn't return. "If you don't come back by the time I count to five, you'll be in trouble," I said angrily.

I began counting, and started looking for the lost child. "Did either of you see where he went?" I asked the other two. I didn't know the boys' names. I should have, I thought in my dream; I couldn't remember who, or even why, I was babysitting.

The landscape of my dream suddenly changed. The children were gone, and I was at a fair or carnival. I saw a mysterious- looking psychic. She wore dark glasses, and a long black dress. "I'll tell your fortune," she said.

"No," I said. "I don't want that."

"You must. Sit," she said, in a harsh voice. I sat down at a table facing her. The fortune teller set down three Tarot cards. "The one you pick will tell your future," she said. I stared at the three cards, and chose the one in the middle. The old woman picked it up, and showed me. "The hangman!" she said, laughing at me. "Death! You've chosen death!"

"No," I shouted, leaving her table. I tried to run, but I couldn't. I was frozen in place.

"Death!" the old woman said again. "You chose death!"

I woke up, and sat upright in bed, not sure if I'd shouted for real or just in my dream. I felt bad. If I'd screamed, I would have woken Terry up. "Terry," I said. I felt the bed next to me, but Terry wasn't there. That made me more scared. Then I remembered. Terry isn't here, I was all alone. I got up, and turned on the bedroom light. I wished I'd had a TV or Internet connection; I didn't want to go back to sleep. It was cold in the bedroom; the gas heater didn't put out enough heat. I would buy an electric space heater, I decided.

I turned on the radio. Although it was tuned to a music station, there was more news of the police chief's gruesome murder. His name was Will Herman, and he had been recently appointed. He was a reformer: the police department had been riddled with accusations of racism and incompetence. The new chief had been chosen to clean things up. They gave a brief biography of Chief Herman, who sounded like a *mensch,* a good man. Although they didn't say as much, it sounded like his politics were progressive. A new bit of information was added; his body, found in a field outside of town, happened to be near a small motel.

I turned the radio off, and thought of my upstairs neighbor. Lisa Gans had known the police chief. I thought of her reaction when I'd mentioned him. What was it that I'd seen on her face? I closed my eyes and tried to remember. It had been more than just sadness.

I wanted to fall back asleep, but I couldn't. I went to the living room, which was even colder than the bedroom. I looked out the window. It was snowing. I took a novel off the bookshelf, and began to read. I grew drowsy, and finally fell asleep.

I woke up groggy the next morning, chilled to the bone. I'd fallen asleep on the sofa, without re-lighting the heater. The window was frost- covered; I looked out. There was a lot of snow on the ground. I searched for my watch, and heard my cell phone ringing. It was Terry. My heart grew warmer just hearing his voice.

"I'm sorry I didn't call yesterday," he said. "Things got crazy at work, and I had to put in some overtime."

We chatted for a while. I told him about Earl and Darrel, the Bible and booklets Earl had given me.

"Geez, Ric, are you living in Nebraska or the Appalachians? Those two sound creepy. I can't believe they're friends of Harry."

"Harry must have changed a lot since he was a child," I said, "or else the twins have. I guess everyone changes." For some reason, my thoughts returned to Sister Eveline and her warning about a dark shadow pursuing me. I grew thoughtful.

"Are you there, Ric?"

I came back to the present, and saw the hunting knife on the book case. "I packed one of your knives by mistake," I said.

"Really? I don't think I'm missing anything. A kitchen knife?"

"No, some kind of hunting knife, like a scimitar. You'll see when you get here." I paused. "When can you come for a visit?" There was silence at the other end.

"I'll surprise you, Rico. When will you come back home? Even if I'm at work on the weekends, we'll have time together at night. I miss that already."

"Absolutely," I said. As good as it was to hear Terry's voice, it filled me with sadness. I love Terry, and I wanted to be with him. "I miss you, Terr-bear," I said. "I love you." I was cold, tired, and emotional.

"Me too," Terry said, "but don't call me that again, OK?" I thought it was cute, but he's touchy that way. We said goodbye. I thought about the old song, that goes something like, "you've got to win a little, lose a little, always have the blues a little… that's the story of love."

Chapter 7

My classes began, and I had less time to feel lonely. My first section of English consisted mainly of Latinos working at the kosher meat packing plant, owned and operated by the Katzenheim brothers. I saw a beautiful sea of dark faces first thing in the morning; there were 22 students. They seemed hard-working and eager to learn. There were some Eastern Europeans there, too, but most of the factory's workers were from Mexico, Guatemala and Honduras. Some of the mothers brought their children with them, and as long as they were well-behaved, it was fine. The Jewish center operated a day care center, but it wasn't in the same building. It is good for little ones to hear English, especially when their families speak Spanish at home.

My mid-day session consisted of political refugees. Many were from Iraq, others were from Africa, chiefly Sudan and the Congo. They represented various cultures, ethnicities and religions. The bond they shared was persecution: before me were sitting the lucky ones who had managed to escape. I knew from what I'd read and been told that this would make many of them more compassionate and understanding. Others would be hardened by their terrible experiences. Most managed to maintain their humanity, though, and I hoped the community center would help them in that struggle. There was limited counseling available for refugees; some had post-traumatic stress disorder from their ordeals.

My last class, in late afternoon, was again workers from the Katzenheim meatpacking plant. They came to me after working a full-day, and they had to fight mental fatigue and physical weariness. I needed to make learning lively; this was at the end of my day, too, when I was tired. I had to keep their attention. Again, some brought their children with them. The children were remarkably well-behaved. Katzenheim brothers were paying my salary, and I aimed to accommodate their workers however possible.

Each day I managed to remember more of my students' names, and by the end of the first week, I had a general idea of who was who. I was starting to learn which students were the class clowns and which were serious.

The meatpackers were a homogenous group. Although most were Latinos, the Eastern Europeans were also family-oriented, hard-working.

The refugees were from different cultures and religions, and I wondered if there was going to be friction. Both the Iraqi and Sudanese students divided themselves into Christian and Muslim, segregating themselves by both country and religion. You can tell a lot about students' attitudes by where they sit. The Christians all sat together, and the Muslims all sat together. It's understandable, I guess. Still, I didn't want the divisions of their former countries to play out in class. In America, we're all supposed to get along.

Teaching is both exhilarating and exhausting. I had only limited interaction with the other staff of the Jewish community center; I wasn't working at the main site. It would take time for me to meet people. It isn't appropriate to befriend the students, even though they were all adults. The teacher/student relationship has certain rules, which I have to honor and respect. The students receive grades from me, and camaraderie could blur the lines.

The staff meetings were first thing Monday morning, and since I taught then, I was excused. There were some gatherings I had to attend; those were all in the new building clear across town. In fact, most of the center's programs were on the lovely new campus miles away from downtown, where I taught. Still, there were other classes besides mine at the school, including some vocational training. Marc, Rabbi Braun, wasn't in my building often.

I liked Omaha and my work; still, I missed Terry. We had been so happy during our month together in Boulder. I wished it could have lasted forever. In addition to my loneliness, the weather in Omaha got me down. The sky was low and gray, and it snowed intermittently. The first couple of weeks I was in Nebraska, I didn't see the sun at all. I couldn't remember ever being so cold.

I bought a space heater for the apartment, and it heated the rooms quickly. I didn't like messing with the gas. I took it from the living room to the bedroom when I went to sleep. The kitchen was small, and the gas heater did the trick in that room. If it failed, I kept the oven on.

Since I was new to the city, I didn't know or understand its politics. But the grisly murder of police chief Will Herman cast a shadow over the community. He was a figurehead as well as a leader, and his death symbolized society in disorder. Chief Herman's death was the main topic of discussion for the staff at the community center, on those occasions when I saw my colleagues. Standing in line at the store, it was the main topic of conversation among the shoppers.

There were various rumors about the killing. The police department released very few details, but there was talk of torture and conspiracy. Since details weren't forthcoming, speculation was rampant. There were no leads, or, if there were, the police veiled it in secrecy. People speculated about the mutilation of the chief's body; it was a gruesome detail that seemed to captivate some.

The assassination had an impact on my upstairs neighbor, Lisa. I ran into her one day when we were both checking our mailboxes. She appeared weighed down by sadness, and I asked her if she was all right. Lisa is a prickly one, and I couldn't tell if she was going to slug me for speaking to her, or if she was touched by my concern. She's difficult to read.

"I'm fine, thanks," she said, dismissively. There was a momentary crack in her veneer. That was the second time I'd seen her look almost human, not like some marble statue.

"Look," I said, "I'm new to town, and I don't know anyone here. Why don't you come up and have a cup of tea and we'll talk? I'm a good listener." I've learned from Harry how to be paternal. Harry is the world's father, and when I was growing up, my friends felt free to tell Harry their troubles, and confided in him more than they did in their own dads.

I didn't think Lisa would accept my offer, and was surprised when she did.

"All right," she said. "I'll stop by just for a minute. Thanks."

We climbed the stairs to my apartment together. "Chilly in here," she said, as we entered the living room. I didn't tell her about the electric heater I bought. I led her to the kitchen, and turned on the oven. The kitchen is the heart of any home, and people feel safe there. Mine was a small room, but there was a table and two chairs.

Lisa sat down, and I plugged in the electric kettle. I washed some fruit, and set it out. The water was soon ready, and I steeped the tea.

"Tell me about yourself," I said. "You've lived in Omaha 15 years. Have you always been a police officer?"

As we talked, I was struck again by her loveliness. Her last name could have been Jewish, but I wondered about her ethnicity. Her features were Asian, with black hair, and almond- shaped black eyes. Her coloring was as dark as mine.

"I was born in a little town east of here," Lisa said, "a little farming community. My parents ran the hardware store."

"Have you heard of a place called Buffalo Crossing?" I asked. "It's about 100 miles away."

"I've heard of it," she said. "It's mostly deserted, isn't it? That's what's happening to most of the small farming towns. People move to the cities to get jobs. They can't all be farmers."

"Are you Jewish?" I asked. "What's that like in a small town?"

The hardness returned to her face. "My parents are Jewish," she said.

It was a strange thing to say. If her parents were Jewish, then so was she. Her tone was unexpectedly hostile.

"I'm adopted," Lisa said, as if that explained her anger. It doesn't matter if she's adopted, not in Jewish ritual. If she was raised Jewish, she is Jewish.

"You had a *bat-Mitzvah*," I said.

"I was 13 years old, I didn't have a choice," she said, bitterly. "It's what my parents wanted."

"Of course it's what your parents wanted," I said, trying to keep my tone soft. I didn't want to be confrontational. She was angry, that much was clear. "Your parents loved you, and they honored their religious tradition by raising you Jewish."

"How the hell would you know about my family life?" Lisa said indignantly.

I refilled her cup with tea, and said nothing. It felt like I was dealing with a disorderly child. If an unruly student is trying to get attention by misbehavior, then it's best to ignore her, and I did. I took a deep breath, and told myself not to take the bait. Her angst wasn't about me, and whatever I said would have been wrong.

Lisa sighed. "Your kitchen is small, isn't it? So is mine. It's dark, too."

"It is dark in here," I agreed. I would have to see if the light fixture could take a brighter bulb. There were no curtains, and I wondered if that would make the room cheerier. The room was painted a stark white, and looked almost institutional.

"I'm Indian," Lisa said, out of the blue.

"From India?" I asked. That explained her exotic complexion.

"Lakota," Lisa said. "Years ago, my people lived in northeastern Nebraska, long before the white man came."

"It's a tragedy how the native people were treated," I said. "Very sad."

Lisa stared straight ahead. She was a lost child, and I felt an instinctive protectiveness. I wanted to rock her and tell her it was going to be all right. She intrigued me, and her pain touched me. Lisa was a like a stray cat that has gone partly wild. I patted her shoulder once, very gently, in the most non-sexual, non-aggressive way I knew. She still recoiled. I didn't understand her particular suffering, but I had suffered, too; everyone does. Pain is pain, it is both specific and universal. Everyone has been crapped on by fate. It's part of the human condition, and you don't grow up till you see that.

"May I ask you something?" I said, deciding to change the subject. "What happened to Chief Herman? Do they have any leads on who might have hurt him?" If a policeman, with all his training, could be assailed, then there was little hope for the rest of us. Was Omaha unsafe? Why was the murder taking so long to solve? Surely the best minds in the city were working on it.

I hoped that changing the topic from the personal to the professional would help ground Lisa, but it didn't seem to.

"Will was a good man," she said, softly.

"You worked closely with him," I said. Then, for a moment, I saw the hardness in her façade break yet again. There was something about her expression that I recognized, but I couldn't quite place. Abruptly, Lisa thanked me for the tea, and told me she had to go. As she left, her eyes wandered again to the knife on the bookcase. She shook her head slightly, and closed the door after herself.

There was something I didn't understand about Lisa, something I was missing. Her hardness was a mask; she was hiding a secret. I was curious. What had Sister Eveline said about someone not being who they seemed to be? Had Sister Eveline been talking about Lisa?

That night, I called Terry before I went to sleep. I told him about my classes, and he patiently listened as I told him about my different students, where they were from, and what they were like. I told him about Lisa, and my puzzling interaction with her.

"She sounds like a psycho, Ric," Terry said. "Geez, between her and those creepy twins, have you met anyone normal? Sounds like your students are OK, though, and that's a good thing. They're lucky to have a teacher like you."

"Thanks, Terry," I said, "Lisa is nice enough. She's just troubled. Imagine how you might feel if you were adopted." I stopped myself before I went any further. Terry had not had an easy childhood. His father was a murderer, and had hit both Terry and his mother. Terry had a rotten childhood. The difference is that Terry doesn't talk about it, and doesn't feel sorry for himself. Unlike Lisa, he doesn't go around with a chip on his shoulder.

Terry talked about his job, which he seemed to like, and some of the trying customers he had to endure. "This one lady was so rude," he explained. "Didn't it occur to her not to be mean to a man with a butcher's knife?" Terry's mention of the knife made me remember that evil- looking dagger on the bookcase, and the way Lisa looked at it.

"So what are we going to do for Valentine's Day?" Terry asked, before we said goodbye. I looked at the calendar. It was just 10 days ahead, and I hadn't even thought about it. I needed to do some shopping and planning.

"I don't know," I said. "It's our first Valentine's together, and we're apart."

"That doesn't make sense," Terry said.

"You know what I mean," I said.

Terry laughed. "There might be a Valentine's Day surprise for you."

"Are you going to have yourself delivered in a cake, Terry?"

"Not a bad idea, Ric," he said. "I'm certainly good enough to eat."

"Except for the bitter aftertaste," I teased.

"Oh, please, Ric, when it comes to bitter, you wrote the book."

"I beg your pardon," I said, feigning outrage. "I'm the nicest man I know."

"Then you should get out more," Terry said.

We laughed, and said goodbye. I missed Terry. It was strange to think of him living in my house, and me living far away. I worried about the future, and wondered if there would be a way for us to be together, or if, like so many couples, we would drift apart. I had to be content in the moment, and not worry about the future. I'm a *kvetch*, a worrier. Terry is younger than me, and better looking. Would he find someone he liked better?

I had trouble sleeping that night, tossing and turning till the early hours of the morning. The electric heater made the room hot, but if I turned it lower, the room got cold. I couldn't get comfortable. My thoughts turned round and round. I remembered the photographs I'd found in Harry's garage. I thought about the picture of the three little boys. Maybe when I found the photo, I assumed they were the children I dreamed about. Maybe I was wrong, and the kids I dreamed of were different. The mind can play tricks.

I thought about the snapshot of my mom and Harry, taken several years before they "officially" met. Harry was living in Nebraska, Mom was in New York City. How had their paths crossed, and where? I recalled the expression on Harry's face in the photograph. He was obviously in love. But Mom had married my father. Love, what a complicated thing it is.

Love--- that was it. I sat up in bad. Love. That was what I had seen in Lisa's eyes when I'd asked about the police chief. What had she said? "Will was a good man," something like that. She hadn't called him Chief Herman, she'd called him by his first name. Lisa had been in love with Will Herman. That first night when I'd asked about her boyfriend, she'd acted so odd. She thought I was asking about the police chief. I tried to remember if her boss had been married.

I got out of bed, and went to my laptop. Fortunately, the cable was configured, though I still didn't have a TV. I powered up, and scoured the Internet. There it was: Will Herman was married with three children. I was thoughtful. If he had dumped Lisa, and returned to his wife, would Lisa have killed him in a fit of rage? Could she have overpowered him? A chill ran down my spine. Was I living in the apartment beneath a murderer?

Of course, the killer could have been the chief's wife. That would explain the mutilation: it was the classic action of a woman done wrong. How had Will Herman been mutilated? I shuddered at the possibilities.

Thoughtful, I went back to bed. Was I being melodramatic? Lisa wasn't a murderer. But she was in love with the police chief. Love is not something you can hide, no matter how hard you try. I thought about Terry. No doubt my love for him was obvious to everyone. If Lisa had been having an affair, she probably didn't hide it as well as she thought. Was Lisa the killer or was it the police chief's wife? I wondered. It could have been either one.

The next day, I had an early call from Terry. He gave me two messages from my home phone.

"This guy named Ted called. He said he'd like to come and get the dresser and the sofa. Does that make any sense to you?" Terry asked. "Why is this guy trying to take your furniture?"

Ted had my cell phone and e-mail address, which he usually used. Maybe he'd called the landline by mistake. "Ted is my first husband," I said, for lack of better terminology. "The bedroom set is his, but I didn't think he wanted it. I don't know why he wants the sofa, it's old. He can have whatever he wants." I paused. "It costs a lot to move furniture. He'd do better just buying new in California."

"He seems like a nice guy," Terry said. "We talked for 15 minutes."

I felt myself coloring. Ted *is* a nice guy, but the idea of him talking to Terry made me uncomfortable. What did the two of them have to talk about? My faults, which are legion? Ted would find Terry attractive, everyone does. I felt a pang of jealousy.

"So you talked to Ted even though you don't know who he is?" I asked, sounding more accusative than I'd wished.

"I remember you telling me about a friend named Ted," Terry said. "I can buy another dresser, and sofas aren't that expensive."

I loved Ted, and we arc still friends. We'd been together for over 10 years, and I wasn't about to check old receipts to find out who had paid for what. By taking the furniture, was Ted severing all ties with me? I had momentary visions of returning to a house completely devoid of furniture. Terry had furniture back in Georgia, or had he sold it all? It would be a lot of work to move to Colorado.

"Terry, it's not my business, but do you still have your father's house in Georgia? Do you have furniture there?" I didn't want anything of his father's in my house, but that wasn't fair of me. It was *our* house, and there was nothing of Terry's there.

Terry was silent. "I should do something with the house in Georgia. I just left, closed the door, and locked up. I don't even have it rented out. It's in the country; there's a few acres, but it's not worth much."

"Does anything back there have sentimental meaning to you?" I'd asked him before, but he hadn't answered.

"You've seen the place, Ric. It's not exactly Versailles."

I didn't like thinking about his house. I'd spent the weekends there, never knowing that it held the mystery to my father's disappearance. I never wanted to go there again. If Terry wanted to bring things from Georgia, I wouldn't go back and help him. I hoped he would understand.

"And Ric, someone named Melissa wants you to call her," Terry said. He'd said nothing about what he wanted to do with the house or its furniture. "I wrote the number down. From the area code, I'd say she's calling from Georgia."

Melissa. The name didn't ring a bell; had she been one of my students? I didn't think so, but I took her phone number anyway. Terry didn't talk anymore about his father's house in Georgia. Instead, he asked about my classes.

I sensed some tension developing in the mid-day refugee class, and it was stressing me out. I told Terry about it; he's a good listener. I told him how the students separated themselves by ethnicity and religion. I worried about two of my students in particular; they were almost at each other's throats. One of the men was Muslim, the other was Chaldean Christian, and both were from Iraq. It had gotten so tense, I almost thought about talking to the rabbi about it. I hated to admit to Marc that I didn't know what to do.

"Can't people just get along?" Terry asked, sounding exasperated. "I mean, they're bringing the conflicts with them, ones that they were trying to get away from. What's wrong with people, Ric? And it's not just the folks from other countries. People who should know better act like jerks. We Americans treat each other like crap."

I thought about the twins, Darrel and Earl, and the strange pamphlet about the "coming race war." If we didn't all learn to get along, there would be conflict. But it was no good just to say the filth is in others; our task is to root out the evil in our own souls. That's the place to start. If we could wipe out the hatred in our own hearts, we would be able to help others. It's a hard task; it's too easy to be bitter and resentful.

Terry rang off, and I headed to work. The first class was great, the students were eager to learn. Sure, they were sleepy, it was first thing in the morning, but they were motivated. It was good of the Katzenheim brothers to care enough about their employees to educate them. Some of the mothers still brought their children with them, the ones that were too young for school. It gave them some time with their babies before day care. The Latinos were all about family, in fact, that was why so many had come to this country. They wanted a better life for their children. What parent doesn't?

My second class was becoming a challenge, like I'd told Terry. Never mind that the refugees were being helped by the Jewish center. One Christian student, Sam, insisted that America was a Christian nation, and he did all he could to antagonize Ahmed, a skinny Muslim kid, who was also from Iraq. I called him a kid, but he was in his early 20's. The other students tried to ignore the conflict. They seemed almost terrified of Sam and Ahmed. Most refugees came to this country to get away from conflict, yet old religious schisms were brewing in my English class. I felt terrible, ineffective. There had to be a way to keep peace in the section. They were here to learn, I was here to teach. It wasn't the place for a religious war.

That day, it started in the beginning of the period. "Teacher," said Sam, "why don't you teach us to say the Our Father prayer in English?"

"That's something you learn in church, Sam," I said. "I think it's somewhere in the Christian Bible, and when your English is good enough, you can read the Bible on your own, or take a religion class at your church."

Ahmed began scowling, and Sam noted his reaction with glee.

"I don't know why you don't tell us," Sam persisted. "Most of us here are Christian. You have democracy in America, and this is what the majority wants, right class?"

It was insufferable for him to address the other students, and to tell me what to teach. I ignored him, and kept on with the lesson. One challenge in the class was that the students were at various levels. If there were two classes, I could have divided the slow learners from those who learned quickly. I had all the levels together. Sam and Ahmed had a fairly good command of English, and their boredom contributed to the conflict.

"America has religious freedom," Ahmed spat. "All you have in this class is Christians." He looked up at me, and added, "and Jews."

I was the only Jew in the class. There were a couple of Buddhists from Myanmar, and they seemed to shrink at Ahmed's raised voice. Ahmed was tall and athletic, and Sam wasn't exactly wasting away: he was downright fat. I ignored Ahmed's outburst, and proceeded with the reading. We were following an easy, well-written text on the government. Each student had two lines to read. I only corrected the worst mistakes in pronunciation.

"Who can tell me what the word 'citizen' means?" I asked. Sam's hand shot up, and so did Ahmed's. I pretended not to see either of them, and asked another student to answer.

"Well done," I said.

We moved on to drills on pronunciation. "Th" was a difficult sound for most of them. Others dropped off the final consonant sounds.

"Everyone repeat 'the,'" I said, and then gave them a list of words starting with "th" to say. "Who would like to begin reading the next set of words?" I asked, and Ahmed's hand shot up. I didn't call on him, and he got angry.

"You never call on me, Mr. Wise," Ahmed said. "You do not like Muslims." He stood up, and stormed out of the classroom.

"Go, leave, terrorist!" Sam called out, as Ahmed left.

"Sam!" I reprimanded. I'd never had behavior problems like this before. Sam and Ahmed didn't seem to realize they needed me. I had to give progress reports on all my students, I was in touch with their case managers. The class was paid for with tax dollars, and Uncle Sam required strict bookkeeping and accountability. If they wanted to keep receiving their benefits while they looked for work, they had to show proof they were taking English classes. There were forms they needed me to sign. It was self-defeating of any student to antagonize me.

"The teacher doesn't like Christians," Sam muttered. "Teacher is a Jew."

"You can leave now, too, Sam," I said. I wasn't going to let that one slide.

Sam rose up, and came over to me. He stood right in front of me. He was taller and much heavier than me. I didn't cower, though my heart was pounding. I was sure he was going to strike me, and if he did, I would have to tell the case worker, and of course Rabbi Braun. I didn't want to think about how much trouble he was putting himself in. Fortunately, another Christian student, Andrew, said something in Arabic to him. Sam looked at me with rage in his eyes, and then stormed out of the classroom.

My heart was still beating wildly when the class finally finished. I felt like an abject failure. I would have to talk to Marc, the rabbi who had hired me. He needed to know the situation. Marc could advise me. In addition, I might even have to talk to the case workers for both of the men. The case workers were overwhelmed with the number of clients they had, but my call would have repercussions. I didn't know exactly what those would be, and it wasn't my problem. Sam and Ahmed weren't being fair to the other students, who were trying to learn a new language and adapt to a new culture.

When the day was over, I drove to the main community center in the suburbs. Rabbi Braun was in his office. He's a smart guy, and sensed something from my expression. "Come in, Rico," he said in a soft voice. He closed the door after me.

"I'm having a little situation," I confessed to the rabbi, feeling my face redden. I was worried he would think less of me. I took a deep breath, and explained the conflict between the two Iraqis.

"It's good you told me," Marc said, matter-of-factly. "I need to share some information with you." He looked uncomfortable, and I worried he was going to fire me. Had the funding been cut? Surely this one incident wasn't grounds for my dismissal.

"I've had a letter from the police department," Marc said. "They believe the person who murdered the police chief is a recent immigrant."

I had a sinking feeling. It was bad for the entire refugee community. They had already been through enough: having a murder suspect in their ranks wasn't going to help foster good public relations.

"Are they sure?" I asked. "Has this information been released to the public?" I still didn't have a television, and I hadn't seen the local news. I wasn't following the story that closely. Omaha wasn't my town yet, I didn't know the names and players well.

"It's a suspicion, no doubt one among many. They know we teach English to immigrants here, and contacted me." He showed me a letter from the police department. It said they had "forensic evidence from the crime scene" which suggested that the killer was a Middle Eastern male for whom English was not the primary language.

I was sick to my stomach. Were Ahmed and Sam suspects, then? They were a pain in the *tuchas*, but didn't seem like murderers. But what did I know? I don't always have great intuition. But if the murderer was Middle Eastern, then many of my students were suspects. I had focused solely on the two I liked least.

I didn't know what kind of forensic evidence suggested that the killer wasn't a native English speaker. I asked Marc, "So why do they think that the killer isn't fluent in English? Did he write a letter?"

"I can't think of anything else besides a letter or note. But read further down," Marc said, pointing to the final sentence. It said that it was possible that the evidence had been planted to incriminate a Middle Eastern man.

"Someone is trying to frame a foreigner," I said. "Who would do such a thing? Are any of my students in trouble, are they under investigation?" I asked.

"I don't know. The police sent me this communication because they know we teach immigrants. They want us to be on the lookout for suspicious behavior, I guess." Marc sighed. "We're installing metal detectors at all our buildings."

"Because of this?" I asked. I remembered that the Jewish center in Atlanta was closely monitored, and had metal detectors. The one in Denver did, too. It was a sad commentary on the times.

"Not because of this. But I'm glad we are, aren't you? Especially if there's any truth to the police's suspicion." He sighed. "As for telling the two men's case workers about their disruptive behavior, I guess you could. But if you do, there will be ramifications."

"I know," I said. "What should I do? I feel rotten, like I can't keep control of the class. I have to tell you, Marc, that in all my years of teaching, I've never had this kind of situation."

Marc didn't answer. "In addition to the metal detectors, the board has approved a contract with a security company. We'll have a guard on your campus 24 hours a day."

"That will be expensive," I said. "The board must think it's necessary. Do they have any specific reason to be worried?"

"The security company is partly owned by the Katzenheim brothers. They're giving us a discount." Marc had evaded my question. It was a typical tactic of management, I thought.

"Nice of them," I said. The Katzenheim brothers owned the kosher meat plant, and were paying my salary for teaching their Latino employees. I had the feeling our doors would close without their generosity.

"As for what to do with your problem students, you can always expel them, drop them from your roster," Marc said.

My anger towards Sam and Ahmed had lessened. I should have been afraid after the police communiqué, but I wasn't. I suddenly felt protective of the men who were aggravating me. Sam and Ahmed were strangers in a strange land. They were recent immigrants, what possible motive would they have for killing the police chief? But Marc hadn't answered my question about who would frame the men. "Why would a recent immigrant be a killer?" I asked. "They just came to this country. They couldn't have any reason for assassinating a police chief," I said.

"Maybe someone paid for the murder," Marc mused. "Or maybe it's the coming race war." He said it wryly, as if it were an inside joke.

96

The coming race war. Where had I heard that before?

"What coming race war?" I asked. Then I remembered: it was the name of a pamphlet Earl had given me. There was a group in Omaha called RaceWars.com. What a world.

Marc sighed. "We have some home-grown nut cases here in the upper Midwest. They're a hodge-podge of nativists, conspiracy nuts, and rednecks. Most of their ilk is in Montana and the Dakotas, but we've got some in Nebraska. They want to get all the non-whites to kill each other. That's the coming race war. Out of the ashes, the great new white race will flourish."

"That's crazy," I said. "Wouldn't the world be a boring place if everyone was the same?"

"It would be awful," Marc said. "They don't care too much for us Jews, either."

I thought about the coming race war, and the *nebbishes* who were trying to cause it. Were there monsters everywhere? In Georgia, I'd encountered the Concerned Brotherhood for Racial Purity. They'd painted graffiti on my apartment. It seemed like these misfits were the northern equivalent. Where did Earl fit in? If he was a closeted gay man, as I suspected, why was he part of such a group? Bigots don't care much for gays.

"Have you heard Duncan Smedley?" Marc continued.

"What's dunking smelly?" I asked, confused.

Marc smiled. "Not what, who. Duncan Smedley is Omaha's right wing talker. He has his own radio show; he talks a lot about the race wars, and the menace of brown people."

I'd never heard of Duncan Smedley. I remembered that Earl had been listening to rabid talk radio down in Buffalo Crossing. Maybe he listened to Duncan Smedley, too.

I left Rabbi Braun's office, and drove home, discouraged. The skies were gray, and it was still bitterly cold. The wind blew, and though the snow had melted a bit, there were patches of white on the frozen ground.

I didn't know what to do about Ahmed and Sam. I'd been so sure I should call their case workers, but now I didn't know. The police would love to get their hands on either Ahmed or Sam. They were perfect murder suspects, made to order. They were

97

both jerks, *schlimazels.* But killers? Of course, if one of them was the murderer, then I had a moral responsibility to do something. But how could I know? I'm neither a psychologist nor a rabbi. It's too easy to scapegoat foreigners; even the police admitted the evidence might have been planted. Who better than a police officer to plant evidence, and again, I wondered about Lisa. She'd try to frame others if she were guilty herself.

I was eager to call Terry and talk to him. My thoughts turned from murder to the mundane. I wasn't sure who Melissa in Georgia was, who'd left a message for me. I rang up Terry, but there was no answer.

I made supper, and watched a movie on the computer. I still hadn't bothered to buy a TV. At nine, I was ready to shower and go to bed. I had no return call or text from Terry, and I felt blue. The weather, as well as the tension in my class, was getting me down. Omaha is a lovely town, but I wanted to see it when it didn't feel like Alaska outside. I wasn't crazy about my apartment; it was always either too cold or too hot.

I called my mother and Harry. We chatted for a few minutes, when I heard a knock on the door. The front door downstairs didn't latch, and anyone could have found their way to my doorstep. "Just a minute," I called. I said goodbye to Mom, and walked over. I wished it had a peephole, because I could never tell who was outside. I wasn't expecting anyone, and I worried for a moment that one of my unruly students had discovered where I lived. I slowly opened it, and smiled.

"Happy Valentine's Day," Terry said. He was wearing a bright red shirt. I'd forgotten all about the holiday--- it wasn't very romantic of me.

"What a great surprise," I said, ushering Terry in out of the cold. "You're a sight for sore eyes. How did you know I'd be home?"

Terry just smiled, and gave me a warm, wonderful hug. It was only February 8th, according to the calendar, but I wasn't complaining.

"Cute place," Terry said, looking around. "It's got character."

"That is realtor-speak for 'old,'" I said.

Terry laughed. "It's old," he agreed. "And chilly."

I'd turned the electric heater off because it had gotten too warm. I turned it back on. "I'd give you the grand tour," I offered, "but you can see the whole place from here. That's the bedroom," I said, pointing, "and that's the kitchen. Have you eaten? They don't feed you on the plane anymore."

"I can always eat," Terry said. The man has a healthy appetite, and it's one of the many things I like about him. Terry is not a picky eater. I looked him over. I thought he'd put a few pounds back on, and I was glad. When he'd first come to Boulder, he looked thin. I like Terry with a few extra pounds on him.

"I can make something, or we could go out," I said, suddenly feeling awake.

"Let's go out," he suggested. "We're celebrating." I went to get my coat, and Terry put his parka back on. We went down the stairs; my car was on the street. I'd been lucky: the car had started every day, so far. It was used to the cold weather of Boulder, but Omaha was even chillier. Outside, it was too cloudy to see the stars. I let the engine idle, and Terry fastened his seatbelt. I drove to Goldman's, one of my favorite cafés. They were open late, and the food was pretty good.

The crowd was sparse. Nine is late for Omaha, and most people were home watching TV, or getting ready for bed, like I'd been doing. Terry ordered a turkey Reuben, my recommendation, and I drank decaf.

"You talk," Terry said, his mouth full of food. "How's your crazy upstairs neighbor? Seen any more of those weird twins?"

"Lisa's not crazy," I insisted. "She's just prickly. I think she was the police chief's girlfriend."

Terry made a slashing motion across his neck, and I was confused. "Yes, the police chief who was just murdered," I said, "if that's what you meant. No, I don't think she killed him, if that's what you're asking, although it's certainly crossed my mind."

Terry swallowed noisily. "No way, you think she killed him? You're living beneath a murderer?" I detected a look of disbelief in his eyes.

Terry had been living with a murderer, his father, for many years. It was something I thought about every now and then, but chosen never to speak of. The past is over. "I don't think she's a murderer," I said. "She's a police officer, too, and she was in love with him."

"How come these things seem to follow you wherever you go?" Terry asked, still eating noisily.

"What the hell does that mean?" I asked, indignant. I had wondered the same thing. Of course, Lisa wasn't a murderer, and nothing was following me around. But I remembered what Sister Eveline said, that sometimes evil gets a taste for someone, and comes back for a second round. But I was paranoid, a little susceptible. Because of my family tragedy, I saw murder and evil everywhere I looked. The assassination of the police chief had nothing to do with me. I was barely even living in Omaha when it happened. It was a local tragedy.

"I need to buy a TV," I said, changing the subject. Nothing good would come out of our current conversation. We'd been through a lot together, and it would be easy to take our anger out on each other. We are both better than that. Terry finished his sandwich, and paid the bill.

"That was yummy," he said. "Good recommendation."

I nodded. I decided not to tell him that my students were suspects in the police chief's murder. That could wait. It wasn't a cheery topic for the short time we had together.

Back at my apartment, I slept better that night than I had in a long time. Having Terry next to me was reassuring, and when I half-woke during the night, I reached out to him. I patted him, and he mumbled something. I didn't have nightmares, but I couldn't credit Terry with that. I had as many nightmares sharing a bed with him as without. I'm not sure what triggers my disturbing dreams; I'm grateful when I don't have them. I couldn't believe what Sister Eveline and Josh suggested, that my dreams were alerting me to something.

Terry had two full days with me in Omaha, and though I had to work one of those days, it was nice knowing he would be there when I got home. The weather was clear, and Terry said he wanted go to Omaha's famous zoo while I worked. He'd read all about it online. Terry drove my car, and dropped me off at school before heading out.

Sam wasn't in class that day, and without him there, Ahmed was better. He glowered during most of the two hour period, but he kept his abrasive opinions to himself. Ahmed was there, after all, to learn English. His language skills were good, and he made no attempt to hide his contempt for the slow students. Still, without Sam, half my problem was gone.

When my final class was done, I called Terry to say I'd walk home. The sun was out, and it wasn't far. I followed my nose up to the apartment. Terry had been cooking, apparently, and it smelled good. I could smell it from the downstairs foyer when I checked my mail box. Lisa was checking her mail then, too, and she looked at me questioningly.

"You have the day off?" she asked.

"No, I had to work."

"I heard someone in your apartment today," she said, ominously.

"It's OK, I have a friend in town. He's a great cook."

"Lucky you," she said, with neither enthusiasm nor pleasure. She walked off without saying goodbye.

"Geez," I muttered, under my breath. "What an attitude." I leapt eagerly up the stairs. I was forgiving of Lisa. If she had been the chief's illicit girlfriend, then she was in hidden mourning. It would be a difficult time for her.

"Hi, baby," I called, entering my apartment. But Terry was not alone.

Darrel looked at me questioningly. He was sitting across the sofa from Terry.

"Oh, hi, Darrel," I said. "Hey, Terry." I went over to Terry, and gave him a hug. I'd kiss him later.

"I was just telling Darrel about Harry and your mom," Terry said. "The latest news."

Well, Darrel knew I was gay now, and that was fine. I shook his hand; he looked uncomfortable. I wondered if Darrel shared his brother's right- wing beliefs. I thought about the strange website, RaceWars.com. Did Darrel listen to Duncan Smedley? Did his brother Earl? I remembered how Earl had given me a Bible, complete with those disturbing pamphlets.

"I'll go now," Darrel said, not looking me in the eye. I hadn't invited Darrel to come and visit, and I wondered why he was there.

"You don't want to stay for supper?" Terry offered. That's Terry, always polite and generous. I wanted Darrel gone, so I could be alone with Terry.

"Terry's a good cook," I offered.

"No, I'll go. Goodbye, Rico." Darrel didn't shake either of our hands, and when he was gone, Terry's face broadened into a smile.

"I guess you've come out to him," Terry said, kissing me hard.

I shrugged my shoulder. "Oh well," I said. "Did you two have a nice chat? Why was he here? He just stopped by?"

"Yeah, just knocked at the door," Terry said. "I thought it was you. He wasn't as creepy as I thought he'd be, from your description. He's an old redneck, that's all. The world's changed, and left him behind."

"Well, you should have seen that farmhouse. It was straight out of a horror movie, like the Bates Motel."

Terry laughed. "You exaggerate, Ric, you always do. God knows what you say about me."

"I tell people I'm dating a man with the face of a supermodel, the body of an Olympic athlete, and the mind of a Nobel laureate," I teased.

"But that's no exaggeration," Terry insisted.

"Ha!" I said. I hugged him. It felt good to be with Terry. "How was the zoo? What did you cook? It smells delicious."

"In answer to your first question, very nice. Second question, penne and tomato sauce," he said. "And I'm going to grill steaks."

Oh, the advantages of knowing a butcher. "Does the corner market have good meat? I've never bought any there."

"I didn't buy it at the corner market. I brought it from home, from the store. It's Nebraska beef, so it's making a homecoming. Seems appropriate."

"You brought it with you?"

"Why not? I didn't know what I'd find here. I don't trust you to pick out good meat," he said with a smile. "Although I'm Grade A- prime.

I smiled, pinched him, and followed him into the kitchen. He got out an iron skillet, and set it on medium heat. He got the steaks out from the fridge, where they'd been marinating in red wine and olive oil. "You're too good to me," I said, as Terry started grilling the meat. I made the salad, and watched Terry as he cooked. I was lucky to have him, I thought, not for the first time. What did he see in me? I'm five years older than him, not attractive, and hardly rich.

He saw me watching him, and came over to kiss me. "You can pay me back later," he said.

I kissed him hard. "Sure thing, Terry," I said. "I'll turn the heat on tonight."

"That wasn't quite what I had in mind, but it would be nice. This apartment is cold."

We ate supper, making small talk. Everything seemed better with Terry there; I didn't feel so *verklempt,* anxious. The world was a good place with Terry in it. I took a deep breath, and kept a mental picture of the moment. It was so right, so perfect. I was happier than I'd been in weeks. I knew it wouldn't last; Terry was leaving the following evening, and my problems would return. But this minute, this very minute, all was right with the world. The police chief's murder and the possible suspects had no place in my thoughts. Even worries about my feuding students disappeared from my mind.

I did the dishes, while Terry sat at the table, talking. He told me about the zoo, describing his favorite animals, what he liked most. He chatted about the market where he worked, and his co-workers. He still liked Boulder, but missed me.

"So what's new with Mom and Harry?" I asked, remembering what he'd been telling Darrel.

Before Terry could answer, there was a knock at the door. Who was it, I wondered. Lisa from upstairs? Maybe she hadn't believed me when I said I had a visitor. Maybe she thought I was being... being what? Held against my will while someone cooked marinara sauce in my apartment?

I went out to the living room, and opened the door, Terry following me. There was a stooped, elderly man in torn coveralls. He was wearing a dirty, worn parka, and looked like a homeless man. This time I knew who it was. "Hi Earl," I said, "come in."

Earl shuffled in, avoiding my eyes. He looked nervous. "I'm sorry to bother you, Rico," Earl said. "I didn't know you had company."

"I'm Terry," Terry said, coming over and shaking Earl's hand. Earl looked at Terry, and something flickered across his face. What was it, desire? Timidity? I

103

couldn't place it. I was having trouble reading these Nebraskans; it had taken me entirely too long to recognize Lisa's lovesick expression for the murdered police chief.

"This is Earl Johnson," I said. "He's Darrel's brother."

"I met your brother earlier," Terry said.

"Oh, he's been here, then," Earl said, with an inscrutable expression passing across his face. What was that look in Earl's eyes, relief? It seemed like wherever Darrel went, Earl followed. I didn't know what it was like to have a twin brother, or a sibling of any kind.

"Yes, he stopped by here," I said. "Did he lose his phone again?"

"I don't know, maybe," Earl said. "He ain't answering. What's the point of having a cell phone if he either loses it or never answers?" he continued, shaking his head in a melancholy way. "I need to talk to him."

"Earl," I said, suddenly remembering my conversation with the rabbi at the center, "have you heard of Duncan Smedley?"

"I listen to him every day, you bet I do. He has his radio program here in Omaha, and Darrel and me come up to watch him tape the show." Earl answered me as positively as if I'd asked if he believed in God or the flag.

I don't know much about radio, but I didn't think most radio hosts had studio audiences.

"Who's Duncan Smedley?" Terry asked. "Sounds like a millionaire's name, like Thurston Howell. Who names their kid Duncan?"

"He's popular," Earl said. "He has a following, here in town and all across the country. You don't listen to him?"

Terry and I hadn't had many political talks, and, while I assumed he was liberal, I didn't know for sure. There was a lot I didn't know about Terry. Now we were living far away from each other. I wondered if some of the feeling I had for Terry was simple infatuation. Did I really know Terry at all? Thoughts of Sister Eveline came into mind. What had she told me, something about a shadow close to me? Someone who wasn't what he seemed to be?

I shook my head "no," and Terry just shrugged his shoulders.

"I thought everyone listened to Duncan. If Darrel comes back by, tell him to call me," Earl said.

"I don't think he will," Terry said, looking at me knowingly.

Earl looked concerned. "If he does, tell him to call me."

"Sure thing, Earl," I said. "It's good to see you again." I hoped he'd take the hint and leave. I wanted to have an uninterrupted evening with Terry.

Earl waited for a moment. Again, a look I couldn't quite interpret crossed his face. What was it? Was Earl a sad, closeted gay man? Did he want to say something to me? Was he homophobic, a fan of right wing radio shows, like Duncan Smedley's? Without another word, he turned and left, closing the door softly behind him.

The rest of the evening passed quickly. My time with Terry was brief, and I was determined to enjoy every moment. I tried not to think about the future. Would Terry move to Omaha? Should I return to Boulder? Those were questions that time would answer. Terry's visit passed quickly, as did the rest of February.

Chapter 8

February was a chilly month, and March came in like a lion. The days were longer, but it was still bitterly cold. I wondered if spring would ever come.

The next time I saw Lisa at the mailbox, she asked me, "Did you and your friend have a good visit? Did you guys go out a lot, see the town?"

"No," I said. "We mostly stayed in."

"That sounds cozy," she said, with a slight sneer.

"It was, it really was," I agreed.

Lisa cocked her head and looked at me. "Oh, I'm sorry, Rico, I didn't mean anything by that."

I shrugged, and started walking upstairs.

"Rico," Lisa called after me, "How long have you two been together?"

I walked back towards her. "Not long, about six months." She seemed to visibly relax. Was she relieved to find out I was gay? Maybe she'd been afraid I'd hit on her, and now she knew I wouldn't.

"Where does he live?" Lisa asked.

"He's back in Boulder, where I'm from."

"Relationships are difficult," Lisa mused. Her eyes had a distant look about them.

"Do you have a boyfriend?" I asked, pressing my luck with the prickly woman.

"No," she said, vaguely, "not these days."

My classes were going well, especially the one with the Katzenheim workers, and I enjoyed teaching. My contract was for five months, and everything depended on funding. Most of my political refugees were hard workers, too, but they were stressed. Sam came to class sporadically, and when he did, he was subdued. I was glad I hadn't talked to either Sam or Ahmed's case manager; things were better. As for thinking one of them was a murder suspect, it seemed ridiculous, and I thought no more about it.

The refugees had left camps to come to a country about which they knew very little. Some had seen American movies, and they had unrealistic expectations. In addition to learning English, they were looking for places to live, jobs, and navigating the health care system. Many were in the process of getting immunizations that are standard in this country. Some were in very poor health. My heart broke for them.

The Spanish speakers learning English were better off than the refugees. They were working at Katzenheim Brother's Meatpacking Plant, and had places to live. Most had been in the country for a considerable time, and were legal immigrants or citizens.

By early March, Sam, the Iraqi Christian, stopped coming to class completely. I was concerned about him, and I sent Marc an e-mail. Marc told me to call the man's case worker, which I did, but I received no return call.

I saw Marc at the downtown campus shortly after Sam disappeared from class. If the police still suspected a Middle Eastern immigrant for the murder of the police chief, they hadn't been back in touch with Marc about it, at least, so he told me.

We still had no metal detector or security guard. "Did the board change its mind?" I asked.

Marc shrugged. "These things take time. It's coming." He had another topic on his mind. "Purim's around the corner," he said. Purim is a minor festival like Mardi Gras or carnival. People wear masks and drink too much. It occurs at roughly the same time, a month before Passover and Easter. Traditionally, the entire scroll of Esther is read.

I wasn't sure why Marc was telling me about Purim; I rarely observe it. It is a minor holiday.

"At Purim, the Katzenheims hold a major fundraising function for the center," Marc continued. "It's a big deal for us. They furnish the meat, and it's a time when we get both publicity and money."

The Katzenheims were paying my salary for teaching their employees English. I would no doubt be expected to attend the Purim festival, but I didn't want to. I'm not big on events. And who would I take? Terry couldn't fly out just for one evening.

"We expect staff to be at the event. You may bring a guest. It is a fundraiser, but we will be able to offer you two tickets for just the price of the meal. You'll need to wear a tux," Marc told me.

"OK, great," I said, trying to muster a little enthusiasm. Purim was the second Sunday in March, and it began to hang around my neck like an albatross. I decided to invite Lisa, my upstairs neighbor. She was Jewish, she was single, and she was friendlier since finding out I was gay. I felt certain she had been seeing the murdered chief of police, though she never spoke about it. It was none of my business, but I was curious. I'd mostly dismissed the idea of her being a murderer. Mostly.

It seemed as though Chief Will Herman's murder would never be solved. People still talked about it, of course, but there were no new leads. A few more details about the slaying were released, but that only fueled gossip. I wondered why Sam stopped coming to class; it no doubt had more to do with him finding a job, or being sick, than hiding from the police.

Terry and I talked almost every day. I missed him. One day when I was cleaning the apartment, I noticed that the strange hunting knife on the bookcase was gone. It must have belonged to Terry. I had forgotten to ask him about it when he'd visited at Valentine's Day, but he must have taken it. Oddly, the silver Star of David Harry had given me was also missing. Had Terry taken it by mistake? Had I inadvertently lost it?

"The knife was yours, then," I said to Terry, one evening when we talked.

"What knife?"

"The hunting knife I packed by mistake. It's gone, so I figured you took it."

"Rico, I have no idea what you're talking about."

I was puzzled. He insisted that he hadn't taken any knife. Why did he deny it? Had I lost it? It wasn't like anyone else had been in the apartment. I didn't have friends in Omaha, no one visited me.

I told Terry about the big Purim event, but he didn't think he could come for it. It was my turn to go to Boulder, anyway.

"So Purim is the Jewish Mardi Gras?" Terry asked, after I told him about it.

"Kind of. You wear a costume, drink a lot, and they read an entire scroll. You know, the whole *megillah*. And we have a special pastry, *hamantashen*."

"Your mom hasn't mentioned it. Do they go to it?"

My mother isn't very religious, and she no longer keeps temple affiliation. Besides, Purim wasn't a holiday we often celebrated when I was growing up; it's just a party, really. It isn't Passover or Yom Kippur.

"Why don't you take your neighbor, the Jewish woman who you think is a murderer?" Terry asked, sweetly.

"Oh, Terry, I don't think she's a murderer. You always put words in my mouth. I think she's the police chief's girlfriend, but I don't think she killed him. And I've already asked her."

"So you asked me to go after you've already asked someone else? That's tacky."

"I didn't think you'd be able to. I hate these things, and I don't want to go by myself."

"You'll have fun, Rico. It sounds nice. I bet the food will be good. That's one thing about your people. They know how to eat."

"Terry, there's more to the Jewish faith than just food."

"Yeah, I know. There's mutilation, too. No thanks, Ric. I'll stay the way I am."

That was the extent of my efforts to convert Terry. I couldn't blame him, what man wants to go through that? I said goodbye, and promised to come to Boulder soon. I would go home for Passover, at the end of the month. Mom and Harry would have been hurt if I didn't.

Lisa agreed to go to the Purim festival with me. I was surprised; it wasn't as if we were close. She kept a wall around herself. I walked up to her apartment the afternoon of the festival. I'd bought a corsage, white roses and carnations. I figured that white would go with whatever she was wearing. I should have asked what color she wanted, but talking to Lisa was never easy. I wore a tux that I'd rented. It choked my neck, and I felt uncomfortable.

"You look lovely," I told Lisa, when she came to the door. She was wearing a low-cut black cocktail dress with a single strand of pearls. Her jet black hair was swept up on top of her head. She was beautiful. I would be the envy of every man at the event; ironic, since Lisa didn't interest me in that way. I couldn't even call her a friend.

"You look nice, too," Lisa said. I doubted her words, but what else could she say? I felt awkward in the suit, and I didn't like wearing a bow tie. It made me feel like I was five years old.

The Purim fundraiser was held at the renowned modern art museum in downtown Omaha. Its sculpture garden and collection of 19th century Indian art are famous. The

Jewish center had the gallery for the evening. I showed our tickets at the door, and Lisa and I walked in. It was very crowded: every Jew in southeast Nebraska was there. There were several hundred people in attendance; many wore masks, and some wore costumes.

The foyer of the art gallery was huge, with a high ceiling. It was decorated with banners and crepe. There was a large blue banner with a *Mogen David*. I thought of the silver one Harry had given me, and again, wondered how I had lost it.

The festival began with a banquet. The seating was assigned, and Lisa and I sat at a large table with six other people. Our dinner companions were nice enough.

The food came out quickly. I looked at the program: there was going to be a reading of the scroll of Esther, the whole *megillah*. After that, there was dancing and a silent auction. The Katzenheim brothers furnished the meat; we had our choice of brisket or roast chicken. Lisa and I chose the chicken. The meal was kosher, of course, and along with the meat they served kasha varnishkes, a salad, and bread. For dessert, there would be a selection of Purim pastries, *hamantashen*. It means "hat of Haman" or something like that. Haman is the villain in the story of Esther.

"What do you do?" a plump woman named Sally asked Lisa. Sally was a banker, and had a hearty laugh. She had red hair, and her cheeks were blushed from the wine.

"I work for the police department," Lisa said, stonily.

"Terrible about the police chief's murder," Sally's husband, Alex, said. "Do they have any leads? Any suspects? Why is it taking them so long to solve the case?"

"I wouldn't know," Lisa said. Her manner was so cold and icy I was embarrassed. It was impossible to draw conversation out of Lisa; there was something robotic about her responses.

"I suppose you can't say," Sally said, as if trying to explain Lisa's behavior. "What do you do?" she asked me.

"I teach classes at the Jewish center," I said.

"Good for you," Alex said. "I'm sure it doesn't pay much, but you're doing necessary work."

It made me feel like answering in a wooden tone, too. Some people always classify others by their income, or lack thereof. Clearly, I wasn't a rich man, but I wasn't impoverished. There were many things I loved and treasured about my Jewish tradition, but the emphasis on material prosperity sometimes makes me uncomfortable. Maybe I would have felt different if I was rich.

"What do you teach?" Sally asked.

"I teach English to immigrants," I replied.

"Duncan Smedley must hate the work you do," Sally said, conspiratorially, and then laughed heartily. "He hates immigrants--- he's such a mean bastard."

I couldn't quite make up my mind about Sally. Maybe she was nice, maybe she was a *yenta*, too soon to tell. It took me a moment to remember who Duncan Smedley was, Omaha's right-wing radio talker.

"I can't stand Smedley," Lisa said. I looked at her in surprise--- she made a spontaneous, appropriate response.

"Times are hard, people are angry," Alex said. "They are looking for someone to blame. I agree with some of what Smedley has to say."

"How can he blame immigrants?" Sally asked. "He probably comes from immigrants himself. We're all immigrants. Everyone sitting at this table, everyone in this room is in immigrant. Our grandparents came here to get a better life. That's what immigrants are doing today."

"I'm not an immigrant," Lisa said, in her dead-pan tone. "My people always lived here."

Sally looked at her questioningly. Lisa's tone managed to be distant and hostile at the same time.

Lisa was clearly suffering, yet I was unsure of the source of her pain. Was she angry about the plight of Native Americans? That was understandable. Was she sad about being adopted, what she saw as her forced Jewish upbringing, or was she grieving for Chief Herman? The problem with some unhappy people is that they are determined to make others as unhappy as themselves: they want to drag everyone down. Lisa was trying her best to ruin the evening for everyone.

"Oh really?" Alex asked. "How's that?"

"I'm a native Lakota," Lisa answered.

"You're not Jewish?" Sally asked.

Lisa glared at her. "I was raised Jewish by my adoptive parents." She spat the words out.

"Well, then, you're Jewish," Sally said. It's what I had said, and Lisa didn't like it.

Fortunately, a waiter brought more bread then, and Lisa took some. Another waiter brought more wine. I was driving, so I wasn't drinking, but Lisa was drinking enough for both of us. That was all right: Purim is a party. I just hoped her drinking would make her talk less rather than more. It is a commandment in the Talmud for Jews to get so drunk at Purim they can't tell the difference between "blessed be Mordecai" and "cursed be Haman."

The pastries were served, and the conversation ended. Sally and Alex talked to other people at the table, and Lisa and I fell silent. At 8:00 p.m. sharp, the reading of the book of Esther, from a scroll or *megillah,* began. There were noisemakers by our plates, and we held them in our hands, waiting. When the scroll was read, we would blow noise makers, boo and stamp our feet whenever the cantor said Haman's name.

The cantor was a short, middle-aged woman with ash blonde hair, and her voice was penetrating and resonant. I didn't remember much Hebrew, but I could tell that her command of that language was excellent. There was something mesmerizing about the way she read, and even if I didn't understand much, I paid attention.

She began reading at a fast clip: she had to, or we would never finish. At the first mention of Haman's name, people stomped their feet and blew the noisemakers, blocking out the villain's name. The book of Esther, it said in our program, is the one biblical book where the word "God" never appears. Still, it isn't a secular book; it claims to be historical, though it's not. It's the prototypical story of racial cleansing, the first pogrom.

Whatever the meaning of Purim, I felt part of something ancient, mysterious and significant. I had no wine, but still, I found myself hissing and stomping whenever the name of Haman was read. There was something about the reading that took me back in time, and made me feel connected with the distant past.

I watched Lisa, and noticed how uncomfortable she seemed. I felt sad for her, and wondered what it was like to be cut off from ancestral traditions. Was Lisa's hostility due to that estrangement, or was there something else? I looked at her, surreptitiously, noting her beauty. Was that lovely face the face of a murderer? She behaved so oddly, it was easy to think of her striking out in an antisocial way. But being anti-social is one thing, killing something else entirely.

The evening ended late, and I wondered how I was going to teach the following morning. Lisa and I said goodbye to our dinner companions, and I escorted her back to my car. She was unsteady on her feet. I didn't count how many glasses she had drunk, but she had obviously drunk plenty. Her eyes looked slightly out of focus, and I worried she was going to be sick.

I drove back through the chilly night, keeping the heater high for Lisa.

"It's so damn cold," Lisa whined. "It's March and it's still this cold!"

"You're from here," I said. "You should be used to it."

I parked the car out on the street, a little farther than I would have liked. It was a definite disadvantage not to have off- street parking. I opened the door for Lisa, and helped her get out. I worried she was going to fall.

"I guess I had a little too much to drink," she slurred.

"Maybe so," I answered.

"I hope you don't think worse of me," she said, a little teary as we climbed the stairs to her apartment. I couldn't think *worse* of her; I didn't think all that much of her to begin with. Hell, I even wondered if she was a murderer. But I hadn't wanted to go to the event alone, and whether or not I liked her was beside the point. I had no other choices.

"Of course not," I assured. "It's Purim. If I hadn't been driving, I would have had a glass or two myself."

I helped her get inside her apartment. She left home with the heater on, and it was nice and toasty inside. All I could think of was how cold my apartment would be. I wondered if it would heat up before I fell asleep. If I stayed in Omaha, I was going to move to an apartment with an actual furnace. Space heaters aren't for me. It was a miracle the building hadn't burned down with just those antiques. And it was either too hot or too cold with the electric heater.

"Lisa," I said, when I was about to leave. "Do you have any aspirin? Any seltzer water? You might want to take a couple of aspirin before you go to bed. You'll have a headache tomorrow."

She didn't answer. "Do you miss your boyfriend, Rico?" she asked. "It's hard being alone."

"Yes," I said, "I miss him. It is hard, I don't have many friends here. But you've lived in Omaha 15 years. You have lots of friends."

I didn't know if she had friends. Lisa was abrasive, and if her behavior at work was anything like her conversation had been at dinner, I wondered if she had anyone at all. She did her best to alienate those around her. It was hard to be near Lisa, she tried to make others unhappy.

"I don't," she sniffed. "I don't have many friends. You're the only one who is nice to me. Thanks for inviting me tonight."

"It was my pleasure," I said. Then, Lisa leaned over and kissed me on the cheek.

"You're cute," she said. "You're a cute little Jew boy."

"Lisa," I said, "you've had too much to drink."

"Well, you are cute. But you probably don't like being called a Jew boy. I didn't mean anything by that. It fits the occasion, it was so damn Jewish tonight."

"Goodbye, Lisa," I said firmly. I wanted to get out of her apartment. "Don't forget to take some aspirin. Do you want me to set them out for you?"

I wanted to leave before she tried to kiss me again. But because I'm not always a nice guy, I decided to turn her drunkenness to my advantage. "You must miss the police chief terribly," I said. "You can't be in mourning for him like his wife is." I said the words, and waited for her to answer.

My comment worked, and I felt ashamed of myself. Lisa began to sob. "I miss him so much," she said, sniffling. "How did you know?"

"I'm sorry, Lisa," I said. I had the information I'd been curious about, but I felt like a *schmuck*. It was none of my business. Why had I needed to know? Just to feel like I'd been right? I'm a curious man; I always have been, sticking my nose where it doesn't belong. Curiosity hadn't done much for the cat. Why had I pried?

114

"They think I killed him," Lisa said, wailing. "Do you know what that's like? I loved him. Why would I kill him?"

"That must be awful for you," I said. I wondered again if she *had* killed him. She was so tightly wound, that at times like this, when she wasn't on guard, she fell apart. Yes, she was tipsy, but there was something else, something I couldn't put my finger on. Whether or not she was a murderer, I didn't know, but she was a little off. Of course, being nutty doesn't make you a murderer. She wasn't likeable, and it was easy to believe the worst.

"Do you know how many adopted children become killers?" Lisa said, taking me by surprise.

I felt a chill down my spine. "No, I don't know," I said. I was anxious to leave. If she was a murderer, I didn't want to be next on her list. "Goodbye, Lisa, get some rest."

"The statistics are very high," Lisa continued. "Did you know that being adopted raises the probability that a person will murder? Freaky, huh. And that's why they thought I did it. That, and the fact that he loved me. He was going to leave his wife."

"But you're not a killer, Lisa," I said, with more confidence than I felt.

"How do you know? They questioned me," she said, triumphantly.

Lisa was many things; she was an *oysvorf*, a social misfit, definitely. But she seemed too selfish to go to the trouble of murdering. I was tired, and wanted to leave. "Good night, Lisa," I said, again.

"You think I'm awful," she said, slurring her words. Her eyelids were heavy, and she looked utterly exhausted.

"No, I don't," I said, turning my back on her. "The police aren't always nice to deal with."

She was a police officer, and my words weren't politic. Then Lisa caught me off guard. "They aren't," she said, her speech no longer slurred. "You know that first-hand."

I spun around. She smiled wickedly at me. I wondered if she had been drunk at all, or if she'd been playing me. How did she know I'd had my own run-in with the cops? Had Lisa been doing research on me? Why?

I stared at her, not sure what to say. I didn't want to admit anything.

"I did a background check on you, Rico. A girl can't be too careful," she said slyly. "They thought you were murderer."

"I was never accused of murder," I said.

Lisa looked triumphant. "They thought you shot your friend, your beloved Terry. Does Terry hold that against you? What a tricky relationship to be in, Rico. I've got to hand it to you. Most people couldn't be lovers with someone connected to a murderer."

I left, slamming the door noisily as she said those last words, stomping down the staircase. To get to my own apartment, I had to go down the external stairs, enter the house, and climb up another set of stairs.

Lisa's words upset me. I'd been a fool to think I could run from my past. Anyone who had a computer could enter my name, and come up with a couple of newspaper articles from the past year. I hadn't done anything wrong, I'd committed no crime. But in the eyes of many, I was a reprobate for having a relationship with Terry. I'd fallen in love with him before I knew about his father.

In my apartment, I cranked up the electric heater, and folded up the tux. What a strange evening. I looked at the clock: it was past midnight, and too late to call Terry. I wanted to tell someone, though, so I powered up the laptop, and checked my e-mail. I decided to write Terry a note, even though he didn't check the computer often. I couldn't tell him exactly what Lisa had said to me, but I'd give him the gist of her behavior. My heart was still pounding from that encounter. I'd provoked it, and received payback for interrogating her.

I was angry at myself. I'd had to pry into Lisa's life, and thought I was such a great detective. How long had Lisa known about me, I wondered, and who had she told? Rabbi Braun at the Jewish center knew all about me, and he had hired me anyway. I doubted the Katzenheim brothers or any of the other donors would be thrilled to know about my past. Was I notorious because of my relationship with Terry?

There was a message in my inbox. Terry had sent me an e-mail message, telling me that Ted had come to Boulder, taken the dresser, the sofa, the kitchen table and chairs. Terry had set up a card table in the kitchen till we decided what to do, and there were a couple of easy chairs in the living room, so there was a place for him to watch

TV. He also told me that there was another message from Melissa in Georgia. I had the number written down on my desk. Since I didn't know who Melissa was, I'd been in no hurry to call.

I typed a message to Terry, telling him about the Purim party, and Lisa's drunkenness. She was a strange woman, and writing the note, I felt angry again. I was fairly sure she was no killer, but what did I know? I didn't tell Terry that she knew about my past. Right or wrong, I loved Terry, he was my friend. Terry had paid a price: he'd taken the bullet intended for me. We had both been bathed in Terry's blood, our ritual bath.

I thought about Sister Eveline. She said something about evil chasing me, and at that instant, I felt like the evil was close. Lisa, a suspect in the police chief's murder, lived upstairs. I'd been warned of the possibility one of my immigrant students was a killer. Now, Sam, the Iraqi Christian had disappeared. Did that indicate his guilt?

But why would Lisa kill Police Chief Herman? Because she was spurned? Was that a reason to kill? I didn't know anything about the psychology of murder. Was it rage that drove people to kill, or something else? To be a murderer, a person had to be unhinged. I couldn't imagine why I would ever kill anyone, no matter what happened. But was there some circumstance that would drive me to murder?

On impulse, I checked the Web for the news and information about the police chief's death. There had been a story about it in the newspaper almost every day, so I had to wade through numerous articles. Lisa's name wasn't mentioned, and there was nothing about the chief's mistress. Maybe the newspapers were shielding his widow. There was no mention of immigrants being suspected, nothing about looking for non-English speakers. My thoughts jumbled, I turned off the computer, and went to bed. Finally, exhaustion overtook me and I fell asleep.

Chapter 9

After the Purim festival, I decided it was best to avoid Lisa. It wouldn't be difficult; we didn't talk often before. If I saw her at the mailbox, I'd be cordial, but nothing more. She didn't stop by to thank me for the dinner. I hadn't expected her to, not really. Lisa was all about Lisa. I wasn't at all sure if she had been drunk, or if she'd used her inebriated state to put the screws on me. I wondered how long she'd known about my past.

The week after the festival, it snowed. It stayed cold, and the snow didn't melt. I was homesick for the mountains. I missed Terry, and I thought of my little house in Boulder. The temperatures were warmer in Colorado, and I wanted to be there for spring. Springtime in the Rockies isn't always as lovely as the song suggests; it can be windy, and the nights are cold. But it is usually sunny, and the days are sometimes warm. I wanted to be there, I wanted to be with Terry. I missed my mother and Harry, my friends Linda, Petie and Josh. I made reservations to go home for Passover at the end of the month, and I looked forward to that trip.

My students seemed weary of learning, and were less enthusiastic. Sam, the Chaldean, still hadn't returned to class, and I wondered about him. I asked some of the other Iraqi Christians if they had seen him, but if they had, they didn't tell me. My Latino students seemed dispirited, too; while they were polite and well-mannered, they seemed to feel the same *veltschmerz*, world-weariness, that I was experiencing. It was almost the mid-point in the semester.

My future in Omaha was still uncertain. I asked Marc about funding for the fall when I saw him on campus; he said he didn't know yet. If the job continued, I would stay on in Nebraska. I didn't know where that would leave my relationship with Terry. Cell phones and e-mail were no substitute for having him near.

I kept telling myself that Omaha would be lovely and green in the spring, if it ever came. The days were longer, but winter seemed never-ending. On a clear but cold Saturday, I decided to go on a road trip. I hadn't been out of Omaha since I'd moved to Nebraska; I didn't want to go back to Buffalo Crossing, though. I looked online, and saw that there was a winery south of Omaha in a little historic town called Brownville.

The road to Brownville followed the Missouri River. Close to the winery, there was a state park. It seemed like a great way to spend the day. I called Terry, and told him my plans.

"I wish I was there to go exploring with you, Rico," he said.

"I do too. I miss you. But maybe you'll move here," I offered, tentatively.

"Hopefully you'll come back home, Rico. Somehow you haven't made Omaha sound so great. Your crazy upstairs neighbor, the redneck twins.... I can't say it is tempting. Boulder is your home, Rico. You belong here. You should be with me."

I couldn't argue with him; I love Colorado. But I have to work. We couldn't live on one person's salary, and why should Terry support me? We belonged together, yes; our love was *beshert*. But how would we manage it?

As if to rub salt in the wounds, Terry added, "It's bright and sunny here. The days feel almost warm. Of course, usually I'm working, but last Tuesday, Linda, Petie and I went snowshoeing up in the peaks."

I thought about the lovely day Terry and I had spent in the mountains. "Did you borrow Harry's snowshoes again?"

"No, Rico, I bought my own. I like snowshoeing and want to do more of it. I hate to keep borrowing Harry's things."

"He likes you, Terry," I said, "he doesn't mind. He hardly ever goes snowshoeing anymore."

"Your parents are great," he said.

"Yeah," I agreed. I couldn't argue that. My thoughts turned to Mom and Harry. The mind travels along its own paths, and for some reason I remembered the pictures I'd found in the garage. I thought of the photo of my mother and Harry taken two years before they were supposed to have met, the picture of Harry with his arm around Mom's waist. They looked so much in love.

I thought, too, of the picture of Harry and the twins when they were children. It had been a while since I was troubled by nightmares, and I was grateful. I don't know why I sometimes have such awful dreams. It doesn't have anything to do with stress in my life. I couldn't really believe they were messages, like Sister Eveline said.

119

"Oh, look," Terry said. "I know you're anxious to get on the road, but that Melissa called again from Georgia."

"The name doesn't mean anything to me, Terry," I said.

"Hold on, Ric," Terry said, and I heard papers rustling. "She said she wasn't sure if you knew who she was, and she said... she's related to Mother Caroline... no, that isn't quite it... I can't read my own writing."

"Sister Eveline," I said, and thought about the old, blind, black woman, who some thought was a prophet. I had my doubts.

"That sounds right," Terry said. "Yes, that's it. Who is Sister Eveline?"

"Someone who knew my father," I said.

"But your dad lived in Colorado, not Georgia," he answered, confused.

"Sister Eveline sees things. She's a prophet. She saw my father."

"Ric," Terry said, "do you know anyone who's normal? Your psycho neighbor, the racist twins, and now a prophet. You collect eccentric people, like some kind of zookeeper."

"Where does that put you, Terry?" I asked, pointedly.

Terry sighed. "I was trying to be funny, teasing you, and you always have to go and be mean."

It wasn't fair of me. Terry was a bit lost these days. He had left his hometown, partly because of our relationship, and partly due to his disgraced father's actions. Terry is sensitive, and his feelings are easily hurt. I am too brusque, and need to be careful with the man I love. I'm snarky and sarcastic. Terry doesn't like that side of me, and I can't blame him.

"I'm sorry, Terry, I didn't mean anything," I said, contritely.

"Sure, Ric, sure," Terry said, as we said goodbye. He didn't sound convinced, and I was angry with myself for my thoughtlessness. Terry's words cut me, though; I did know a lot of outliers. I've never been part of the mainstream. Terry was a high school football player; he'd been married and was a star in his hometown. His town turned against him, partly because he was gay, but also because of his father's notoriety. He'd been caught off guard by rejection. Terry knew nothing about being an outsider,

120

but I'd always been one. My religion, my profession, everything about me was against the grain. Until now, Terry had always been part of the mainstream.

I decided to call Melissa before I left. I had two previous messages from her, and I would have called sooner if I'd realized who she was. I didn't believe in prophets or psychics, but Sister Eveline had been right about some things. I dialed the number, and it rang several times before anyone picked up.

"Yes?" a young woman said.

"Melissa? This is Rico Wise, a friend of your grandmother's." I wasn't exactly a friend, I hardly knew the woman, but I didn't know how to introduce myself.

"Thanks for calling, Mr. Wise," the young woman named Melissa said. "My granny's been sick."

"I'm sorry to hear that," I said. "I hope it's nothing serious."

"She's been in the hospital, the doctor thinks she had a stroke."

"I'll keep her in my thoughts, Melissa."

"Thank you, sir. They expect her to recover. She was doing poorly, but she's a little better. Granny's a strong woman."

"Yes," I said. "She's been through so much."

"Mr. Wise, she wanted me to give you a message."

"Really?" I asked. I couldn't imagine why Sister Eveline had a message for me. I'd only met her once, and we had talked briefly on the phone. Still, there was a mysterious link between us.

"She was worried about you. She's been sick, not feeling good, and she kept saying she had to get in touch with you. She didn't have your number, and neither did I."

I couldn't remember whether I'd given her my phone number. I'd called her, but Sister Eveline is blind, and couldn't have written it down.

"The pastor made a few calls, and he found your number. I hope you don't mind that I called you," Melissa said.

"Of course not," I said. I didn't know what I could do to help the old woman or her granddaughter; I'd send a card, but that didn't seem like much.

"Granny had been seeing you in her visions, like she does, and she was worried."

"She doesn't need to be," I said. "Everything is going well."

"I'm glad to hear that, I'm so glad to hear that. But she wanted me to tell you to be careful."

"All right," I said. I felt aggravated. Was the old woman trying to frighten me? Why? She probably meant well, but I wanted her to leave me alone. Everything was fine, things were going well.

"Granny said, let me think… she made me memorize it so I'd get it right. She told me that the shadow was getting bigger, that it was growing stronger. She said, she said that the old lie was being told again, and that you must be careful. She said that things aren't what they seem."

I was puzzled. What did Sister Eveline mean by all that? It was a bunch of gibberish. A shadow, a lie; I doubted she even understood what the "old lie" meant to me. The old lie, for us Jews, is the myth that we have some kind of bizarre ritual at Passover that involves sacrificing Christian children. It was unbelievable, ugly, but Hitler had exploited that old wives' tale very effectively against us. And to say a dark shadow was growing--- well, that was generic. "Things aren't what they seem" is a truism, it isn't insight.

I didn't know what to say, so I thanked Melissa, wished her grandmother well, and rang off. I wondered why I'd bothered to call.

I packed the car for the day, printed out directions and a map, and began to drive. I went south, past the city limits of Omaha, and reached the highway. I felt a sense of relaxation as I left. My life wasn't tense, but I felt confined; there were no mountains to go to, and I needed to leave the city and let nature do its healing work. As I drove, following the Missouri River, it occurred to me that while Nebraska isn't dramatically beautiful in the way Colorado is, it is pretty.

I drove over gently rolling hills; the fields were brown and unplanted, but I imagined they would soon be lovely and green. The trees were sparse, and there was a sense of openness that touched my soul.

There were few other cars on the road. It was mid-March, and Nebraska isn't a spring break destination for college students. The freeway that followed the Missouri

River meandered between Iowa and Nebraska. After an hour, I decided to take the state road instead of the highway.

The sun was trying to break through the clouds, but it was chilly. There were patches of snow on the ground. I passed old abandoned houses, and unpainted barns. The scenery filled me with sadness, and I became reflective.

Lisa, that odd creature, was haunted by some demon I couldn't understand. She was young, beautiful, but miserable. Her boyfriend had been murdered, and that was a tragedy. But it was no good falling in love with a married man. Surely her friends, if she had any, could have told her it wouldn't end well. I'd been so determined to find out about Lisa and her relationship to the murdered chief. I thought I had tricked her, taking advantage of her tipsy state. But she had the last word. She knew all about my past. Lisa was cunning, even manipulative. Did that make her a killer?

I thought briefly about my students. My work was meaningful, and I was helping people, doing my little bit to make the world a better place. Most of the students were wonderful and hard-working. Ahmed was a pain, and Sam had disappeared. It wasn't plausible to think that one of them was a murderer. Still, it was odd that Sam went missing. Was he in hiding? What possible motive would he have for killing the chief of police? Even as an act of terrorism, it was misguided.

I wondered about my call to Melissa, and Sister Eveline's words of warning. I was sure she meant no harm, and I should have been grateful that anyone in Georgia still cared about me. But Sister Eveline's advice was generic and ominous. Everyone has a dark shadow at their side. The previous autumn had been harrowing, but I had to deal with things and move on. And something good had come from my experiences; I'd met Terry.

My father's death, I worried, might never be solved or avenged. In Georgia I'd searched for the solution to that mystery. Now there was a murder in Omaha, and strangely, I was close to a couple of the suspects, Lisa, and my foreign students. If Sister Eveline saw a shadow beside me, it was understandable. Was murder following me wherever I went?

My thoughts turned to Terry. He was a good man, a *mensch,* almost too good to be true. Why did he love me? He could have found someone more handsome, smarter, someone who wasn't always so damn confrontational and sarcastic. Terry had grown up living with a man I was sure was a murderer, his own father. Had Terry ever suspected?

I arrived at the picturesque little town of Brownville, on the Missouri River, and parked my car. It was a small town, with just the one street. There were lovely, historic, red-brick homes; it was one of Nebraska's oldest towns, full of 19th century charm. As I walked around, I was grateful for the wool trench coat I was wearing. A cold, mean wind blew off the river and chilled me. Brownville was frozen, not just by the cold weather, but by the past.

I reflected on my own life, and how I always fought to keep things the same. I was happiest when there was no change. Life rarely accommodates. I want all my loved ones to always be together: Linda, Petie, Josh; Mom, Harry, Terry and me. I want things to stay the same, but they don't. When I return to Boulder, it won't be like it was. Everything changes.

Chilled, I went back to my car. I drove past the vineyard, and was pleasantly surprised to find the winery open. I parked, and went inside. I was the only guest, and a heavy set woman invited me to taste some of the vintner's offering. She poured a small glass for me. I'm not a wine snob, and I liked it. I smiled at the woman, and thanked her. I bought a bottle, deciding to take it home at the end of the month.

A couple of old mansions nearby were open as museums, and I visited them. After an hour, I'd pretty much seen all of Brownville. I got back in my car, and decided to drive on to the park. It was past lunch time, and the wine wasn't sitting well in my stomach. I was hungry, and needed to eat. I passed a roadside drive-in café. I parked out front, and went inside.

The café was small and dark. There was a kid working at the grill, and he looked impatiently at me, as if I was interrupting him.

"Are you still serving lunch?" I asked. The radio was on too loud, and a man's voice made the speaker's vibrate. The young cook was sullen.

"I have hot dogs and onion rings," he sighed, as if serving me was a Herculean task, a grave inconvenience.

"Beef hot dogs?" I asked.

"Yes," the kid sighed, sourly. "Nebraska beef."

"I'll take a hot dog and a side of onion rings, then."

"Oh, we have mushrooms, too, if you'd rather."

"Sure, make that a side of fried mushrooms instead." I sat down at an uncomfortable little table. The young man turned the radio down slightly, and that allowed me to understand the speaker's words. The radio announcer had a low, calm voice, and there was something hypnotic about his phrasing. I wasn't really paying attention; my thoughts were elsewhere, with Lisa, Sister Eveline, Terry. But that changed suddenly.

"Just think about it," the radio voice said, in slow, carefully enunciated tones. "All the bankers are Jewish. A small cabal of wealthy Jews runs the entire financial system of the country, the world, really." I felt my heart beat more rapidly. What kind of *drech* was this? This is the 21st century; who still believes that Jews control the world?

"They have brought down the entire world economy," the voice droned on. His tone was so sincere, so non-threatening the message almost sounded reasonable. "Their nature never changes. Jews have always, only been interested in finance. They are wreaking revenge on the world. A lot of them are homosexuals, as well, vicious ones."

"Excuse me," I said to the young man who was frying mushrooms. He didn't seem to hear me, so I tapped the steel counter twice. The kid turned and looked at me.

"Yeah?" he said. "Did you change your mind? It'll just be a minute more, I promise."

I'd lost my appetite, food was no longer important. "Who is this on the radio?" I asked.

"Duncan Smedley," the young man said, as if I was an idiot. "Saturday afternoons are the rebroadcast of Friday's show. Turn it up louder?"

"No," I said, "it's vile. Turn it off, please. How can you listen to that ridiculous shit?" So this was Duncan Smedley I was hearing. What a disgusting, homophobic anti-Semite. I kept learning more about Nebraska, but not necessarily things I wanted to know. Rabbi Braun hadn't told me that Duncan Smedley was an anti-Semitic homophobe.

"You don't like it?" the kid asked, surprised. I doubted if he'd ever been sworn at by an adult, and I felt bad, just for a moment. He walked to another part of the counter, and flipped a switch. Rap music began booming from the radio, shaking the walls of the little café. It was better than hate speech.

My hot dog and mushrooms were ready; I paid, and left. In the car, I turned on the radio. I wanted to hear more from Duncan Smedley. Had he really said what I thought? It was unreal; surely I had misunderstood. If he had said those things, the anti-defamation societies would be all over him. I scrolled up and down the dial, and finally found the soothing, hypnotic voice again.

"I know it's not politically correct," Smedley droned. "But I have an obligation to speak the truth. My listeners expect it from me." I pulled away from the curb, and made my way back onto the state highway, continuing towards the park. "These internationalists, this homosexual cabal, are wreaking havoc with the world's financial system. They are committed leftists, and are determined to make America fail. Russia wouldn't tolerate the Jews, and now they are in this country, scheming to cause our downfall. Any time you hear someone say we have to accept people of all faiths, all lifestyles, run the other direction," Smedley blathered on.

I drove slowly, nibbling at the hot dog. It wasn't doing much for my stomach. I turned the radio off. I took a deep breath, and tried to calm down. I wanted to cleanse my mind. The hateful words I'd heard on the radio disturbed me.

I could no longer see the wide Missouri River. I was going uphill, very gently. I saw the turnoff for the state park, and went in. The road continued, twisting and turning through beautiful, frosty fields. Abruptly, I saw the river again, and the road ran parallel to it. I parked my car at the road's end, and got out. I threw out the rest of my hot dog and mushrooms.

I followed the trail, and was soon rewarded with a lovely view of the river behind me. A sign pointed to a wooden stairwell. I climbed up. There were round, shallow caves that had been used as shelter by the Indians. This far south, Nebraska no longer bordered Iowa, but Missouri. When the latter had been a slave state, escaped slaves would swim across the river to freedom, and hide in the shallow caves till it was safe for them to continue on. The caves were covered with mysterious, ancient drawings as well as more modern graffiti.

I was alone in the park; although it was a Saturday afternoon. A cold gust of wind chilled me, and I shivered. I wished I'd brought gloves. In spite of the beauty of the place, my thoughts were troubled and jumbled. I was upset by Duncan Smedley's hateful words. There was a dark shadow nearby, Sister Eveline said. She was right: the darkness was called Duncan Smedley.

My mind drifted as I walked about the park, walking along the escarpment, looking at the shallow caves. I wished Terry was here to enjoy the park with me, to calm me down.

I took a deep breath, and tried to call my meandering mind back to the present. I concentrated on the sun over head, which was trying valiantly to bring the springtime. I shivered from the cold wind, occasionally gusting up from the river far below. As I concentrated on the present moment, I felt peace and calm return to my heart. I forgot Duncan Smedley's hate speech, and I let go of my worries.

Nature did its healing work. It did me good to be outdoors, away from the city, away from the routine. There was a lot of uncertainty in my life, as there is in everyone's, but I felt happy. Maybe happiness wasn't the right word; as I grew older, I experienced more contentment. I loved, and was loved. I had meaningful work. Those are the things that matter.

The park was peaceful. As I walked about the trails, I ran into only two other people, a couple about 20 years older than me. I nodded hello as we passed. I had the cliffs on the banks of the river almost to myself. It grew colder as the afternoon wore on, and I finally decided to head back home. Getting out of Omaha, and seeing open country had done me good. I got back in the car, buckled up, and started home. I decided to take the interstate. It took me to the Iowa side of the Missouri River.

As I drove, I thought about Duncan Smedley. Sister Eveline may have been right. The old lie had come back. It was two weeks till Passover, and the hateful old lies had returned. The economy was bad, and people wanted someone to blame. They blamed immigrants, they blamed the president, they blamed minorities. Jews are a minority, a community of outliers, and suspicion frequently fell on us. Gays, too, aren't part of the mainstream, and that made us a target.

Back at my apartment, I powered up the computer. There was no message from Terry or my mother, but I did have an e-mail from Rabbi Braun. It was a forward from the Jewish center, decrying the recent anti-Semitic rant by Duncan Smedley. The town's Jewish leaders, including the Katzenheim brothers, urged a boycott of Smedley's sponsors. Smedley's hate speech hadn't gone unnoticed.

I turned off the computer, and called home in Boulder. I wanted to talk to someone who would understand.

"Hi Mom," I said, when she picked up.

"Rico, good to hear from you. It's just a couple of weeks till your vacation, and you'll be here. We can't wait."

"Me either, Mom. What are you making for Passover?"

"Terry is helping me. I'm sure we'll start out with matzo ball soup, we always do. Then we'll have brisket."

"Sounds great." I was silent. "Mom, there's this radio guy here in Omaha. He's saying that there is a cabal of Jewish bankers deliberately wrecking the country's economy."

"That's novel," Mom said, sarcastically. "I've never heard that one before. You'd think if these *schmendriks* had to target Jews, they'd come up with something new, wouldn't you?"

"I guess that's too much work. These ideas have been out there for hundreds of years, and whenever anyone wants to stir something up, they go back to what's tried and true," I said. "This radio guy says the Jewish bankers are all homos."

"I'd like to say people aren't stupid enough to buy that kind of talk," my mother sighed, "but I'm not that hopeful. Promise me you'll be careful. Do you think you're in danger?"

My mother was concerned, mothers usually are. I'd been wrong to call her, now she'd worry. But I was in no danger. Still, I remembered Sister Eveline's eerily prescient words about the old lie and a black shadow near me.

"Mom, if they start rounding up Jews in Omaha, they won't have anywhere to put us all. There's a lot gays, too; we're everywhere."

My mother was silent on the other end. "Be careful, OK? There's not always safety in numbers," she finally said. "Maybe you should take a self-defense course. And you're so short, I wish Terry was there with you."

Mom was worrying unnecessarily; I'm perfectly capable of taking care of myself. My mother knew that Terry had saved my life in Georgia. It didn't matter to her what Terry's father had done, because Terry had sacrificed himself to protect me. In her eyes, Terry can do no wrong. I was incapable and incompetent in her eyes, and Terry was my only salvation.

"I miss Terry," I said, trying to re-direct the conversation. "Does he come over much?"

"Harry and I adore him," my mother said, almost reverently. "He's such a nice man. So much nicer than" she lowered her voice, "Ted ever was."

"Is Terry there now?" I asked. They'd liked Ted just fine.

"As a matter of fact, he is. He and Harry are watching the game. Shall I put him on?"

"No, don't bother, I'll call him later," I said. I said goodbye, and rang off.

I powered the computer back up, and scoured the Web for a movie to watch. I was tired from driving, but I didn't feel like going to bed. I wished I had a friend in Omaha to do something with. That friend would never be Lisa, and certainly not the twins.

I checked my e-mail again, bored, and looked for something to do. Omaha had theater and movies. I don't like going places by myself. It takes time to make friends, and I'm impatient. Teaching doesn't provide companionship. Unlike other jobs, the only people you are around most of the time are your students. You can't be friends with them, it blurs the boundaries. Finally, my eyes burned with fatigue, and I decided to go to bed.

I took the heater into the bedroom, and cranked it up. The room grew warm, and I fell asleep quickly. My sleep was troubled that night. In my dreamscape, I found myself in a green field. I wasn't sure where I was. It wasn't a mountain meadow, it was flat. There were some tiny wildflowers, and the grass grew up to my knees. I was lost, and couldn't see any buildings or signs to tell me where I was. I became anxious; I didn't know how I'd gotten there.

The air was suddenly still. I could no longer hear the birds sing. The sky was cloudy, but it didn't look like rain. Something was terribly wrong. My head began to ache, and I felt a sinking in the pit of my stomach. The stillness ended abruptly, and the wind began to blow. It was wind like I'd never felt before, like a hurricane or typhoon. I heard noise like a freight train, and the wind blew harder still. I knew with a terrible certainty that I was going to die. I shouted out in fear, and woke.

I sat up in bed. I was drenched in sweat, and felt disoriented. Where was I? My heart was pounding, and I tried to figure out my dream. I had been in a terrible storm. Why did that frighten me? I took a deep breath, and tried to calm down. I wished Terry was there. I wanted to call him; I looked at the clock. It was 2:30 in the morning. I couldn't call. He was working, and needed his sleep. I looked at the bedside table, and stared at the phone, willing it to ring. It didn't.

The next morning, I got up late. I was tired, groggy from my nightmare. I hated those awful dreams, and wished I could flip a switch and turn them off. Just after 9:00 a.m., I called Terry. He was heading to work.

"Hi Terry," I said.

"Hey, you," he said. "Why didn't you call last night? I was over at your folks. Your mom said you called. What happened?"

I fought the urge to say that the phone worked both ways, and he could have easily called me. "I didn't want to interrupt the game," I said. "Mom said you were watching hockey with Harry."

"It was great," Terry said, with pleasure. "We don't have hockey in Georgia. It's a lot of fun."

"It's all right," I said.

"All right? How come you don't like it better? You have a home town team, both hockey and football. It's great."

"I'm not a jock like you are," I said. "Sorry."

"You've got other qualities," he said.

"I look like an international model?" I asked.

"You're OK. But you're no sex symbol," Terry said, laughing.

"Terry, aren't you blinded by love?"

He sighed. "Blinded, but not blind. I miss you. How long till you come home?"

"Just about 10 days. It's lucky I work at the Jewish center. Most people don't get off for Passover. What's the weather like?"

"It's gorgeous," he said. "The days are sunny, the nights are cold. It's perfect sleeping weather." He paused. "Are you having nightmares again? You sound tired."

"Every now and then," I said, vaguely. I didn't want to tell him about my recent dream. "I miss you, *hartse*," I finally said.

"I miss you too. I'm anxious to see you. How is your job? Will you be staying on there, do you know?"

"I don't know anything. The semester's just about half over, I should know soon. I haven't seen much of Rabbi Braun. He's a busy man," I added.

"Rico," he said, softly, "I'm nervous about this holiday dinner. What do I have to do?"

"What do you mean?" I asked. "You don't have to do anything. You just eat. It's nice of you to help Mom, I'll help too."

"I'm not Jewish. I don't know anything about Passover. I don't want to look like a fool; I don't know any of your Jewish language."

"Relax," I assured him. "Just eat a lot, OK? There's something called the *Haggadah*, it's a prayer book. We read some prayers, and then we eat." I paused. "Don't be anxious, enjoy yourself. You know the story, right? It comes from Exodus. You probably read it in Sunday school."

"I guess," Terry said. He didn't sound convinced. "Your religion is hard, did you know that? Harry said you only get forgiven once a year. You're not supposed to mix meat and cheese, you can't eat bacon. And you have that horrible thing done, you know, down there."

"Don't be squeamish, Terry," I said. "You make it all sound so bad. Think of it not like a burden, but as something you do for love. There are things you do because it honors the past."

Terry didn't sound convinced. "The past is over, Ric. Should we stop taking penicillin because our ancestors didn't use it?"

I didn't answer, thinking. "You do things because you love God. It's not like you go to hell if you eat a piece of ham. We don't believe that. And God gave us a brain, and that intelligence invented medicine."

"I think my religion is easier," Terry said. "I'm glad you don't expect me to change."

"Yes, Terry, but ask yourself, whose food is better? Yours, or ours?"

He paused. "Actually, Ric, that is your best argument so far. Your mom's brisket is great. Of course, my side has Southern fried chicken."

"And there you have it," I said. "My missionary efforts are over. Brisket vs. fried chicken, it's a draw."

Terry laughed. "Come back soon, OK? I miss your twisted perspective on the world. You make me feel so sane."

"Terry!" I reprimanded. "Be nice. Besides, sanity is boring."

"I love you, Rico," he said, seriously. "Things are less fun without you."

"Terry, that is the nicest thing you've said to me." We said goodbye, and I was pensive. He was right. Life is less fun alone. I was lonely. Did I really want to live without Terry? I didn't know where our relationship was going, I couldn't see the future. Although Terry and I had been through rough times together, I loved him. I wanted to be with him. We'd gone through fire, and come out still in love. Not everyone can say that.

I felt more kindly toward the world after talking with Terry. I looked out the window, and was glad to see the sun shining. The weather mirrored my happy mood. The snow was mostly gone from the yard. I opened the window, and was surprised. It was warm--- it was actually *warm* outside. I put on a sweatshirt, no jacket, and walked downstairs. I stepped out in the yard, and was even happier. It was a lovely day. I took a deep breath. It felt like springtime. I went back inside, and decided it was time for action. I combed my hair, and got ready to go out for a walk.

I heard footsteps above me, and thought about Lisa. I hadn't seen her lately. I was lonely, but Lisa wasn't going to be a friend.

It was gorgeous outside, and I wanted to savor every moment. I heard birds singing, and there was a warm, gentle breeze. It was Sunday afternoon, and children were outdoors playing. My neighborhood was residential, and the houses were well-maintained, for the most part.

I walked. It had been cold since I'd been in Omaha; winter had lasted so long. Now the sun shone brightly, and I was certain summer was around the corner. The days were longer, and, in the sunlight, I could see buds on the branches. Walking confirmed my first assessment of the city; Omaha was a pretty place.

Someone had failed to pick up their newspaper from the sidewalk, and I glanced at the headline. "Smedley Angers Jews," it said. I hadn't thought about Smedley all morning. Just seeing his name made me feel lousy.

The Jewish community would stand up for itself. My thoughts turned dark and hateful, and for an instant, I hoped someone would teach Smedley a lesson. Where was the murderer of the police chief, I wondered, and why couldn't he have killed Smedley instead? Smedley was just using up oxygen, not contributing anything but hatred. I tried to put him out of my mind.

Still, I wondered about Chief Herman's murder. Why hadn't it been solved? Was the police department in Omaha so incompetent? My hometown had been rocked by murder; the police had made every conceivable bureaucratic mistake, and a little girl's death was never solved. I wondered if that would happen with Will Herman's murder.

The sun was warm, and I couldn't stay anxious. I thought about Terry, and felt happy. Spring was here, and better things were on the way. The police chief's murder would be solved, and whatever happened, it had nothing to do with me, no impact on my life. Events, though, would soon prove me wrong. I was close to the fire, but I didn't know it at the time.

Chapter 10

At work the next day, I had to master a new routine. The security system was finally in place, and I was asked to show my driver's license before a guard would let me in. He checked my name against a list, and had me pass through a newly installed metal detector.

"I'm sorry, Mr. Wise," the man from Katzenheim Security told me. "It's a new system, there are still some kinks. Once you get your new ID, the process will be quicker." His name tag identified him as LeVon. He was a tall, husky African American, and looked to be in his mid 30's. Marc hadn't mentioned anything about new identity cards.

"I know you're doing your job. But I have students waiting. I wasn't expecting this," I said, trying to keep my tone pleasant, glancing at my watch.

"Your students will be late, too," the guard said. "We just got the system up and running yesterday. Luckily there haven't been too many glitches."

When I entered my classroom, I had another surprise. It was spring break for the public schools, and parents who hadn't been able to find a sitter or day care for their school age youngsters brought them to class with them. Normally there were a few toddlers in the classroom, someone's child was always sick, or their sitter was ill. Today was different. At the center, our vacation was during Passover, after the half-way point of the semester. This week, the schools were out.

"I'm sorry," Marisa, one of my students said to me. She had three little ones with her, a girl and twin boys. The little girl was probably about eight, the twins were maybe four or five. "I try the day care, they full," she said, looking dejected. "My babies are too little to be alone, I must take to work with me."

Marisa wasn't the only one with youngsters. There were about 10 children in my class, far more than usual. I was going to have to figure out something or the entire period would be derailed.

"Could the moms and dads take turns with the kids?" I asked. There was an extra table in the back of the class, and if at least one parent watched the children, they wouldn't disturb the other students much. One of the adults would have to miss the work of the class that day, which was too bad, but it would be worse if the entire student body was disrupted. The parents talked among themselves, and worked out a system.

I asked the adults to open their textbooks, and began my lesson. We were still on prepositions, something that perplexed my students. Just as we got underway, the class was interrupted. Marc walked in. He had never done that before, and all I could think was that I must have done something wrong. For the life of me, though, I couldn't figure out what.

"Rabbi Braun," I said. It wouldn't be right to call him by his first name in front of my students. He looked tense as he walked over to me.

"I'm sorry to interrupt," Marc said, softly. "There is a meeting of all staff at noon. You need to be there, over at the main campus. It's important." He turned and left. My heart was pounding. What was going on? Was this about the new security system?

When the boss summons you, you don't ask questions. I began teaching, still wondering about Marc's visit. Why was this staff meeting so important? I was distracted, and tried to focus on the class. I kept losing my place in the textbook.

The noon meeting was during my class for immigrants. It would take half an hour to get over to the new part of town; at 11:30, I asked the students to turn to the person next to them and practice some drills. I told them they were free to leave at the usual time, 12:45, and were on the honor system to stay till then. I hurriedly walked out of the classroom. I wished Marc would have just sent me an e-mail.

I got in my car, and drove over to the main campus. I parked my car in the lot, which was almost full. The campus was large, and I didn't want to be late. I headed toward the staff lounge, where the meetings were normally held. A sign on the door redirected me to another room, one I had never been in before. I finally found it, and walked in as quietly as I could.

I was surprised at the number of people there. Every single person I'd ever seen at the center was in the conference room, along with a couple of rabbis I'd never seen. Marc nodded his head at me, and I sat down. I had most of my interactions with him, and consequently, I didn't know the pecking order of the center. Marc isn't technically my boss; my paychecks are signed by the board president. The Katzenheim brothers, who owned the kosher meatpacking plant, were on the board, as well as muckety-mucks, or *k'nockers* from the Jewish community.

"I'm glad you are all here," a well-dressed woman said. "I know you have responsibilities, and we have all been under great duress." She had black hair that was swept up on top of her head, and very few wrinkles, though I thought she was probably about 50. Oh, the miracles of plastic surgery or injections. "I'm Marjorie Zebar, the center's board president, for those of you who don't know me," she said.

Everyone around me looked nervous.

"As you are no doubt aware," Ms. Zebar continued, "our new security system is up. "We are grateful to the Katzenheim brothers for helping us with this. There have recently been some threats against the center. Because of those threats, the board feels the system is necessary."

A low twitter went through the assembly, and I looked at Marc questioningly. He shrugged his shoulders. Ms. Zebar gave no indication of the nature of the threats, and I wondered if anyone would ask. Had there been suspicions of a bomb, warnings of violence?

"These threats," Ms. Zebar continued, "came last week, when a certain right-wing radio host decided to engage in inflammatory, anti-Semitic rhetoric." Duncan Smedley, surely. Unstable people heard his *drech* on the radio, and took their clues from what they heard.

"The board, along with community leaders, has met in special session to address the situation with Smedley," Ms. Zebar continued. "We have written him a letter, which we also sent to the Omaha newspaper. We contacted the station owner, and are urging our friends in town to boycott the businesses that support Smedley. In addition, rabbis have met with non-Jewish clergy in the community, who will ask Smedley to consider his words more carefully." She said the name "Smedley" with evident disgust.

Ms. Zebar gave us each a copy of the letter which had been sent to Smedley, as well as a list of his sponsors. If he didn't apologize by the end of the week, there would be a rally in support of the Jewish community. When I thought most of the important work of the meeting was done, I looked at Marc, and tapped my watch. He nodded, and

I left, returning across town. I was sure Marc would let me know about the rally, which had tentatively been scheduled for the Sunday before Passover, if Smedley made no apology. I thought it would be tricky to organize a march that quickly, but since no one asked my opinion, I didn't share it.

I tried to focus on my classes the rest of the day. My purpose was to teach English, and I tried not to be depressed by Smedley, and the threats the center had received. Smart people were working on the problem, and they would know what to do. I admired the restraint and tact of the community leaders in the letter they wrote to Smedley. They had kept the tone pleasant but direct. I wanted to find Smedley and kick him in the shins, or somewhere more painful.

When the day was over, I drove home, thinking about the children in my classroom that day. For the most part, they'd been very well-behaved. I'm not particularly paternal, but I sometimes wish I'd had children. Somewhere deep inside me, there was the desire for traditional domesticity. I longed to be with Terry, and live in my little house in Boulder. I wanted children, a dog, and simple happiness. But that didn't seem possible. I was middle-aged, and circumstances had taken me far from home. The dream of life with Terry seemed distant, far-away.

That evening, I called Terry. He answered, even though he was at work. I was a little surprised he picked up. He usually doesn't when he's behind the butcher's counter. I didn't mention my hopes about living with him forever, and raising children. It suddenly seemed saccharin.

"It's slow tonight," Terry said. "I guess no one wants my meat."

"I do, Terry," I offered. When there was little else to say, we resorted to our little corny jokes.

"That's what you're supposed to say," Terry said with a laugh. "I can't wait to see you."

"Me either," I said.

"What is it you're not telling me, Rico?" Terry asked.

"What do you mean?"

"You don't sound like yourself. Your mom says someone there is giving you a hard time."

"Not me in particular," I said, sorry I'd mentioned it to my mother. "Nothing like that. There's a guy on the radio that hates Jews and gays. Because of him, there have been some threats against the center. Now we all have to pass through a metal detector."

"Why do people hate Jews?" Terry asked, not waiting for my answer. "Are you sure you're safe? Come back home to Boulder, Rico."

"I'm fine, don't worry. People hate anyone who's different, Terry, you know that. It's human nature, whether you're in Omaha or Boulder. That's why people hate gays." My words weren't completely true; Omaha was homogeneous, compared to Boulder. In Boulder, people mistrust you if you *aren't* different.

"A security system? It's sad that you need that. Be careful. I wish I was there with you."

"Look, Terry, lots of Jewish community centers have metal detectors. The one in Atlanta did."

"Really? That's terrible. I mean, it's terrible that you guys need that."

I was silent. There was nothing else to say. It always throws me off when anyone calls Jews "you guys." It's a way of distancing us, of making us into the Other.

"Rico, you have Arabs in your class, don't you? Are they the problem?" Terry asked. "Are they terrorists?"

"I have Muslims in one of my classes, but they aren't terrorists. They've come here trying to make a better life for themselves and their families. They don't want trouble." I thought about Sam and Ahmed. Of the two, the one I suspected more was Sam, and he was Christian.

The police had said there was evidence that the killer of the chief of police was an immigrant. The people who moved here came here with nothing, no one. If someone offered them enough money, would they commit a crime?

You might as well suspect anyone. If someone paid me a lot of money, would I do something unscrupulous, something violent? I hoped not, I didn't think so, but I had never been that desperate, and no one had asked me. There are many desperate people. Who wasn't a suspect, if that were the criteria?

My refugees came from violent countries. They say some people who are oppressed and tortured become oppressors and torturers, the Stockholm syndrome. Was that the case with some recent immigrant? Was someone mimicking the terrible behavior he experienced?

"You're quiet, Rico," Terry said. "Are you sure everything's OK?"

"I miss you, that's all," I said. "Just a little more than a week and I'll be home." My thoughts turned from murder to dreams of a quiet home life and little children. Maybe even a dog. Of course, we had Sid the cat, but I wanted a dog, too. Why not? It was my fantasy—so I might as well add a picket fence and a new car.

"Gotta go," Terry said, abruptly, and I assumed he had a customer. I ended the call, and turned on the computer.

I logged on to an Omaha news Web site. There was nothing new about the murder. There was a brief blurb about Duncan Smedley, and how "controversial" he was. Controversial? He was a racist, an anti-Semite, a homophobe. Why were journalists afraid to say that? Did they worry about offending him? Was he making someone a lot of money? I turned off the computer, discouraged.

I looked on my desk, and re-read the letter from the center's board president. She'd included a list of Smedley's sponsor to write or boycott. There were about a dozen companies, both local and national. Omaha is a hub of Midwestern commerce, home to a number of business magnates. I was glad to see none of them supported Smedley. I made a mental inventory of the products I usually bought. I would have to check the manufacturer's labels.

I thought, too, about Ms. Zebar's talk of a rally. Had she mentioned where it would be held? And how could they organize a march so quickly, in just a week? Maybe they could get Smedley to back down and apologize. I wanted more, though, I wanted vengeance. There was a part of me, a part I'm not proud of, that would have like to see people like him disappear. I wouldn't shed any tears if Smedley met the same fate as the police chief.

That night, my sleep was troubled. I was in a lovely, green field again, the meadow that I didn't recognize. It was springtime. I looked around, and tried to find some marker, some distinguishing aspect of the field. I couldn't find anything. I listened intently. If I could hear traffic noise, I could find the road. I heard the sound of running water, and realized I was by a river. If I was close enough to hear it, then I could find the stream, and maybe that would help me.

I began walking. The air was still, and it unnerved me. The sky was grayish-yellow, and there was the heavy feel of humidity.

I heard the sound of crying. My heart froze. What was it? I listened intently. I turned toward the noise. It was nothing frightening: I saw two little boys. I walked toward them. They looked alike. Were they the sweet little twin boys I'd had in my class that morning, Marisa's children? Where was their mother?

"Joselito, Juan," I said. "Don't cry. Your mother will be back soon." I came closer to the little boys; the dark clouds overhead parted, and I saw their hair was not black, it was blond. The boys turned towards me, and it took me a moment to recognize them. I recognized the boys I'd seen in Harry's old, sepia picture. I walked closer to them. The yellow cast of the sky gave my dreamscape the feel of an old-fashioned photograph.

One of the little boys was hitting the other. "Stop that!" I said, running toward them. I saw a look of sheer hatred on one boy's face. Something about that look was evil, and chilled me to the bone. I tried to pull the fighting boys apart, and I heard a terrible noise. It was loud, deafening, like a freight train. The boys looked at me. The noise grew louder still, and I knew we were all going to die.

I woke up, disoriented. Where was I? There was indeed a terrible sound. What was it? It sounded like a very loud train, or maybe a piece of heavy machinery. But there was no train track near the apartment in Nebraska. It was night, so there was no road work being done. What was it? It was some kind of siren, I realized. What did it mean? It wasn't the sound of an ambulance passing, it was too loud for that. I got up. It was cold: I hadn't turned on the heater. It had been so warm that day.

I went to the window to see where the noise was coming from. Rain was pounding against the glass, and the wind was blowing fiercely. I saw a flash of lightning, and a loud clap of thunder came almost immediately after. That wasn't good, it wasn't good at all. The terrible sound I heard wasn't the thunder, though.

I didn't have a TV, so I turned on the radio. "Warning," the announcer said. "A tornado has struck just outside of the Omaha city limits. Residents are advised to take shelter immediately. This is a tornado warning, a tornado has been seen."

The siren kept going. What did a person do in a tornado? We don't have them in Colorado, so I had no idea. I went back to the window, and looked out. Again, I saw a flash of lightning, and thunder followed immediately. I had never heard thunder so loud. Between the thunder and the siren, I could hardly hear myself think. I didn't know what else to do, so I pulled the chair out from the desk, and crouched down under it. If there was flying debris, then maybe the desk top would protect me. I grabbed my cell phone, and held it in my hand.

After a few minutes, the siren stopped. The thunder wasn't as loud, though it was still raining hard. The radio said the tornado warning had been downgraded to a tornado watch, with the possibility of flash flooding. My heart was pounding, and I wanted to call Terry. It was my first tornado, hopefully my last, and I needed to tell someone. I looked at the bedside clock. It was three in the morning, and Terry wouldn't welcome my call. Still, it wasn't every night that there was a tornado. Although I'd talked to Terry earlier, I decided to call him. It was selfish, but I told myself he'd want to know that I was all right.

"Yeah?" a groggy voice said on the other end of the phone. "Rico? What's wrong?" I felt bad for waking Terry.

"We just had a tornado. There was a siren."

"A tornado? Are you all right?" Terry sounded awake now.

"I'm fine. I was sleeping, and I heard this siren go off. I turned on the radio, and they said a tornado touched down."

"Crap, Rico, that's terrible. Are a lot of people hurt?"

"I don't know anything yet," I said. "It just happened. I sat under the desk in case there was flying debris," I added.

"It sounds scary," Terry said. "Does your apartment have a storm cellar?"

I didn't know. Terry and I continued to chat, and I felt calmer. It helped to talk with someone. I was lucky to have Terry in my life.

"I'm sorry I woke you up," I said, finally, beginning to feel drowsy.

"Don't worry," Terry said, kindly. "I'm glad you're all right." We said goodbye, and I put my head back on the pillow. I couldn't fall asleep, though; I remembered the strange nightmare I'd had. In my dream, I had been startled by the savage look on one of the children's faces.

Tired, I managed to drag myself through work the next day. We talked about the tornado in class; my students weren't as frightened as I was. The difficult lives of my students made me realize just how good my life had been. For most of them, the destructiveness of nature was a given. Storms were the least of their problems. Most came from countries where the government was corrupt and in some cases repressive; others had come from war- torn areas, and spent years in refugee camps. My life had been easy in comparison.

The week passed; the time for Passover and my trip back to Colorado drew near. I was happy about seeing my family and friends. I was anxious to see Terry.

Duncan Smedley refused to apologize for his anti-Semitic rants. He continued blaming Jews for the country's economic woes. His rhetoric often included African Americans and gays; his lies were tired and old, but his talk resulted in more threats against the center. A bar where gay people sometimes went was burned down. Fortunately, no one was inside at the time.

Marc sent me an e-mail. "There will be a rally on Sunday afternoon," he wrote. "It's being organized by leaders of the religious community here in Omaha." The march would start at the Episcopal cathedral, pass Smedley's radio studio, and end up in front of the art museum.

"I'll be there," I wrote back. I was leaving for Boulder Sunday evening; Passover began the next day. I could pack on Saturday. I'd hoped to leave Friday after work, but I needed to be at the rally on Sunday afternoon.

The next day, Marc was at his small office in my building. He handed me some fliers promoting the rally.

"I hope we don't have a tornado the day of the march," I said, with a smile.

"This is the time of year we get them."

"Really?" I asked. Tornadoes were a new phenomenon for me. Fortunately, no one had been hurt when the storm had touched down, but some homes and businesses were damaged.

"Yes, spring is the time for twisters. Normally we don't get too many; Nebraska is north of what they call 'tornado alley.' But we still have them."

"You sound like a meteorologist," I teased. "If you ever get tired of being a rabbi, maybe they'll hire you at Channel 10."

Marc smiled, and I was glad he liked me enough to allow some gentle teasing. I have a sarcastic tongue, and should have been a little more careful around the man who was, for all intents and purposes, my boss. But humor sometimes breaks the ice; after the tornado, and in light of Duncan Smedley, I thought a little levity was in order. Things had become so darn serious.

"Will you go home for Passover?" Marc asked. "Does your family have a Seder? If not, you're welcome to come to our home. My wife, Liz, makes great matzo balls."

"Thanks," I said, "I'll be going home. I'm glad the center is closed. I'm grateful." Passover comes before Easter; increasingly, schools had vacation in the midway point in the semester. The Jewish community center took the Passover week off, regardless of when the holiday fell.

My students were waiting, but this was the longest I'd talked with Marc since my first day in Omaha. It was an opportunity to get information. "Is there any word yet about next year?" I asked. "Have you heard if my contract will be extended?"

"We have a grant application for the English as a second language class, but this year we have some competitors. Your funding comes from two sources, you know. The government pays for the ESL for immigrants, and the Katzenheim brothers pay for your other two classes. I can't tell you anything for certain yet, but as soon as I know, I will tell you."

"Thanks," I said. I needed the job, and maybe Terry could find work here in Omaha.

I thanked him, and went back into the class room. Marisa's children had come back again with her; she couldn't find a sitter. I looked at the three little children, the little girl and twin boys. Again, I had the longing for children of my own. As I watched the twins, though, I remembered my nightmare, and the murderous look on the little boy's face.

"Mr. Wise, was that the right answer?" Mario asked.

The student's question brought me back abruptly to the present. My mind had been wandering. I hadn't heard the young man.

The class ended, and I began to get ready for the next section. I waved goodbye to the children as they filed out with their parents.

Attendance in the ESL class for refugees was more sporadic. Although the students had to be there, they were busy with so many things. They had children, they were looking for jobs, they were getting vaccines.

That day, Ahmed was in class, and I had a surprise visit from my Iraqi Christian, Sam. It had been weeks since I'd seen Sam, and I assumed he'd dropped out, or maybe found a job and was taking night school somewhere else. I wasn't the only English teacher in Omaha, and other agencies besides the Jewish community center offer English as a second language to immigrants. I'd even wondered if Sam had been hiding after killing the chief of police.

Problems began right away. Ahmed scowled at Sam, and said something in Arabic. Naturally, I didn't understand. Sam understood, though, and he bolted out of his chair. He stood next to Ahmed's desk, towering fiercely, and then Ahmed stood up and faced him. I thought there was going to be a fight, and I wasn't sure what to do. I'd never had violence in class before.

"Gentlemen," I said, in my firmest school teacher voice. "This is not the place or the time to discuss your differences. You are here to learn English."

I made my way over to them. Both men were bigger than me, and I didn't want to get in the way of blows. But it was my classroom, and I had an obligation to my other students. School is a place to learn in safety. I stood slightly away from Ahmed; I worried that if I got too close it would make things worse. Men are skittish, insecure creatures.

"Teacher, this does not concern you," Sam said to me, dismissively.

"Teacher, Sam is right," Ahmed said, looking at Sam murderously.

"This is my classroom," I said, firmly; my voice came out a little louder, a little more shrill than I would have liked. If I was as tall and heavy as Terry was, I wouldn't worry about how I sounded. If wishes were horses…

The other students stared at the two men, watching expectantly. They were anticipating a fight. I was so angry, I could have throttled them both. This was a classroom, not a battle field. Sam lunged at Ahmed, and I tried to grab his shoulders. All I succeeded in doing was tearing his shirt, and Sam looked at me in surprise. Miriam, one of the Iraqi women, yelled something. Whatever she said did the trick. Both Sam and Ahmed froze in place. At least there had been no blows. The only damage came from me, I'd torn Sam's shirt.

My heart was pounding. I insisted that the men separate that very minute. As if a genie had heard my silent wish, or as if he was psychic, LeVon, the security guard, was walking by outside classroom. Maybe he'd heard Miriam's shout; LeVon strode in with a sense of purpose. Both Sam and Ahmed were startled by his approach. LeVon is a big guy, and looked very official in his uniform.

"What's going on here?" the guard asked. "Is everything all right, Mr. Wise?"

Sam and Ahmed continued to stare at each other, but they didn't make a move. I was frozen in place, too, but I was supposed to be in charge.

"These men were arguing and disrupting the class," I said, my voice sounding high-pitched, my words too fast. I sounded more like the class tattle-tale than the instructor.

"Anyone hurt?" LeVon asked, looking at Sam's torn shirt.

"No," I said. Time seemed to stand still; I realized how fast my heart was beating. I took a deep breath.

"I'm leaving," Sam announced.

"No, you ain't," LeVon said, in a deep voice which I wish I could have emulated. "You and me are going to talk first. This is not a boxing ring. You're both in real trouble."

"I can't get in trouble with police," Ahmed wailed. "I will be deported."

The fight had gone out of the two men, and they looked ashamed and deflated. The room stunk with testosterone.

If I wasn't so angry, I would have felt sorry for Sam and Ahmed. What was the trouble between them? One was Christian, one Muslim. But it was so much more than that. They were frustrated, and felt powerless. They were in a new country, and I doubted that they were receiving a warm welcome from my fellow American citizens. I'm sure the people of Omaha are no worse, no better than anyone else. Still, there is prejudice and xenophobia.

"You want me to take these two tough guys outside, have a talk with them?" LeVon asked, ominously. He towered over Sam and Ahmed, and I wanted to hug him in gratitude. I felt calm, back in control.

"That won't be necessary," I said confidently, "Thanks, LeVon."

LeVon looked at me, and an expression I couldn't quite interpret crossed his face. Pity, maybe? Compassion? Anger? I didn't know him well enough to tell. "Just doin' my job, Mr. Wise," he said. "Let me know if there's more trouble from either one." LeVon strode away, leaving me with the two gladiators.

"Please, Mr. Wise, I don't like police," Ahmed said, and I wondered if he was going to cry. I had no reason to feel sorry for the two men. They had caused me nothing but aggravation, disrupting my class. I owed them nothing, so why did I pity Sam and Ahmed?

"Here's the deal," I said, speaking quietly. "This is what's going to happen. You're going to leave the center permanently, and you're going to take English somewhere else. I don't want to see either of you on this campus ever again. I won't turn you in to your case workers. But I'll be watching you, believe me. If I hear you cause problems for another teacher…"

Without waiting for another word from me, Sam bolted. Ahmed at least had the grace to thank me. "I thank you, Teacher," Ahmed said, giving me a little bow. "I thank you." He, too, was gone. Was I being too kind, was I a *schlemiel*? I took a deep breath, and turned back to my class. The other students tried to pretend nothing had happened, and didn't stare at my reddened face. The class had just begun; I continued teaching, there was nothing else to do.

As I drove home that evening, again I wondered about the two men. What if one of my two quarreling students had been the police chief's killer? I thought of the strange letter Marc had received, saying the police were looking for a Middle Easterner. It seemed farfetched to think either Sam or Ahmed killed the police chief. I didn't believe it for a moment, and was sure someone had tried to frame a foreigner.

I hadn't been home for long before I had a visit from someone else I'd suspected as a murderer.

"Hello," Lisa said, when I opened the door.

"Lisa, what a surprise." I hadn't seen her since the disastrous Purim festival.

"I hear there's been trouble at the Jewish center. Is everything OK? Some threats? A new security system? Does it have anything to do with Duncan Smedley?"

"Do you want to come in?" I asked. Lisa made no move. "There have been threats, that's all I know. I don't know anything else. Some *schmuck* is taking Smedley's words to heart," I said.

Lisa looked at me, doubtfully. "You don't know the specifics?"

"No, do you?" I asked. I had the feeling she knew something. Was this her idea of friendship, taunting me? She had information she wasn't going to share, and thought her knowledge gave her power.

"I really can't say anything," Lisa said, turning to leave. I was sure she wanted to tell me. I was curious, but I didn't want to beg. "We're not supposed to comment on an ongoing investigation. At least no one has been hurt so far," she added ominously, walking down the stairwell.

The woman was maddening. What did her colleagues think of her, I wondered. I'd been about to ask what she was doing for Passover, but I no longer cared. She could spend the days alone. I would be with my family, who I loved, and who loved me.

Chapter 11

The week ended quietly. My English as a second language class for immigrants was subdued. Neither Sam nor Ahmed returned to school. I'd dealt kindly with them, and wondered if I'd done the right thing. Terry accused me of being too soft, and said I'd better be that forgiving of him next time we had an argument.

"Terry," I said, "we won't have any more disagreements if you'll just admit that I'm always right."

"In your dreams," he scoffed. "What if one of them was the killer?"

"Terry, that isn't likely. Why would one of them have done it?"

"You're no detective, Ric. Let the police decide."

"They don't seem to be doing a good job, Terry. It's been a couple of months, and still no word."

"Strange. What's the problem? Maybe you should tell them about those two jerks."

I was silent. I didn't remind Terry that his father had been a law enforcement officer, a probable murderer, and that no policeman or detective had ever solved my father's tragic death. Terry and I pretend that the past never happened. He does a better job of it than I do.

"Terry," I asked, "have you ever wanted children?" I had to stop thinking about his dad, so I changed the subject.

"What? Where did that come from? Kids? That's impossible. We're both men. Don't tell me you're thinking about a sex change."

"Funny, Terry. I know we can't have our own children, I had biology in high school. There are children out there who need a good home. We could be foster daddies, or adopt a child from a third world country."

"Ric, I've been there, done that. I have a daughter, you know. I love her. Kids are a lot of work, and we're both old."

I'd forgotten about Terry's daughter. I'd never met her, so she didn't seem real to me. Terry's daughter lives with his ex-wife. I'd never met the wife, either, though she

148

and Terry are still friends. It took me a minute to come up with his daughter's name. "How is Karen?" I asked. "Do you hear from her?"

"When she needs money," he sighed. "Every now and then she sends me an e-mail."

"Maybe Karen wants a little brother or sister," I offered. And that was the extent of our conversation. Terry didn't seem anxious to have more children. But I was just getting started, and I pride myself on my powers of persuasion.

Neither my nightmares nor the tornadoes returned that week, and I was grateful on both counts. The weather stayed lovely and warm, and I was ready for spring vacation. Saturday morning, I packed.

I was excited by the prospect of seeing Terry. We talked every day, sometimes twice. But that wasn't the same as being together. I missed him. Our relationship was new, and we had already been separated. Part of me wanted to quit my job and scurry back to Colorado. It was a childish impulse. I'm a grown man, and have to work. Maybe Terry would move to Omaha. Omaha is nice enough. But it wasn't home, and I missed the mountains.

Terry said that in Boulder, the days were warm, the nights cold. Getting ready for my trip home, I packed clothes for hiking; Terry wanted to explore some mountain trails. There would still be snow, at least, patches of it, even though Passover was late that year.

My mind drifted as I got organized for my trip. Something on the local news radio caught my attention, and I listened. Duncan Smedley, the local shock jock, had appeared at a meeting of a group that "some considered racist," according to the bland reporter. I wasn't surprised that Smedley addressed a racist gathering, but I was disgusted by the broadcaster's neutral language. I paid attention as the newscast continued; I wanted to know the name of the group. When the host identified the meeting as one held by the group "Coming Race War," I wasn't surprised. Smedley would have a lot in common with those crazies.

I finished getting my things together, and was about to go out for a walk when someone knocked on my front door. I wondered if it was Lisa again, with some new information she wanted to dangle in front of me. I decided to ask her about the police chief's murder the next time I saw her.

Two men were at the door, and it took a minute for me to recognize them. One looked young and in good health, the other was sickly and hunched over. They were so unlike, it was hard to believe they were brothers, much less twins.

"Earl, Darrel," I said. "Nice to see you, come in." It was a surprise to see them. I didn't think they would be back. I thought they were too shocked after meeting Terry.

Darrel strode in, and Earl shuffled in after.

"Hi, Rico, we were in town, and thought we'd stop by," Darrel said.

I wished they had called first, but here they were. I couldn't be rude; they were Harry's childhood friends.

"Nice to see you," I said. "What brings you to the city?"

Earl looked fidgety. Darrel answered, "A meeting."

My mind was on my trip home, and seeing Terry, my mom, and Harry. I didn't ask what kind of meeting; it probably had something to do with farming, and I didn't want to be bored with the details. "I'm going back to Boulder tomorrow," I announced.

"You're moving home? You just got here," Earl protested.

"For a vacation," I clarified.

"Oh, that's right, it's almost Easter," Darrel said. "You have time off from work?"

"A week," I answered, not bothering to say it was for Passover. They might not know what that was, and why embarrass them?

"Earl and me are going out for a runza," Darrel said. "We thought you might like to have one with us. Have you eaten a runza yet?"

A runza, I had discovered, is kind of like what New Yorkers call a knish, a little meat or cheese pie. I'd had runzas here in Omaha, and they were good.

"Yes, I've had them," I said. "Sure, I'll come along. Do you two have a favorite place?" There were runza cafes all over town, they were as common in Omaha as pizza or hamburger stands are in any other city.

"We do," Earl said. "We'll take you there, if you don't mind riding in the truck."

I didn't, and I followed the two down the stairs. Midwesterners are nothing if not practical, and they favor utilitarian vehicles; the twins were no exception. Their pickup wasn't new, but it looked sturdy. The lower half was covered with dust and mud.

Darrel drove, and Earl opened the door for me, expecting me to ride on the middle seat. I wished we'd taken my car. Then the two large men would be as cramped as I was going to be. Earl had a little difficulty getting in. I remembered Darrel saying Earl had arthritis, and that's why his room was on the first floor of the creepy old farmhouse.

We headed towards downtown, and Darrel parked by a small fast food café that had a sign which read: "Omaha's Best Runzas." We got out, and I followed the twins inside. I looked at the menu above the counter where the cashier stood. Runzas, like knishes, could be filled with different things: potatoes, meat, chicken, cabbage. The little café was crowded inside; the clientele was mostly older, and very white. We placed our orders: Darrel and Earl ordered ground beef, I ordered chicken. We found an empty booth; Darrel and Earl sat facing each other, so I sat next to Earl, since he was smaller, and there was more room.

A girl brought the runzas we'd ordered to the table, and they smelled delicious. They might have been Omaha's best, I didn't know.

The three of us ate in companionable silence. The runzas were tasty. It was nice of the twins to stop by, but we had little to talk about. I didn't know about farming, and they didn't know about teaching.

"How do you like Omaha?" Darrel asked, finally. Darrel was outgoing. His politics were disgusting, but he was personally charming, and not a bad-looking man. Darrel was Harry's age, mid-60's, but he looked 20 years younger. He had a full head of gray hair, and piercing blue eyes. Like Earl, he was tall, but he was heavier than his brother, and it suited him. I wouldn't want to get in a fight with Darrel; farm life had made him strong.

"I like it fine," I answered. "I love this warm weather. I was getting tired of the cold."

"Cold front coming through tomorrow," Early said sourly. In contrast to his brother, Earl seemed sullen and unhappy.

I'd heard that on the radio. I hoped it wouldn't interrupt the rally against Smedley. Or rather, the tolerance rally. The organizers had asked us not to use Smedley's name. The man was such a media whore, we didn't want to give him attention. Also, the Jewish center didn't want the march to be negative, so instead of being against racism, we were marching *for* tolerance.

"I hope it doesn't interfere with your flight home," Darrel added.

I hadn't even thought of that.

"Darrel and me don't much like Omaha," Earl said. He glanced at his brother, and Darrel nodded in agreement.

"Oh really?" I asked. "Why is that?"

"It's too big," Darrel explained. "There's too many people."

"And the wrong kind of people," Earl added.

I was trying to be polite. I knew where the conversation was headed, and I didn't like it. I didn't want to argue with two old men. Terry says I'm too confrontational, but I don't know how to be any other way. You have to stand for something in life.

"There's gangs in Omaha," Darrel continued. "Lots of crime. Lots of traffic. Some of the people who move here don't even speak English."

Here we go, I thought. I decided to play stupid. "I noticed. Harry took me to the Czech Café. A lot of the menu isn't in English. I heard an older couple speaking Czech, or maybe Russian."

The twins were silent, and I was pleased with myself. I'd scored. Sometimes you can make your point by just playing stupid. It's not hard for me to do, and isn't always an act.

Darrel wanted another runza, and I offered to get it for him. I walked over to the counter, and stood near the cash register. A tall, heavy set man came in and stood behind me in line. I ordered a sauerkraut and beef knish, and while I waited, I chatted with the clerk. She was friendly enough; Nebraskans are pretty good-natured. When the runza was ready, I took it and turned to go back to the table with the twins.

"Queer," the tall man in line behind me muttered.

I was surprised, and my face reddened. I didn't know what I'd done to merit the hostility. Duncan Smedley was poisoning the whole town. I don't look much like a

Nebraskan; I'm not tall and blond. I decided to ignore the comment, since he was bigger than me. Because I looked different, the guy decided I *was* different.

Darrel ate, and the brothers said they needed to be on their way. "Darrel don't much like to drive after dark," Earl explained. "You come out and see us anytime," Darrel said. "I know there ain't much to do on the farm, but we'd be glad to see you."

"Thanks," I said, terrified by the prospect. I didn't want to see Buffalo Crossing ever again. Still, Darrel and Earl were nice, friendly guys--- discounting their racist politics. I promised the twins I would say hello to Harry from them; they dropped me home, and we said goodbye.

I called Terry, who didn't pick up. He was probably working. I wanted to tell him about the nasty comment at the runza café, but I wasn't going to leave a message. What makes people hateful like that? I doubted if anyone ever called Terry a name, he was bigger than me.

I called my mother, and we talked for a few minutes. Next, I checked my e-mail, and was glad to see a message from Linda, my childhood friend. I answered back, and added that I would be glad to see her and her mother at the Seder.

My mind drifted, and I thought about Darrel and Earl. They had said they were at a meeting earlier that afternoon; I remembered the newscaster saying that Duncan Smedley had addressed a meeting of the group that was linked with the racists in the "Coming Race War." Is that where the twins had been, was that why they had come to Omaha? They seemed too nice to be racists. But just because someone had nice manners didn't mean they weren't bigots. Earl had given me some strange pamphlets when I first moved to town.

That night, my sleep was troubled. I dreamed that Terry was in a canoe on the Blue River, near the farmhouse where Darrel and Earl lived. I was standing on the shore, watching him. The wind was cold, the sky was dark.

"Come with me," Terry said.

I had never liked the water. I stood where I was. I couldn't make myself get close to the river's edge.

"Come on," Terry repeated. "The current is quick, I can't wait much longer."

"No, Terry," I said, woodenly. "I can't." Part of me wanted to go with Terry, but another part of me was too afraid.

"You have to come now," Terry said. "I can't wait any longer."

"I'll come," I called, suddenly frantic. The banks of the river were very steep, and I had trouble climbing down. When I got to the river, Terry's canoe had drifted far away.

"Come back, Terry!" I called. But Terry didn't hear me. His face was turned from me, and, in my dream, I knew I would never see him again.

When I woke up, my face was wet. I'd been crying. My bedroom was cold. I hadn't run the heat in several days; it had been so warm. I went to the living room, and got the little electric heater. I'd left the window open, and it was making the apartment chilly.

Earl said that the weather was changing, and he was right. It was 20 degrees cooler than it had been during the day. I closed the window. The moon was full, and the skies were clear. I wondered if there was going to be frost. I hoped the blooming flowers and budding seedlings wouldn't be harmed. I brought the little heater in the bedroom, and turned it on medium heat. In a few minutes, the room was toasty and warm, and I fell back to sleep. Terry was on my mind; as I drifted off I wished I could reach over and touch him. In another 24 hours, I would be able to.

The next morning, I put a bagel in the toaster, and called Terry. He sounded groggy.

"Hi, Terry," I said. "Did I wake you up?"

"No," he lied, weakly. "I was up."

"I'm looking forward to seeing you tonight," I said. "Can you pick me up, or do you work?" I asked.

"I work till seven," he said. "When do you get in? I've got it written down somewhere."

"I get in just before nine," I reminded him.

"I'll be there," he said, sounding a little more alert. "How's your weekend so far?" he asked.

"It's just party, party, party all the time," I answered, with gentle sarcasm. "Why, Omaha is more exciting than New York City. And I'm young, tall, blonde, and rich."

"That's why I love you," he said, giggling. "I wouldn't want you if you were short, middle-aged and middle-class." He paused. "It's so boring here; we just have the Rockies; skiing, snowshoeing, hiking."

"Oh, rub salt in my wounds," I said. "But we'll go hiking this week."

"We'll do whatever you want," he said. "I have to work some days, but I have Tuesday and Wednesday off. Maybe we'll just stay in bed, and catch up that way."

"I want to, Terry. I'm lonely without you."

We talked a few more minutes. My bagel was dark brown, the way I liked it, and I munched on it while we chatted.

"I gotta get ready for work," Terry finally said, with a sigh. "See you tonight, baby."

"OK," I said. "I love you." I hadn't told him about the hurtful comment. Talking with Terry, everything seemed all right, and it no longer mattered that some guy hated me just for being different.

"Me too, Ric, me too."

It was the day of the anti-Duncan Smedley rally, as I thought of it; it was technically the March for Tolerance. Although Omaha was white-bread and conservative, I believed Duncan Smedley was an aberration. Sure, there were people like the man at the runza stand; guys who had rotten beliefs. Omaha was also home to the group that talked about the "coming race war." But there were good people, kind folks, and I would see a lot of them at the march.

I made coffee, and shaved. I don't like shaving on the weekends, but I needed to look respectable for the march. I looked online for directions to the Episcopal cathedral, where the rally began. The event was going to be held downtown, assembling at that church, after the services were over, and marching to the radio studio where Smedley broadcasted. It would end at the sculpture garden of the art museum.

I got ready to make my way to the rally. I didn't live far from downtown, and even though it was cool, I decided to walk. As in most rustbelt towns, the center of town was usually deserted, especially on the weekends. Walking gave me time to think, and I let my mind drift and wander. I anticipated seeing Terry in a short time.

The wind began to blow, and I was glad I'd worn a sweatshirt. I was pleased to see a fairly large crowd in front of Trinity Church, the Episcopal cathedral. The street had been cordoned off, and I saw several police officers. That wasn't a bad thing. Tempers can flare at even the most peaceful gathering, and there was the possibility there would be fans of Smedley's, causing problems. Would they stage an anti-tolerance, pro-racism rally? I didn't put anything past them.

The Gothic-style church was lovely. I stared at the Victorian structure, my eyes drawn to the stained glass windows. Then I wandered around the crowd, hoping to find someone to walk with. I recognized a few faces from the community center, but no one was especially friendly. I didn't see Marc, Rabbi Braun. There were Jews, Christians, African Americans, and a gay organization attending. In the time I'd been in Omaha, I hadn't met any other gay people.

I found a couple of women standing by themselves. They looked a little masculine, with short hair and no makeup. I assumed they were lesbians, and I smiled at them.

"Hi," I said, walking over to them.

"Hello," the red-headed one said. She seemed friendly, and had a nice smile. She had green eyes, and was on the plump side. Her friend looked to be a few years older, with short gray hair.

"I'm Rico," I said, reaching out my hand. She shook it, and introduced herself as Carol.

"This is Judy," Carol said, introducing her companion.

The march started promptly at 1:30, and many people carried signs. I had forgotten to make one; Carol and Judy didn't carry a sign, either. I was glad to walk with the women. It wasn't far to the radio studio, just about four blocks. The art gallery, where the event ended, was just a block from the church. At the gallery, there would be various speakers.

"How long have you two been together?" I asked Carol.

Carol looked at me with a puzzled expression.

"We've worked together for about 12 years," Judy said. "I worked there first, and then about two years later, Carol came."

"Where do you work?" I asked, curious. Maybe I'd seen a relationship between the women that didn't exist; maybe they were just friends or colleagues.

"Boys' Town," Carol answered. Boys' Town is a large, Catholic orphanage just outside Omaha city limits.

"Oh," I said, "that must be challenging. Good for you, helping troubled youth. Are you teachers?"

"We're sisters," Judy said. "Carol is in accounting, I teach. We live in the same house, of course."

"Sisters?" I asked. "You don't look alike at all." It was my day to be stupid, I guess, but the ladies were too kind to laugh at me.

"Not biological sisters," Carol explained. "We're nuns."

"Of course," I said, as if that's what I'd thought all along. First I'd taken them for lesbians, then when they told me they worked at a Catholic institution, I still hadn't understood.

I needed to use the restroom, and it seemed like a good time to cease bothering the nuns. The march had gone about two of the four blocks, and we were walking very slowly. I excused myself, and went to look for a public toilet. I made my way back to the cathedral; I figured it would have a restroom. It would be open in case people wanted to pray. Churches are different than synagogues, which are locked up tight after services.

I found a side door that was open, and quietly made my way into the sanctuary. It was beautiful; massive, dark, mysterious. The colored glass in the windows cast filtered light into the space, illuminating paintings and statues. I paused, and looked around, struck by the peacefulness. A crucified Jesus hung over the altar, with his arms outstretched.

I walked as quietly as I could, afraid I would disturb someone praying. I needn't have worried; the sanctuary was empty. I slowly made my way down a side aisle toward the front doors of the edifice. There was a discrete sign pointing to a restroom, near some stairs. I made my way down the dark staircase. It smelled musty and damp, like a room that has been closed off for a long while. I tiptoed, hoping the doors at the bottom would be unlocked. They were, and I quietly opened them and proceeded to the basement.

I felt light-headed, and realized I was holding my breath. I shook my head at my timidity. The statues weren't going to come to life and chase me, and the building was quite empty. Still, for some reason, I moved as quietly as I could, and even thought about taking off my shoes so they wouldn't make any noise on the tile floor. I felt like an intruder in someone else's house. I was committing no crime, I wasn't trespassing. The church doors were unlocked, and if anyone asked me, I could say I had come in to pray.

"I know," I heard a man say. I froze. I wasn't as alone as I thought. I almost jumped out of my skin with surprise. My eyes took time to get used to the dark basement; I couldn't see anyone at first.

I kept walking on tiptoes, making my way down a dark hall toward the voice. There was a slight turn, and the passage opened up into a larger room that looked like a nursery. There was a crib, a changing table, and several chairs. The gloom was barely broken by a small window, which let in little light.

Standing under the window, a tall, dark-haired man was speaking excitedly into a cell phone. He spoke loudly; maybe the connection was bad, but more likely he assumed he was alone, too. Who makes phone calls from a church basement? I pressed myself against the wall, sneaking around like a criminal. My instincts alerted me to be wary. I'm not a particularly intuitive man, but for some reason, I felt afraid.

"I told you, I know who did it, Duncan," the man said, agitation in his voice.

My heart began to pound. Was this man calling Duncan Smedley on the cell phone? It wasn't likely. Duncan can be a first or last name, and isn't uncommon. I listened intently. The man mumbled something in to the phone, and though I was standing close by, I couldn't make out his words. Maybe I couldn't hear him over my pounding heart.

"Sure, I've been keeping an eye on these losers and their pitiful little parade," the man sneered. I stood motionless, wanting to hear the rest of the conversation, or at least, his side of it.

"Yes," the man continued, talking slower. "I told you I know who the killer is."

Did this man know who killed the police chief? How could he? Why would he be calling Smedley with that information? Why not turn the murderer in? Was he going to try blackmail? Was that how Smedley augmented his income? Anything was possible. Of course, I was probably misinterpreting the whole thing. I didn't know who he was calling, or what he was talking about. I only heard snippets of a one sided conversation.

"That's what I'm trying to tell you. The killer played for our team!" With that, the man snapped his phone closed. He sighed, and began to walk towards me. If the man was talking about what I thought, he wouldn't be happy knowing he'd been overheard. What did he mean, "played for our team?" I remained motionless. The man was coming closer, walking with great strides. I was dead, surely. Curiosity killed the cat, and I was going to get my desserts.

The man on the cell phone walked so close I could smell him. He was a smoker. He assumed he was alone; he was pre-occupied, lucky for me. He walked right past me without turning his head. I was in a cold sweat, and if I could smell him, I was sure he could smell me. I wasn't smelling too good, the way I was sweating. I stayed still, till I heard the man reach the top of the staircase. I didn't even want to move then, but I was nervous, and had to use the restroom.

I took a deep breath, and made my way quietly to the bathroom. Inside, I flipped on the switch. An exhaust fan came on, and I quickly flipped the switch off, in case the man was close enough to hear it.

I made my way to the toilet, in the dark, and sat down. My legs were shaking. I went over the whole thing in my mind. The caller had been keeping an eye on the rally, and was talking to a man named Duncan. He said he knew who the killer was, and that the "killer played for our team." What on earth did that mean? The only time I'd ever heard the expression before, it was an allusion to being gay. Was Smedley gay? If so, that news would rock his right-wing audience.

I got up, and felt my way to the sink, not daring to turn on the light. I rinsed my hands. I waited a few minutes, then quietly made my way through the nursery, up the stairs, and back into the dark, mysterious sanctuary.

I went back outside, and walked to the sculpture garden of the museum. I'd missed most of the walk. I wasn't sure how long I'd been gone, but I must have taken longer than I thought. There were several speakers at the rally, but I had trouble paying attention. I was confused, trying to make sense of what had happened. The truth was, I had no idea who the dark-haired man was calling, and or what he was talking about. On the other hand, when he talked about a killer, that could mean only one thing. Who should I tell? If I went to the police, would they think I was crazy? Did I really know anything, or was I just guessing, putting pieces of a random conversation together? My hands were shaking.

There were several "counter-protestors;" happily, not too many. They called themselves the "rally for free speech," wanting to defend their beloved Duncan. Smedley himself was not there, but his lackeys were.

I finally saw Marc, and waved ostentatiously at him: as long as he had seen me there, that was all that really mattered. I waved goodbye to the nuns. I told myself I'd misinterpreted the phone call, and left the rally, making my way home. The temperature had turned downright cold, and a chilly wind began to blow. It would soon be time to catch a cab to the airport, and fly back to Boulder for Passover.

Chapter 12

The plane from Omaha to Denver almost didn't leave. By the time we departed, it had begun to snow lightly, and a blizzard was predicted. We left, though; the flight was short, and I tried to put Smedley and the police chief's murder out of my mind. I was going home, and it was a wonderful feeling. Everything seemed more manageable when I was safely in Terry's arms, and he was in mine.

The Denver airport is huge, and I worried Terry would get lost. But he was there, waiting for me when I got off the plane. I almost didn't recognize him at first: his hair was shorter than I'd ever seen it, like he was enlisting in the army. All his curly blonde frizz was gone.

"Your hair," I said, before I even hugged him.

"What hair?" he asked.

"Exactly," I agreed, putting my arms around him and squeezing as tight as I could.

I drew back hurriedly; I'd forgotten about his wounded shoulder.

"What's wrong, Ric?" Terry asked. "Are you ashamed to hug me in public?"

"No, or course not," I said. "I didn't want to hurt your shoulder, that's all."

He kissed me on top of my head, making me feel like a child. "It doesn't hurt much anymore. And besides, a little 90 pound weakling like you couldn't hurt a great big manly man like me."

With that comment, I pinched him as hard as I could on his behind. He looked startled, and for a minute I was worried he was in genuine pain.

"You'll pay for that, Ric, when you least expect it," he threatened, softly, menacingly.

It was chilly in Denver, too; Terry drove his truck, fortunately the top was still on. We made our way out of the confusing parking structure, and then got on the highway north to Boulder. We didn't talk much during the drive. Omaha was suddenly very far away, and Smedley a distant nightmare. I was happy just being near Terry, and I hoped he felt the same.

When we got to the house, Sid came lunging at us as Terry opened the door. It startled me.

"Is he all right?" I asked. "He hasn't done that before." Then Sid bolted quickly away, after I scratched his ears. Cats are unpredictable creatures.

"He's excited to see you, that's all," Terry said.

It was late, and I was tired. I took my suitcase and backpack into the bedroom. The house was neat and clean, and that made me happy.

"Did you eat?" Terry asked.

"I had a sandwich before I left Omaha," I said. "What about you? Did you eat? How was work today? Thanks for getting me. Remind me to give you a tip, driver."

"Yeah?" he said, a glint in his eye. He came at me with hunger in his eyes; it was reciprocal. Afterwards, we both lay on the bed, exhausted. Part of me wanted to talk, and tell Terry my news, but part of me was content just lying next to him. I realized how much I missed him. Still, in the back of my mind, a voice nagged, warning me not to confuse desire with love.

Terry got up, and turned off the light. We fell asleep holding each other. I tried to get used to my soft mattress again, and realized that even if I tried to stay on my side of the bed, I would roll towards Terry, since he lay in the center.

"We need a bigger bed," I whispered, before falling asleep.

"No we don't," he answered. "I like this. You can't get away from me."

I was in a green, grassy field. It was beautiful, peaceful and calm. I was alone, I thought. Then a voice startled me. I couldn't tell where it was coming from.

"A storm is on the way," someone whispered. Suddenly, I saw a shadowy figure by a tree. It was a man talking on an old-fashioned rotary phone. "A terrible storm is coming," he said, louder, into the telephone receiver. The light shifted, and I could see the man more clearly. His features didn't look familiar, but he recognized me. He looked right at me, staring, and began to laugh. A chill ran down my spine.

It started to rain. There was a torrent of precipitation, a hard, fierce downpour. The man was gone, and the lovely green field was in shadows. I looked down at the ground. The rain was red, and had a strange, mineral smell. Blood. It was raining blood. I held out my arms, and saw that I was covered in thick globs of the stuff. My clothes were turning brown from the gory mess. I could feel blood on my hair, running down my face. I began to shout. I shouted as loud as I could.

"Rico," someone said. "Ric, stop." It took me moment to wake up. Where was I? I felt a sense of panic, not sure if I'd just had a nightmare, or if it had really happened. Something about the man talking in the phone seemed real, but I felt confused.

"You're having a nightmare, Rico," Terry said, his voice thick with sleep. "Wake up, OK? It's a bad dream, that's all."

I was sitting up in bed, and my throat was hoarse. Geez. How long had I been yelling? Poor Terry. I hoped I hadn't woken the neighbors, too. How loudly had I shouted?

"Terry," I croaked, "I'm sorry." I was awake, and I could see Terry was fully alert too. There was alarm in his eyes.

"Are you all right?" Terry asked. "You really scared me. I've never heard you yell like that before. Must have been a terrible dream."

"It wasn't that bad," I lied. "Just strange, that's all. I'm sorry. I probably woke up half the neighborhood."

"If someone calls the cops, tell them I wasn't trying to kill you, OK? Because that's what it sounded like."

"Oh, Terry, I'm sorry," I said, again. I didn't know what else to say, so I just kept apologizing.

"You're not doing it on purpose," he sighed, then added, "are you?"

He lay back down, but I didn't trust myself to fall asleep again. Sweet Terry. I felt guilty; the man needed his sleep. So did I, for that matter. Should I sleep in the guest room, I wondered? I couldn't get the feel and smell of blood out of my mind, and I got up and took a shower.

Terry looked tired the next morning, and I was sure I did, too. He didn't mention my nocturnal antics, and I felt too bad to even apologize again. I remembered my old friend Josh, and how he had suggested he could hypnotize me if I wanted. Would it help? My nightmares almost made me dread falling asleep, especially when they were as awful as they were the previous night.

163

Taking my shower that morning, something nagged at the back of my mind. What was it? I had lost something, something was missing. It was something small, but somehow it linked all the strange things that were happening to me. I reached around my neck and remembered. My father's cufflinks were there, on the chain where they always were. Harry had given me a silver *Mogen David*, star of David. What had I done with it? Where was it? I wasn't wearing it. I'd lost something else, too, but I couldn't remember what. I felt exhausted.

I toasted a bagel, and opened the fridge door to get the cream cheese. Taking up space inside was the largest brisket I'd ever seen, marinating in wine, garlic and pepper.

"This is for tonight?" I asked.

"Oh yes," Terry said. "Your mom said she trusts me enough to bring the meat."

"Well, you are a butcher, she ought to." I stood by the fridge, with the door open.

"Do you mind closing the refrigerator door, Ric?" Terry said.

I was trying to think of what else I was missing. I started, and came back to the present. How long had I been standing there with the door open? My face and chest felt cool from the refrigerator.

"I'm distracted, Terry," I said. "Probably 'cause you're so good-looking."

"I am good-looking," Terry mused, "but I don't think you're quite yourself, baby. What's up?"

I hesitated for a moment, and then I decided to tell him. For a relationship to work, there has to be communication. I told Terry about the man I'd overheard at the Episcopal Cathedral. I told him about Duncan Smedley, and the twins' possible connection to the Coming Race War group. I talked about the three boys I dreamed of. I wasn't telling things in order, but I explained the things that bothered me most. When I was through, I felt better. Our time together was so rare and precious, I didn't want to tell him what was surely trivia. But it's the little things that make up our lives.

Terry looked at me, surprised. "Some of this you've told me, but some you haven't. Why didn't you tell me all this was going on? Baby, I'm your friend." He paused, and sighed. "I was thinking you didn't love me anymore, and that you wanted away from me. I worried you were having nightmares about me."

"Never, Terry. I love you." I kissed him on the cheek. "I didn't want to tell you because I was afraid you'd think I was crazy. Besides, this is all trivia, *schmegegge*."

"Look," Terry said, "I never said you weren't crazy. We both know you're not quite normal," he said, with a smirk.

"Terry!" I said. I looked at him, and he winked. He was teasing.

"Oh, Ric, who's to say what normal is? Not me. You know my story."

I didn't answer, but looked him directly in the eyes. There was a flicker of understanding between us. Yes, we both knew Terry's story. It didn't need to be discussed.

"You have this friend Josh, the counselor," Terry said. "Maybe you should run some of this by him. I don't know what to say about your nightmares. I can listen, though. And you think that somehow all these weird things are related, the police chief's murder, Duncan Smedley, the phone call you overheard?"

"I do. I think it's all connected, but for the life of me I can't say how. It's just a feeling." I sighed. "You're a good man, a great listener, thanks."

"It works both ways," Terry said.

"There are things that you need to talk with me about?" I asked, with a sense of concern. I'd been so wrapped up in my own drama, I hadn't been listening to Terry.

"There's things we need to talk about," Terry repeated, simply. "But not right now, OK? I've got to work on the brisket."

"I'll help," I said, and Terry got a large pan out. He turned the stove top to high heat, and put some oil in a large pan. When it sizzled, Terry put the brisket in to brown. He turned to me, and said, "Do you think these dreams of yours mean something, can they predict events? Maybe you could dream about the lottery."

The question caught me off guard. I didn't want to have that conversation; I finished eating my bagel noisily, and swallowed. "Maybe I'm wrong to think these things are all related. I don't see how they could be." I said nothing about my dreams, and my belief that they were warning me.

Finally, the meat was browned, and Terry put it in the oven. All day long, it smelled delicious. I called my mother, and we spoke briefly. She was busy and distracted, and I assured her I would be over early to help.

"Who's coming tonight, Mom?"

"There's you and Terry, of course, Linda and her mother, Gloria; Harry and me. I thought we'd keep it small this year."

"That's nice. What do you want me to make?"

"Terry's doing the brisket, so you don't need to bring anything else. Come early and help me, we can chat," she said.

I promised to, and rang off. Then I called my grandmother. We hadn't spoken much since the fall. She was my father's mother, and her health wasn't good. She lives in a Jewish retirement center in New York, and I was sure her facility would do something nice for the holiday.

"Hi Bubbe," I said, when she answered.

"Hello, Rico," she said. Her voice was soft. "I dreamed about your father," she said, before I had a chance to say anything. "He's at rest now."

Instinctively, I fingered the cufflinks I always wore around my neck, thinking of my dad.

"They remember him down South," I said. "A pastor there said they are grateful for his good work."

"How do you like Iowa?" she asked.

"Nebraska, I'm in Nebraska now," I corrected.

"Oh, I get all those Midwestern states confused. All I know is New York and Florida."

My grandmother was born in Romania, and had spent most of her life in New York City.

"The dead don't need our pity," she said, presumably in reference to my father. Her conversation jumped around. "It's the living we should be concerned about," she continued. "I worry about you, Rico."

"Don't worry, Grandma, everything's all right," I assured her.

"No, it isn't," she insisted. For a moment, she was silent. "I'm an old woman, Rico, and I've seen many changes. I know what I believe seems old-fashioned to you. But I was born in the old country, and I hold fast to the old ways."

I wasn't sure what she meant. My grandmother practices a more traditional form of Judaism than the rest of the family does; she's very religious.

"There's nothing wrong with tradition," I said.

"I'm glad to hear you say that," she said simply. "The past year was hard for you. You need to be made whole, pure."

I was startled. Was she condemning me for being gay? That wasn't a taboo in our tradition. Was it because Terry isn't Jewish? How, and why, should I be purified?

"Because of Terry?" I asked, incredulous. "He's a good, loving man."

Terry looked up at me. He had been fussing with the brisket.

"Listen to me, darling. Anyone who comes in contact with the dead must take *mikveh*. When your friend was shot, his blood was on you. Rico, you must have a ritual bath."

I'd been to Hebrew school, but I didn't remember anything about ritual impurity, *mikvehs*. Orthodox women use a *mikveh* before they marry, or maybe after their menses. I never heard of a man going to the *mikveh*; it's old-fashioned, something we no longer do.

"Bubbe, men don't do *mikveh*," I protested. "No one does that at all these days."

"You think I'm a superstitious old woman. But ritual bathing can cleanse the trauma from you. It can be healing."

If a *mikveh* was necessary, surely Marc, Rabbi Braun, would have suggested it. *Mikveh* was a vestige of the past, when people didn't bathe regularly. It was no doubt a good idea when people didn't have running water or bathtubs in their homes.

"It must be done, Rico. Promise me you'll talk to a rabbi about a ritual bath."

That was easy to do, and I promised. I wasn't sure what to make of her talk. I rang off, after we had wished each other a happy Passover.

The day passed quickly. Terry was thoughtful, but I was chatty. Once you start confiding, it can be hard to stop, and I told him about my experience with Sam and Ahmed, and how LeVon had come to my rescue. I told him about the rally, and eating runzas with the twins. He listened, good-naturedly.

At four, I headed over to my mother's. The guests were coming at six, so there was time to help my mom with the last minute details. The table needed to be set, and there were a dozen other things. The meat needed to cook for an hour longer, so Terry was coming later.

The day was sunny and crisp; there was no snow on the ground this late in the season. The days were getting longer. I inhaled the clear mountain air with gusto, as I walked the two blocks to my mom's. Behind me, the mountains loomed; their peaks were still lightly dusted with snow. The Flatirons are the symbol of Boulder, and their jagged peaks tower over the town. I've lived almost all my life near them, in their shadow.

The smells in my mother's house were wonderful. Chicken soup was simmering on the stove, and potato kugel was just out of the oven.

"Hi Mom," I said, giving her a peck on the cheek.

"Rico, happy Passover. I'm so glad you're here. Harry! Ric's here." Mom's face was red with excitement, or maybe from cooking. Harry came out from the kitchen. He was wearing a white apron.

"Rico, good to see you. Where's Terry?"

"He'll be along," I said. "Don't worry." I gave Harry a hug, and accompanied them into to the kitchen. Things were in a state of controlled chaos, which is always the case before a holiday dinner party. The strange conversation I'd had with my grandmother lurked in my thoughts, and I wanted to tell my mom about it.

Harry went into the dining room, and I was alone with my mother. The snapshot of Harry and my mother, taken years before they were supposed to have met, danced at the edges of my mind. I stirred the soup, and put the chopped liver in a serving dish.

"Mom," I began, plunging in, "when did you meet Harry?"

My mother was distracted, and catching her off guard might be to my advantage. I didn't think she had ever lied to me, but she hadn't told the entire truth. Maybe I'd never asked. I always assumed she met Harry after my father's disappearance, but I can't say that she had told me that.

My mother got a far-off look in her eye. She seemed to be looking out the window, but I wasn't sure. We heard the rattling of china in the dining-room.

"Haven't I ever told you?" she asked.

"No, not really," I said tentatively.

"I've known Harry a long time."

I waited for her to say more.

She looked at me thoughtfully. "I think the matzo balls are almost done," she said, looking at the clock.

I opened the lid of the pan. They were huge and fluffy, just like they needed to be. I poked a fork in one. "They're done, I think," I said. "But you make sure."

I turned off the burner, and looked for something to take them out of the water with. I found a little strainer, and began fishing them out. "So how did you meet Harry?" I asked again.

She sighed, and looked at me. The phone rang. "Harry, can you get that?"

Wherever he was, Harry hadn't heard her question, the phone kept on ringing. Finally, my mom walked over to pick it up. From that moment on, we never stopped moving till we sat down at the table. The moment was lost, and I would have to find another time to ask.

The meal was delicious, the company was cordial. My mother had streamlined the readings and prayers; we each took our turn reading the Haggadah, even Terry. His voice trembled a little as he read, and I felt bad that he was nervous. When he was through, I reached over and squeezed his hand.

Linda and I sat next to each other, and chatted. Terry sat on Linda's other side. I'd known Linda and her mother, Gloria, all my life. We were neighbors and friends. It was obvious that Linda was smitten with Terry. Her face lit up any time he spoke to her. How could anyone not love Terry? He is everything a man should be, and I'm lucky to have found him. He's a *mensch*.

We all ate and drank too much. Terry's brisket was a hit, and everyone asked for his cooking method. At the end of the meal, we vowed to meet the "next year in Jerusalem!" We opened the door wide, to welcome Elijah and the hoped for Messianic era. I wasn't sure of my beliefs, but at that moment, after four glasses of wine, I didn't think any future age could be better than the present moment was. Terry and I were together, and I was with my family and friends. It was heaven on earth, and I didn't need a future paradise. The night was cold, and we soon closed the door.

Holidays are a time of good food and cheer, but they are also a time of memories. As the evening went on, my mother seemed reflective, pensive. Maybe she was thinking about my question, when she first met Harry. Maybe she remembered my father.

"I'll never forget my first Passover at my mother-in-law's," Mom said, with a wry smile.

Gloria looked at her. "Harry's mother? He wasn't raised Jewish."

"No," Mom said. "My first mother-in-law. Harry's mother passed away before I got a chance to meet her." She smiled at Harry, and got the far-off look in her eyes I'd seen earlier.

I'd heard the story many times before; it came up frequently at the holidays. I listened again; it always made me smile.

"Stephen was in seminary, and we were newlyweds," my mother began. "I'd met his parents at the wedding, but I didn't know them well. They had some friends over, who insisted we read the entire Passover prayer book in Hebrew. That meal lasted till one in the morning. All I could think of, is what have I got myself in for? How can I make sure we never do this again?"

Gloria, Linda's mother laughed. "I'm glad you keep the prayers brief, Sheila."

"I talked to Grandma today," I said.

"Your first mother-in-law?" Gloria asked my mother. Mom nodded.

"She thought I should have a *mikveh*," I continued.

"Whatever for?" Linda asked. "At your age, you aren't having any more periods." Linda's mother laughed loudly. Linda is a nurse at the women's ward in the local hospital.

"Oh, you," I said, pointing my finger at her. "She thought because…" I didn't finish the sentence. I realized I'd just talked myself into a corner. It wasn't festive holiday talk to mention how I'd inadvertently come across human remains, and been covered in Terry's blood. Terry felt uncomfortable enough; the past didn't need to be drug up. I didn't know how to extricate myself, and sat with my mouth open, thinking.

My mother looked at me, waiting for me to finish. When I didn't, she said, "A ritual bath is everything that's wrong about our religion. It implies that women are unclean. Men don't have to have *mikvehs*, it's only women."

"I had a ritual bath," Harry said, "when I converted. It was like being baptized. Believe me, that was the least painful aspect about becoming Jewish."

"But I'm worth it," my mother said, smiling.

Harry told us about growing up on a farm, and what they did at Easter time. "My best buddies were these two twins who lived down the street," he said.

"I've met them," I said, trying not to roll my eyes. They were Harry's friends, after all.

"I have too," Terry said.

"They're nice enough," Harry said blandly.

"They're polite, but they're bigots," I said. "They like this Duncan Smedley creep."

"Who's that?" Gloria asked.

I explained. I told them about the threats we'd had at the Jewish center in Omaha, and the March forTolerance. I told them how a gay club had been burned to the ground.

"Who wants dessert?" my mother interrupted.

"Sorry," I said. "It's not cheery talk, I know."

"No," Harry said, "but it does kind of fit the Passover theme. It's about persecution. So much of what Jews and other minorities went through in the past gays are experiencing today."

That started a lively debate about the meaning of the holiday. I glanced at my watch, wondering if the evening was going to last as late as my mom's first Passover at my grandmother's. The topics of conversation became lighter, and eventually, we all grew tired.

All good things come to an end, and our gathering did too. The kitchen was a mess, and Terry and I stayed to help Mom and Harry clean up. Even Linda stayed, good- hearted woman that she is--- or maybe she stayed to be close to Terry. She stood next to him as they washed and dried dishes, hanging on his every word.

"Break it up, you two," I teased, when they giggled at some joke the rest of us weren't privy to. The dishes were eventually washed and dried, and order was restored. We said goodbye, then Terry and I started for home. The shiny, full Passover moon lit our way.

I took Terry's hand, and a couple of students, driving by, yelled "right on!" at us. I laughed, and Terry was embarrassed, at first.

"Boulder isn't Georgia," he marveled. Emboldened, he kissed me. Four glasses of wine had affected him.

"Did you have a nice time?" I asked. "Your brisket was delicious."

"I liked it all right," he said. "Passover's a violent story, don't you think? All those plagues. Blood on the doorpost, and killing first-born babies." He shuddered.

"It is, now that you mention it. Surely there was another way they could have left Egypt without killing the children," I said.

"And the animals? What did those poor creatures have to do with anything? I'm glad Sid the cat wasn't there. He would have been traumatized," Terry said, with a grin.

We got home, exhausted, and barely got our clothes off before falling into bed. It was cold that night, and I snuggled next to Terry, grateful for his warmth. The bright moon shone in through the window, and even though I was tired, I had trouble falling asleep. I tried not to toss and turn; I didn't want to keep Terry awake. Maybe the wine hadn't agreed with me, but sleep wouldn't come.

I thought about the expression on my mom's face when I'd asked her how long she had known Harry. I felt pensive, melancholy, and reflected on Harry's connection to Buffalo Crossing. At times, especially in the space between wakefulness and sleep, everything seemed linked. I was seeing pieces of a puzzle, but wasn't sure how it all fit together. Right before I fell asleep, I remembered the knife, the crescent-shaped dagger that Terry had taken from my apartment in Omaha. Why had Terry said he hadn't taken it back, when he had? As important, how had I managed to pack it by accident with my books? Puzzle pieces, puzzling pieces.

I was walking in a peaceful meadow. The sky looked troubled, and I wondered if it was going to rain. The air was heavy and humid. I was by a stream. I looked down at my hands, and saw they were dirty. I dipped my hands in the water. It was cool and fresh; I wanted to roll up the cuffs of my pants and wade in. There was no one around, so I took my pants off. The water felt cold. I stepped gingerly, and felt my feet sliding in the muddy bed of the creek. I heard thunder, and looked up.

The sky had grown dark, and the wind began to blow. I needed to get out of the water, but my feet were stuck. I couldn't move. Rain and hail began to pelt me. My feet wouldn't move. The wind blew ferociously, and the sky became so black I couldn't see. I heard a terrible sound like a freight train. I knew I was going to die.

"No!" I cried. "No!"

"What is it, Ric, another bad dream?" The voice was heavy and thick. I didn't know who it was. "Wake up, you're all right."

I tried to make sense of the words, but I couldn't. My feet were still stuck.

"Dammit, Ric, quit kicking the covers," someone said.

I woke up, and realized I was in bed, lying next to Terry. It was Terry who was speaking. Pale light came in the window, and my feet were tangled in the bedcovers. Terry was trying to pull the blankets off my feet, and back onto his legs. Sid was loudly meowing by my ear. I sat up, and got the twisted covers off, putting them on Terry. He looked at me sleepily.

"My head hurts," he said. "I had too much wine last night. And my stomach—why did I eat so much?" he groaned.

I wasn't feeling all that great, either. I looked at the clock, and saw we'd just been asleep a few hours. My dream had put me in a panic, and I was tired. I made up my mind then and there to talk to Josh about my nightmares. They were disrupting my life, not to mention Terry's sleep.

"Should we get up?" Terry asked. "I have the day off, and we could go hiking."

"Let's sleep another hour," I suggested. "I don't feel like hiking just now."

"OK, suits me," Terry said. "Just don't have any more bad dreams."

"Whatever you say," I agreed. I put my arms around Terry, and we both fell back asleep. A while later I woke up again, and kissed Terry on the back of the neck till he was awake, too.

"Geez, Ric," he mumbled. "You treat me like a sex object. At least Linda likes me for my mind."

"Don't fool yourself," I said. "Linda wants you for the same thing I do, and it isn't your brilliant wit."

He laughed, and turned over to kiss me back. When we got up, we showered and made our way lazily to the kitchen. I sat down on a folding chair, and realized that the table cloth was covering a card table. Ted had taken the kitchen table. I'd liked that solid oak table.

"You think we need to buy some furniture?" I asked, while Terry made coffee.

"Eventually, I guess. We can do it when you move back here. We'll have more time."

"What if I don't move back?" I asked. "Will you come to Omaha?"

Terry sighed heavily. The playful mood of the morning changed instantly. "Never mind," he said.

I was silent. The issue was important. It wasn't the time to pursue it, maybe, but then, when was? At some point, we would have to decide. "We'll have to figure it out," I persisted.

Terry was silent. "You want a bagel?" he asked, finally. He wasn't going to be drawn in. I nodded, and held my tongue.

I had a stack of mail to go through, and we had chores around the house to do. We'd slept late, and by the time we were ready to leave the house, it was after two.

"Do you still want to go hiking?" Terry asked.

"We could go for a shorter walk," I said. "It's a beautiful day." It was clear and sunny, the wind was brisk and crisp. We took our jackets, and Terry and I drove up to the Chautauqua ranger station at the base of the Flatirons. There are trails inside the Boulder city limits, and we opted for a trail that skirted the foothills. We didn't talk much, both of us tired from the previous evening.

I'd said everything I needed to say the day before, and wanted to give Terry space to talk about what was on his mind. I wondered if he was angry with me for suggesting he move to Omaha. Maybe he was tired from me waking him up.

We walked in silence. I took in the beauty of the mountains, and wanted a mental picture of the afternoon to take with me. I love Boulder, the Flatirons, and the Rocky Mountains. We walked higher and higher in elevation, and the air was cool. The trail wasn't long, and it eventually circled back down. We came to a clearing we'd passed on our way up, and Terry motioned to a wide rock. "Let's sit," he suggested.

I didn't mind, but it wasn't like Terry to need a rest during a hike. We were still close to town, and because the days were longer, more people walked late in the day; it was light when they got off work. Spring break had ended several weeks earlier; still, there were students and out hiking. Walking and bike trails are part of what makes Boulder such a livable city; the natural beauty of the mountains is another draw.

I basked in the rugged charm of the foothills, scanning the landscape. The Rockies were still snow-covered at their peaks. Some of the highest ones would have snow till June or July; on some, the snow never melts. I wanted to remember what I saw, how the cool air smelled and felt against my bare face. I wanted to remember being with Terry. I knew the magic moment wouldn't, couldn't last, but I treasured it.

"We're not far from the continental divide," I said, breaking the silence. "It's just a few miles west of here." I gestured to where I thought it was.

Terry nodded. He was wearing a cap and sunglasses, and I couldn't read his expression.

"Are you angry at me?" I asked, finally.

A young hiker and his girlfriend walked by, and Terry nodded "hello" at them.

"I'm frustrated," he said, when they had passed. "I don't know how much longer I can live like this."

I braced myself. My heart began to pound. Was Terry going to leave me? Had he found someone else? I wondered why he'd stayed with me as long as he had. He could have anyone he wanted. Why had he chosen me at all? Did he feel guilty because of what his father had done? Was he loving me out of regret?

My eyes welled with tears. "Don't stay with me just because you feel sorry for me."

Terry looked at me in disbelief. "Feel sorry for you?" he asked. "Sometimes I want to strangle you. I swear, you like to torment me, like I'm a toy. You're such an ass."

I was surprised at his anger. It's not like Terry to be irritable. We weren't starting off well. If Terry needed to bare his soul, I had to keep my mouth shut. That

175

was a challenge. "I'm sorry, Terry." I wasn't sure how I'd angered him, but apologized anyway. I took a deep breath.

The sun had shifted. It was getting late, and the dry desert air was getting cold. I didn't want to be in the foothills during twilight. It's easier to take a misstep and sprain an ankle when you don't see well.

"We've been through a lot together," Terry began. I took his hand, and held it firmly. Terry looked at me, and squeezed my hand back. Maybe he sensed the change in the air, the encroaching evening. "We should make our way back home," he said, and I nodded. He didn't move, though, and seemed about to say something more. Some hikers passed us.

I sat patiently, and almost thought I saw a tear trickle down his cheek. "You know me better than anyone, Rico."

A gust of wind blew, and I took my sunglasses off. Because the sun had shifted, we were sitting in the shade. "You ran away from me once," Terry said, ignoring the tiny drop that made its way down past the corner of his mouth. "I don't blame you for that. You had your reasons to be angry."

"Terry, you tell me to forget the past," I protested. "But I left Georgia, I didn't leave you. I wasn't angry with you." As I said the words, I wondered if they were truthful.

"I couldn't let go of you, though. I needed you," Terry said, as if I hadn't spoken. "I still need you. I wish I didn't, God knows." He sounded angry. "So I came here to be with you," Terry continued, "I couldn't stand the thought of living without you. You're the best thing that's happened to me."

He turned his face towards me, and got close enough to kiss me. He didn't, but just sat there with his face so close to mine his features began to blur. I heard footsteps, and another couple of hikers passed by. Terry didn't seem to notice.

"And then you left me again," he said plaintively. "You ran off to Omaha. You're stronger than me, Rico. You're always ready for the next fight, while I'm still licking my wounds from the last one."

"I'm not strong, Terry," I protested.

"You are, Rico. And I follow you wherever you go, like a lost puppy dog. You move to Boulder, and I follow you to Boulder. You move to Omaha and God knows I'll probably follow you there, too. But, Ric," he warned, pausing, "someday you'll run, and I won't follow."

Chapter 13

Being home in Boulder did me good; my thoughts seemed clearer in the high altitude. I was glad the community center and the students were far off. I was temporarily rid of Duncan Smedley, and my suspicions about the police chief's murder.

Terry and I took walks together, and spent time with Linda and Petie. We talked; we cooked, we ate, we drank. It was perfect, and I couldn't have asked for anything better. There was only one thing that I wish could have been different: nightmares bothered my sleep, as they had in Nebraska. When Terry was at work, I called my old friend Josh in Denver and scheduled an appointment. Once again, I drove into the city, and parked in front of the old Victorian house.

Josh was prompt. I'd barely picked up a glossy magazine in the waiting room, when he invited me into his office.

"So what's up?" he asked.

I told Josh that the nightmares were troubling me still. I asked him if hypnosis might help.

"I can't promise anything," Josh told me. "Dreams are complex, we don't fully understand them. It's possible that hypnosis will end them, maybe just temporarily, but I can't promise. It's your decision."

I was there for help, and Josh offered it. I wanted to at least try. Josh told me to close my eyes.

"I want you to focus on your breath," he instructed. "Pay attention as you inhale and exhale. Now, starting at the top of your head, feel warmth envelop you. Let your scalp relax. Allow the muscles of your forehead to unwind."

The sky was sunny, and I felt good. I was walking along the green banks of a stream. The air was warm and dry, and I could hear birds singing. I took a deep breath, and smelled freshly cut grass. I decided to sit on a blanket spread out under a tree. I stretched out, and the rays of the sun shone down on me. I closed my eyes, and fell asleep.

When I woke up, the temperature was cooler. The sky had turned cloudy, and I smelled ozone, heralding rain. I stood up. It was time to head inside, and I wondered how long I had been asleep. I looked at the horizon; it was dark and ominous. I needed to hurry, or I would be caught in the storm.

The wind started blowing hard. Clouds of dust were moving around me, and I was scared. I tried to run, but my feet wouldn't move. I was immobile as the wind blew harder and harder. Rain began to fall, pounding me so hard it hurt. The rain was thick and runny; I looked, and saw that it was not water drops falling on me, but blood.

The grotesque storm was spinning around me. Dirt, sticks and pebbles were caught up in the air. I stuck my hands out, wanting to protect my face and eyes from the air- borne debris. Something was in my right hand. I looked, and saw I was holding a sharp, evil-looking knife. It was dripping with blood. Where had the knife come from, and why was I holding it?

"Rico, wake up." The words made no sense to me. I wasn't sleeping. I was being torn apart by the fierce wind, and there was a knife in my hand.

"Rico, wake up." The voice was insistent, and I tried to process the words. Who was speaking? "Open your eyes now, you're safe in my office."

I was tired and confused, but I couldn't fight the command any longer. I did what the voice ordered. I found myself in Josh's office, and it took me a moment to realize where I was, and what had happened.

"I'd like you to say something, Ric. Do you know where you are?"

I sighed. "Josh, what happened?"

"You entered a deep hypnotic state. I was worried you couldn't hear me. You are one of the most suggestible patients I've ever had. You were easy to hypnotize---if only all my patients were like you. What do you remember?"

What I thought I'd experienced was fading like a dream. "There was a storm," I said. "The wind was fierce, and…" I closed my eyes, remembering, "there was blood. There was all this blood. And I had a knife, I was holding a knife." I remembered the crescent-shaped knife that Terry had taken back from my Nebraska apartment, though he didn't remember. I almost told Josh, but it seemed too trivial.

"You find blood disturbing," Josh said.

"It's disgusting. I hate blood, it's gross."

Josh looked at me. "Interesting. You had a recent trauma that involved blood."

"I did?" I asked.

Josh had a confident expression on his face, and flipped through a note pad. "You told me that when Terry was shot, you were covered with his blood."

"Yeah," I answered. I wasn't sure where Josh was going.

"Is it possible that you suffer from tremendous guilt? It was you who should have been shot. Maybe you have survivor's guilt. The shooting involved blood, and it's an image you can't get out of your mind."

It was possible. "I'm Jewish. Of course I feel guilt."

"You told me that when your father's remains were found, the press did some unflattering stories about your relationship with Terry."

"My grandmother thinks I should have *mikveh* for the ritual impurity of coming in contact with death and blood." I didn't answer his query directly.

"I can't advise you on religion," Josh said. "But it seems to me that you have guilt and shame to work through. Are you ashamed of your love for Terry?"

"No," I said too quickly.

"Do you blame Terry for what his father did?" Josh asked.

I shook my head "no." "The past is over and done with," I said.

"The past is never over," Josh said. "Time isn't a straight line. There's no dot you can find and say 'here the past ends, and here the present begins.' There's no point on a line where the present ends and the future begins. We have all of it, past, present and future inside us. It's all here and now; time's a circle, not a line."

"No," I protested. "Oh, maybe we have it inside us, I don't know. But if time isn't a line, then I don't know what's real and what isn't. You might as well tell me my nightmares are true and this conversation is a dream." I felt a rising tide of anxiety. "I have to believe in something, I have to believe my own senses."

Josh said nothing, and neither did I. He looked sad, distant. After a few moments, he glanced at his watch. "I'm sorry, Rico, we have to finish, I have another patient. Let me know if the hypnosis eases your nightmares. Keep in touch."

I gave Josh a hug goodbye, and made my way out of his office to the sun-drenched Colorado day. I wasn't sure the hypnosis had accomplished anything, but I did feel relaxed.

My week in Boulder ended too soon. Terry and I didn't come to any resolution about our future together. I remembered what he said about not always following me wherever I would run. In light of the issues he and I faced, a lot of things seemed trivial. A missing knife was nothing. Finally, our visit was over.

"Come back to Boulder," he said softly, as he dropped me off at the airport. "I miss you, Rico. You belong here in the Rockies. You belong with me. You don't have to work. I make enough to provide for both of us. We're simple people, Ric, and don't need a lot of money."

"I love you, Terry," I said. I hugged him as tightly. All the way to the airport he had been singing a slow, sad rendition of "Silver Wings."

"Call me when you get in," he said, and then he drove away. I was running late, and needed to hurry. Watching him leave, though, I felt like I was going to cry. I needed Terry, I love him.

My classes wouldn't last much longer; because Passover was so late this year, it was just a few weeks till the end of the semester. Hopefully, I would soon know if my contract at the Jewish center in Omaha was going to be renewed. Terry and I would have to decide where to live at that point. Terry's offer was sweet, but I wasn't going to retire at 43. I wasn't sure exactly how much Terry made; it didn't seem like my business. Still, he was union, and had great benefits.

The city of Boulder has domestic partnerships for gays; it's a "live and let live" place. Terry and I weren't registered as domestic partners, and there was nothing holding us together, except for love. Is love enough? Ted and I had never bothered registering, and I wondered if that had made it easier for us to separate.

My thoughts were ruminative during the flight back to Omaha. I had been free of nightmares since I'd seen Josh. Maybe I did have issues of guilt about Terry. Leaving him behind in Colorado wasn't doing much to assuage my anxiety. Still, I think the hypnosis helped.

I'd waited till the last possible moment to return to Omaha: I flew back on Sunday night, my classes started bright and early the next morning. The closer I got to Nebraska, the more the cares which preoccupied me came to mind. Omaha is a lovely city, but the presence of Duncan Smedley was a stain on the town. I wondered, idly, if they had made any progress on the police chief's murder. I thought about my students, and looked forward to seeing them. Most of them, at least. I can't say I missed Sam or Ahmed.

I took a cab back to my apartment. I ran into Lisa on my way upstairs to my apartment; she was checking her mail. She wasn't overly-friendly, and I was past caring. Lisa was never going to be a friend, she had too many issues. I thought about my friends in Boulder, Linda, Petie, and Josh. It had taken me a lifetime to find them, and I wasn't going to make new friends overnight. Friendship takes time. Still, I wish I had some buddies in Nebraska.

It took me a few days to get back into the swing of teaching. I liked my work at the Jewish community center; I wished it was in Colorado, though. I had relaxed in Boulder, and I'd enjoyed walking in the mountains with Terry. I missed him already, and I longed for a hike in the Rockies.

By Friday I was back in my routine, and the rhythm of life in Nebraska. That day, though, things took a startling turn. All the peacefulness of my Colorado vacation vanished.

I sensed something was up the minute I stepped foot on campus. I saw several of my colleagues chatting excitedly in the parking lot. I rarely saw anyone I worked with.

"Hi," I said, and they nodded politely. Because of my teaching schedule, I wasn't able to go to staff meetings; the other employees didn't know me, and I didn't know them. Whatever they were gossiping about they chose not to share with me. They whispered to each other, smiling.

When I got to the metal detector, I noticed a smirk on LeVon's face.

"What's up, LeVon?" I asked. "Everyone's acting funny."

"You didn't hear?" LeVon asked, his face breaking into an open grin. "Someone finally killed Duncan Smedley."

"No!" I said, trying not to smile myself. He was a rotten person, and, I am ashamed to admit, I'd even wished him dead. The murder didn't surprise me. Smedley had made a lot of enemies. "Who did it?"

"No one knows," LeVon answered, "but that racist bastard had it coming."

I nodded. I didn't disagree with that. I needed to get a TV, or just turn on the radio more often. I hate being the last one to find things out. In my classes, Smedley's death apparently made no impact. My students had other concerns. I doubted if any of them had even heard of the right-wing shock jock.

At lunch time, Marc stepped into my room. He was on my campus that day.

"Did you hear the news?" Marc asked, soberly.

"About Smedley?"

"Yes."

"So what happened?"

Marc looked concerned. "He was murdered. They found him at home, and he was mutilated. There was another man with him who was also killed, but his name hasn't been released. It's horrible, almost unbelievable. This is Omaha, not Mogadishu."

"It's awful," I said, trying valiantly to mask my glee. I couldn't shed any tears for Smedley. Still, no one deserves to be murdered, and mutilation was a final indignity. Whoever the killer was, he was angry. "The police chief was mutilated, wasn't he?" I mused.

"Yes, I think he was," Marc said. "They haven't said if there's a connection. I don't see how there can be." He sighed. "Omaha is a quiet town. We don't have this kind of thing here."

"The police chief was a liberal," I said, trying to come up with some link between the murders. "Why would someone kill a liberal police chief and a conservative talk show guy? It can't be the same murderer, at least, if there's a political motivation."

"They're completely unrelated," Marc said. "We live in strange times. Smedley's murder isn't good for us."

"I don't understand," I said, but I was afraid I did. The Jewish community center had organized an anti-Smedley rally. We called it a March for Tolerance, but everyone knew how angry the Jewish community was. Smedley had gone out of his way to target us. We might become suspects in his grisly murder. Smedley ridiculed gays, African Americans. I wondered if those groups would fall under suspicion, too.

"They will look at us carefully," Marc said. "Especially because of the rally."

I remembered the man on the cell phone I'd overheard at the Episcopal cathedral. What had he said? Something to the effect that he knew who the chief's murderer was, and that he played on the home team. That wasn't quite right; what had he said, and what did his words mean? I tried to remember. Did it have anything to do with Smedley's murder? Then I remembered a conversation I'd had with Marc much earlier that winter.

"Marc," I said, "you got a letter about the police chief's murder, a while back. They suspected a recent immigrant. They notified you, because they knew the center has classes for Middle Eastern refugees."

"Yes," Marc said. He looked serious, and his intensity worried me.

"Marc, you don't think it was... a Jewish person who killed Smedley? Is it possible the murderer was a student here?" I asked. "Will the police interrogate us?" I was a Jew, a gay man, and I worked with immigrants. Fortunately, I was well below the radar; no one in Omaha had ever heard of me, and that made me glad. If the cops made a profile of Smedley's potential killer, a guy like me would fit all the criteria.

"I don't know what to think. But we should all be very careful."

Marc looked at me, and I was puzzled. "Why? Smedley's murder has nothing to do with any of us here," I said. But why couldn't it have been someone from the center? I remembered my strange, hypnotic trance at Josh's, the storm of blood, holding that grisly knife. Had my unconscious sensed this murder was about to happen? As many enemies as Smedley had made, foreseeing his death required no special skill.

"Marc," I said. "What if someone wanted to frame one of us, make it look like someone here is the murderer? It would be a good way to throw the police off the trail."

"That's improbable," Marc said, dismissively. "No criminal is that capable. Killers make mistakes. Even if he tries to frame one of us, it won't work."

I wish I shared his confidence.

Then Marc added, "I'm asking everyone who works here to be circumspect. Mind what you say, all right? I don't want you discussing this with anyone, especially your students. Comments can be easily misconstrued."

"OK," I agreed. "I wasn't planning to talk about it in class. It would only alarm the students, and make them remember the violence many of them fled."

"I know I can count on your discretion," Marc said. He was about to leave, and I wondered if there was a subtext to his discussion with me. I looked at him. Did Marc suspect me? For that matter, did I suspect him?

How well did I know Marc? I'd never spent any time with him outside of work. I was grateful to him for getting me this job. What if he'd engineered my move to Omaha to cover up what he was doing? Oh, that was too paranoid. The thing about violence and murder is that it makes you lose perspective. You suspect anyone with a possible grudge.

Marc was a rabbi, a man who'd devoted his career to the life-affirming principles of religion. But why not Marc? Rabbis aren't all saints, they are flesh and blood. Marc worked with Middle Eastern immigrants, indirectly. If someone wanted to frame a refugee, Marc would know how to do it. Marc knew Lisa, my upstairs neighbor, the police chief's mistress. What if he was jealous of Will Herman? Maybe Marc was after Lisa; she was beautiful, desirable. My thoughts went round and round.

I was worried and anxious the rest of the day. I tried to concentrate on teaching, and not Smedley's murder. Even in death the man was aggravating. I wanted to be home in Boulder, with Terry. Colorado seemed a whole lot safer than Nebraska. We probably had the same number of murders, but the violence in Omaha seemed worse, maybe because I was indirectly affected. Mutilation of the dead was barbaric, an added sacrilege. Whoever the murderer was, he, or she, was sick.

The conversation I'd had with Marc unsettled me. I probably should have told LeVon to be careful with what he said, too, but it wasn't my place. If Marc warned me to be careful, then no doubt he had advised all staff members.

I wondered if Marc thought I was the killer. Marc knew my past. Maybe he thought I'd finally snapped. I remembered the thoughts I'd had when Josh hypnotized me. I was holding a bloody knife. Was I the murderer? Was I so insane that I blocked the killings out of my mind? If I kept thinking bizarre things like that, I would make myself go crazy.

That evening, I called Terry. I wanted to tell him about Smedley's murder. Terry didn't answer, and I began leaving a message on his phone, when someone knocked on the door. The day had been warm, so I was sitting in my undershorts. I went to the bedroom to put on a sweat suit, when whoever it was knocked again.

"Just a minute," I called. Who was it? Lisa? The twins? The knocking continued, getting louder. I was startled. Who was so impatiently pounding on my door? A homeless person? Downstairs, the outside door didn't always latch, and anyone could have come in off the street. I slipped on a T-shirt, and went to see who was so worked up.

Three men in uniforms were standing there. It took me a second to process their identity, but they didn't give me time for questions.

"Rico Wise, step out of your apartment," a policeman ordered.

"What for?" I asked. Why were the cops there, and why should I leave my home? What was going on? Lisa was an officer, were they looking for her? If so, they had the wrong apartment.

"Step outside, we have a warrant to search your apartment," the policeman ordered again. "Hurry up now. We need to ask you some questions."

"I don't get it," I said, but that wasn't a good enough answer. Two of the officers practically lifted me up by the elbows, and brought me out into the hallway. Someone shoved a piece of paper in my face.

"This is the warrant," one of the cops said. He was holding it so close I couldn't read it. Three people in white uniforms went into my apartment. They looked like medical technicians, with gloves, booties, and masks on their faces.

The two cops still had me firmly by the elbow, and before I could take another breath, I was being whisked down the stairs. In front of the building, there was a journalist with a camera. He snapped a picture of me being escorted.

It felt like I was in a Kafka story. Nothing made sense. A search warrant for my apartment? What were they looking for, drugs? I didn't have anything like that. Had they confused me with a different Rico Wise? Had they come to the wrong apartment? What should I do?

At the foot of the outside stairwell of the apartment, I saw Lisa. It was dark outside, and shadows covered her face. Lisa was a cop. Maybe she could help, at least explain to the cops who I was, that I didn't have any contraband.

"Lisa, what is going on? Tell these guys to let go of me. I don't have any drugs, tell them."

Lisa looked at me with distaste. "You're a sick bastard," she said, and walked away from me, like I was filth. Why had she called me a name? And then it occurred to me: whatever was happening, Lisa had a hand in it. What did Lisa tell her fellow officers about me? She knew I wasn't a druggie or a thief, just a quiet, middle-aged teacher.

The drive to the police station downtown wasn't far, but it seemed to take place in slow motion. "What is this about?" I called to the cops riding in front. The two policemen sitting there didn't answer. I wanted to call Terry, but I had been so surprised I didn't think to get my cell phone. But Terry couldn't help, I needed someone local. Should I call Marc? They give you a phone call, don't they? Was I being arrested? For what? My head spun.

I was escorted swiftly into the police station. At least there were no journalists with cameras here. They ushered me into a small room, and left me by myself. I was sick to my stomach with fear. Something bad, really bad, was going on, and I was the last to figure it out. Why was my apartment being searched? What questions did the police have for me? Did this have anything to do with my father's death? What was Lisa's role in this?

A fresh-faced young man in a suit came in to the room, after I'd waited for what seemed like hours. Maybe it had only been minutes, but I wasn't wearing a watch, and there was no clock in the dreary little room.

"I'm Detective Swenson," the man said, introducing himself. His smile seemed forced, and didn't quite reach his eyes. "Thanks for coming down."

I stared at him in disbelief. "It wasn't my idea. I have to go to the bathroom." I did, too. Being scared always does that to me.

"Can it wait?" he asked, his smile fading.

"No."

Swenson left the room, and an older officer in a uniform entered, and escorted me wordlessly to a restroom down the hall. My stomach always betrays me when I'm nervous. Cramps were seizing my guts.

I took care of business, and came back outside, where the uniform was waiting. He took me back to the cheerless room, saying nothing. He looked so unfriendly I didn't even bother to ask him questions. I waited for what seemed like another hour, and the nice-looking man in the suit came back.

"I'm Detective Swenson, remember?" he asked.

"I remember," I answered. Did he think I was dim-witted? "What the hell is all this? Do I need a lawyer? Why are they searching my apartment? If you think I have drugs or stolen merchandise, I can assure you, I don't."

Detective Swenson didn't answer. He pushed a button on his side of the table. "I'd like to record our conversation," he said, cheerily.

I said nothing.

"Is that all right?" he asked.

I just stared sullenly, and that seemed to bother the detective. He was young, probably inexperienced. I'd just discovered how to annoy him; it was the only power I had. I decided to continue the silent treatment.

"Say yes or no," he said. "Or are you being uncooperative? That doesn't look good. Makes it seem like you've got something to hide."

"I'll speak when you tell me what this is all about," I said, sounding more confrontational than I'd intended.

"This doesn't have to be difficult," Swenson said, with exaggerated patience. "I hope you were treated well on your ride down here. Would you like something to drink?"

I sat silently, since that seemed to upset him. I was angry. If he was hoping for rapport, I wasn't going to make it easy. As far as I was concerned, this was police harassment. Lisa had told some lie about me, and I was paying the price. Would Lisa plant evidence? Had she planted drugs in my apartment while I was out of town? Why would she do that? I'd always been nice to her. Of course, I'd secretly suspected her of murder, but she didn't know that.

My mind began to consider possibilities. I thought of my troubled students, Ahmed and Sam. Would they break into my home and put bomb-making stuff inside? Oh, surely not. That would be elaborate vengeance for dropping them from class.

Detective Swenson left the room abruptly. A few minutes later, a much older man with thinning red hair and a mustache came in. His bald head shone slightly. He seemed more morose than Swenson. It was just like TV, I thought, with the cops playing good guy and bad guy. He didn't introduce himself, but brought a small carton, about the size of a shoe box, and set it on the table between us. I wanted to act cool, not to even look at him, but I was desperate to find out what was going on.

He put on a pair of vinyl gloves, snapping them with a flourish. He put his hand in the box, and brought out a small book in plastic envelope. I looked at it, in spite of myself.

"Recognize it?" he said, tiredly.

It was a paperback Arab-English dictionary.

"It's a foreign language dictionary," I said.

He looked at me like I was an idiot for stating the obvious. "Is it yours?"

I'd bought several online. A couple of them were on the bookcase in my apartment. I'd taken one of them to my classroom. It looked like one I'd bought, but they are fairly common.

"I have a couple of dictionaries like that," I said, before thinking about my words.

"Thought so," he said, putting the small book back in the box. Then he took out a couple of snapshots.

The first snapshot was of an evil-looking knife, with a blade that was crescent-shaped. The second was a silver Mogen David on a keychain. I couldn't hide my expression of surprise. The knife looked familiar; it was the one Terry had taken back from my apartment, the one he said he hadn't have. The star of David was exactly like the one Harry gave me. I didn't know where I had misplaced it. Why did the police have pictures of my things? Was that my Arab-English dictionary?

I looked first at the picture of the knife. When I'd moved into my apartment, I'd found it in a box of books. It wasn't mine, and I assumed it was Terry's. Terry had taken it back when he'd visited, but when I'd asked him, he denied it. I knew that whatever the knife and pendant were involved in, it was bad. Did Terry have something to do with it? Was Terry hurt? Had the police brought me to the station to give me bad news?

"Is Terry all right?" I asked, unable to keep my silence.

"Who's Terry?" Red-headed mustache asked.

"Please tell me what this is about, then," I pleaded. "Please."

Detective Swenson magically re-appeared. He must have been listening. Whatever was going on, I felt powerless. I had a bull's eye painted on my back, and was caught in the cross hairs of something I didn't understand. I was confused and frightened, considering all kinds of dire scenarios.

"Who's Terry?" Detective Swenson asked the same question Red-head had. Swenson placed another snapshot in front of me. It was a photo of a man's face, a man who was clearly dead. "Is this Terry?" Swenson asked.

"No," I answered truthfully. I couldn't keep from staring at the dead man's face. He had thick black hair, and had been nice-looking. I felt a sinking in the pit of my stomach. I was staring at the guy I'd seen on the cell phone at the Episcopal cathedral, I felt sure. His face was disfigured by death, but it was the same man.

"You know him, though," Red-head said. "Did he go by another name, or just Terry?"

I turned my head away. My cramps were back, and I thought I was going to throw up. What did the man on the cell phone have to do with the knife and the star of David? Why was he dead?

Before I could answer, both men left the room. I was upset, confused by all the coming and going, the language dictionary, the snapshots. I wanted to know what they were searching my apartment for. Nothing made sense. There was a link between the dead man and my things. I had no idea who the man was.

I felt another wave of nausea. A young woman came in to the room with a white card and an inkpad. "I'd like to take your fingerprints," she said.

I am a teacher, my fingerprints are on file. The DMV had them, too. I didn't see the harm in letting them take more. It was a mind game, but I was past caring. I let her print my fingers, which she did without speaking. There was no expression on her face. I sighed, and tried to get control of my nausea.

She left the room, and I waited a long time. I was thirsty; my mouth had gone dry from nervousness. I had to go to the bathroom. I thought about letting myself out, and walking down the hall. Should I, did I dare? Finally, Swenson and Red-head entered the room.

"Sorry about the wait," Swenson said. Red-head glowered.

He wasn't sorry. I was desperate to understand. It was getting late, and I was tired. They had knocked on my door around 7:00 p.m., and I was sure I'd been in the tiny little room for several hours. I was sleepy and nervous at the same time.

"You really hated Smedley," Red-head said, finally.

"I never met the man. I hate what he said, what he stood for." Why were they asking me about Smedley?

"You hated him enough to kill him," Red-head said.

I snorted. "Oh, give me a break. A lot of people hated him. He was a racist, a jerk. Did you ever listen to him?" Smedley was on the radio all the time, I was certain they'd heard him. In Nebraska, it seemed like you couldn't avoid it.

"Look," Swenson said, with his phony smile. "You're Jewish, you're gay. Smedley said a lot of bad things about Jews and gays. It's not surprising you murdered him."

"I didn't kill him," I said. I was exhausted and confused. Why would anyone think I killed Smedley? What did Smedley's murder have to do with the dictionary, knife and the star of David? How did the cops know so much about me, anyway? Who told them I was Jewish or gay?

"You have quite a temper, Mr. Wise," Red-head said.

"I do?" I asked sweetly. "Everyone has a temper, Detective."

"You have a lot to be angry about," Red-head continued. "Your father was murdered. You had some trouble with the police in Georgia. Do you have a problem with law enforcement? Is that why you killed Chief Herman? Must make you uncomfortable to be here," he taunted.

"I didn't have trouble with the police in Georgia," I said, trying to keep my anger in check. "As you say, my father was murdered. The killer was a policeman," I said. "A retired sheriff." My words were neither politic or circumspect. Belatedly, I thought about Marc's cautious advice. Had Marc been trying to warn me? I wished Marc was here with me now. But that was foolish. I'm a grown man, and have to fight my own battles.

"Could we just start from the beginning?" I asked, reasonably. "What am I accused of?"

The two men looked at each other, and Swenson said, finally, "You haven't been *accused* of anything. We have some questions, that's all. We appreciate your cooperation."

"And let the record show," I said loudly, wanting to make sure it was caught by the microphone, "that I am answering your questions of my own free will." I took a breath, and tried to calm down. I thought about hiking with Terry, and when I had that picture in my mind, I looked at the two men.

"As you know," Swenson said, "Duncan Smedley was killed this morning, along with another man we can't identify. He was cut up with a knife, which was found at the scene, along with that piece of jewelry. We think the same person killed Chief Herman. What do you know about all these murders, Mr. Wise?"

Red-head put a snapshot in front of me, and I cringed. Smedley had been castrated. I wished they hadn't shown me. I would never get it out of my mind. Had it been done with the knife that belonged to Terry?

Red-head looked coldly at me. "A witness saw both these items in your home. The knife and the necklace were found at the scene of the murders. Your fingerprints are on them." He set down the pictures of the knife and the star of David, and looked at me triumphantly. He was very pleased with himself.

"Your dictionary was found when Chief Herman was killed," Swenson added. "He was clutching it his hands."

I felt light- headed and sick to my stomach. I had been set up. But by whom? Who had even been in my apartment? I had no friends in Omaha. I tried to think, but I was tired and overwrought. But I knew who the "witness" was. Lisa had been in my apartment. She had called me a "sick bastard." I was no murderer, but at that moment, I could have choked Lisa. Lisa was surely the killer, and had taken my things to plant as evidence by her murder victims.

Was Lisa the only possibility? It could have been Sam or Ahmed; it might have been Marc. But Lisa had the easiest access to my apartment. The thing was, I didn't even know the dictionary was missing, and I wasn't sure exactly when the knife and Star of David disappeared.

"You think the person who killed Smedley and this other guy is the same person who killed the police chief." I said the words slowly, with dawning realization. The only reason I hadn't been charged with the crime was that I had barely been in town when the police chief was killed. If they had evidence I was at the crime scene, they would have arrested me. Maybe, I thought, my fingerprints weren't on the knife and necklace. They were trying to psyche me, trying to get me to incriminate myself. I was innocent, but innocent people go to prison all the time.

"What possible motive would I have for killing Chief Herman? I'd just been in Omaha one day when he was murdered. Why would I kill this guy with Smedley, since I don't even know his name?" I thought my questions were reasonable.

Swenson and Red-head stared me down.

"When was Smedley killed?" I asked. Had the dark-haired man, the one on the cell phone, been at Smedley's house? Had they been killed at the same time? I wondered.

Red-head looked at Swenson, and Swenson said, "Around five this morning. Do you have an alibi for that time?"

At 5:00 a.m., I was at home in bed, just getting up. I had no witness.

"You're a strong guy, you work out," Swenson said, eyeing me. He was appraising my appearance. Something didn't add up for him; I could tell that much from his expression. Swenson was a young guy, and easy to read.

"Me, a strong guy? I'm five foot five, and weigh 135 pounds. I hike a fair amount," I said. "But I don't go to a gym." Then I realized what he was trying to figure out. The man I'd overheard at the church had been larger than me; I'd never seen Smedley, but he was probably bigger than me. If that was case, then they must have

193

wondered how a runt like me could have overpowered two big guys and a police chief before that. For once, I was grateful for my scrawniness. But who would be strong enough to commit the murders, I wondered. Who could take down a police chief and two men at the same time? The killer would either have to be very strong or very clever. I wasn't either one.

"How old was Smedley?" I asked. "Was he a large man? I never met him."

Swenson seemed to consider something, then he spoke. "Smedley was 53. He was just over six feet tall, about 200 pounds."

Surely the detectives could see it would have been difficult for me to overpower two bigger men. I felt a sense of relief. I wasn't out of the woods, but maybe I had a reprieve. The only way to save myself was to figure out how someone had taken possessions from my apartment, and who that person was. I had to buy time.

"So how did a skinny little guy like me overpower Smedley and this other man? Surely they fought back. You can examine me yourself," I said, "but I'm not covered with cuts and bruises from a fight." I was wearing a short sleeve T-shirt, and I held out my arms. "How did I kill the police chief? And why? You say I hated Smedley, but I never met him. I didn't know Chief Herman or this other guy."

"There's plenty of ways it could have been done," Red-head said, with a sneer. "We're running toxicology. You might have drugged your victims. Know anything about poison?"

I wanted to say something sarcastic, but that wouldn't help. The murderer had to be Lisa. She was a cop. She had figured out how to break into my apartment and take my things. Who else had a motive to kill her lover, the police chief? Lisa might know about drugs. Poison is a woman's tool, I'd once read. But what linked all three men together?

I asked the question out loud. "What's my motive?" I asked. "I didn't like Smedley's message. But who is this guy with the dark hair? Why was he killed?" Then it came to me. I'd heard him tell Smedley he knew who killed the police chief. I had overheard the man, and someone else had, too. Was anyone else in the church that day when I'd heard him phone Smedley? Had the killer seen me at the church, too, and followed me in order to frame me?

Neither detective answered my question. "I need to use the restroom again," I said. The men sat silently, and Detective Swenson motioned toward the door. I wasn't going to be accompanied. I needed to play my cards right, I was winning this hand. I went to the restroom, trying to think, hoping to clear my head. It felt good just being out of the cubicle for a few minutes. I hadn't been charged, and that was in my favor. I had to figure out who the killer was, and how, why he had framed me.

I used the restroom, and walked back to the cubicle. I was exhausted.

Detective Swenson was still in the room, but the red-head was gone. "Thanks for coming in," he said. Was I being dismissed just like that? Swenson sounded tired, too. Whatever information they'd been hoping to glean from me, they now had. Maybe they hadn't heard what they'd wanted. "You haven't been charged yet," Swenson warned, "but that can change. Don't leave town, don't do anything stupid."

"I can leave now?" I asked.

"You haven't been charged, you could have left any time you wanted," he said.

It was close to midnight, according to a clock I'd seen in the hall. The detective didn't offer to give me a ride home. My apartment wasn't far; although I was tired, I didn't mind the walk. It gave me time to think.

The late night air was cool. Lisa, it all came back to her. But why? Why had she set me up? Just to throw suspicion off herself? If she wanted to divert scrutiny, she should have picked someone across town. But I happened to be close by. I thought about her strange behavior. She was a lunatic, plain and simple. The mutilation of the bodies was the indication of a sick mind.

I'm a scrawny guy, and the police realized I could not have overpowered two men who were larger than me. But if I couldn't, how could a woman? Lisa had police training; did she know some special technique? Had she drugged them? If the two guys had been poisoned, then I was a suspect again.

I walked quickly. Downtown Omaha isn't dangerous, but I felt susceptible. Someone had deliberately set me up, taking my dictionary, knife and star of David. I put my hands in my pockets, and realized I didn't have my house key or cell phone. How was I going to get inside when I got back to my building? I would have to pound on Lisa's door and have her call a locksmith. She was the last person I wanted to see.

I shouldn't have worried. When I got home, my front door was wide open. The apartment was in shambles. The drawers had been pulled out of the desk and dresser; books were pulled off the shelves. My computer and cell phone were gone; either the police took them, or some thief had seized the opportunity. I picked up the land-line telephone, and thought about calling Terry. It was past midnight, and I thought better of it. Terry needed his sleep, and so did I.

I switched the radio on to distract myself, and turned up the volume. I hoped it would wake Lisa up. Why had I ever tried to be her friend? She had chosen to repay my kindness by casting suspicion on me.

I lay down on the bed. I would have to call Marc in the morning. He needed to know what had happened. What should I say? By the way, Rabbi, I've been accused of murder? If I needed a lawyer, he would know who to get. I slipped off my sweat suit, and fell asleep. I had no dreams.

Chapter 14

Although I was tired, I slept poorly. The longer I lay in bed, the angrier I became. Who had framed me? Lisa had obviously told the police about the knife and the star of David, maybe even the Arab-English dictionary. If she was the murderer, then she had reason to implicate me: diversion from herself. When had those things been taken from my apartment? I had no security system, and I'd told no one but Terry what was missing. I hadn't even noticed an Arab-English dictionary was gone. Nothing taken was of value.

Lisa had been inside my place, but who else? Harry had been here, briefly, when I first moved in, and then Terry had spent a few days in February. I tossed and turned all night, my troubled thoughts going round and round. I thought about Sam and Ahmed. Had one of them committed the murders, and chosen to frame me? They could easily have taken a dictionary from school. It wouldn't be hard to find out where I live; they could have followed me home from work without my knowing.

The morning sun streamed in. I wasn't sure how long I'd slept. I looked around the messy apartment. I would have my work cut out trying to bring order back to my home. What had the police found? Nothing, I assumed, or they would have charged me with murder. The dictionary, knife and the Star of David were damning. The knife was most mysterious; I didn't know where it had come from. I assumed it was Terry's, but he said it wasn't. I should have believed him. He hadn't taken the dictionary, or Mogen David. Who had? It had to be Lisa.

I decided to phone Terry. I needed to call Marc, too. It was Saturday, our Sabbath, and I hated to disturb the rabbi. Marc might be at services, anyway.

"You hung up in the middle of your message last night," Terry said, answering the phone. "What's up?"

I tried to stay calm, but I had to fight down the rising hysteria inside me. I told him everything that happened, about the search warrant, being questioned by the police. I explained how I'd been framed, the things taken from my apartment.

"Oh, Ric, I'm so sorry," he said. "Why do these things happen to you?"

"What's that supposed to mean?" I asked. I was feeling paranoid. Sister Eveline's words came back to mind; she said that once darkness got a hold of a person, it didn't want to let go. I felt like I was being swallowed, tainted by evil. It had found me, and I worried it was winning.

"Nothing, I don't mean anything," he assured me. "I don't know what to say, that's all. What rotten luck. Should I come out?"

"Aren't you afraid I'll kill you, like I did Smedley and the police chief?" I sniped.

Terry sighed. "I'm not the enemy, Ric. I'm on your side."

It was true, but Terry was easy to fight. I didn't know how to take on the detectives, and a murderer who seemed intent on framing me. I suspected I would lose my job, when the news came out. My life was going to hell.

"I'm going to confront Lisa," I said. "She's the one who turned me in. I think she's the murderer."

"Be careful, Ric," Terry warned. "Don't confront her by yourself. If she's the killer, she's dangerous, and she's got nothing to lose. You've got to be cautious. She's gone to a lot of work framing you. Promise me you won't talk to her. I wish I was there."

"I wish you were, too, Terry," I said.

"Can you talk to your rabbi friend? Maybe he'll have advice for you." Terry paused. "What about those brothers you know? Could you get one of them to help you?"

"The twins? They live an hour and a half from here. They're old," I said. "What can they possibly do?"

"Well, both brothers aren't old. One of them's younger, right?"

"No, Terry, they're twins. Twins, you know, are born at the same time."

I was being snarky. I couldn't blame Terry for thinking the brothers were different ages; they weren't identical twins. Darrel looked a lot younger than Earl. Terry was offering support. Why was I fighting him, he was trying to help. Terry wanted to come out, but I told him not to. "It's just a hassle, really, that's all this is." It was more than that, but there was no need for Terry to disrupt his life. He didn't need to risk his job by taking time off work. I asked Terry not to tell my parents unless it became necessary.

I said goodbye, and called Marc. He wasn't home, and I debated about whether or not to leave a message. What would I say? By the way, Rabbi, I'm implicated in the violent murders that are on everyone's mind? I kept my voice calm, and asked him to please call at his earliest convenience.

I set about straightening up the apartment. I felt tired, and still angry at Lisa. I heard footsteps upstairs, and I knew she was home. It sounded like she was jumping up and down. Lisa wasn't usually that noisy. She was letting me know that she was happy about what she'd done. She was doing a victory dance, raising a ruckus. That was just like her.

I righted the books, and picked papers up off the floor. The morning was humid; the weather seemed unsettled. Sun alternated with clouds, and it felt like a storm was on the way. Maybe I projected my own mood on the outside world. Marc didn't return my call. It was Saturday, and if he wasn't at temple, he was probably spending time with his family.

It finally got quiet upstairs; Lisa had calmed down. I wanted to ring her neck. It was time to confront her, in spite of Terry's warning. He'd wanted me to promise not to talk to her, but I didn't. I planned on being careful. I looked down at the street; her car was still parked outside. Although she was quiet, she was home. I made my way up the outside stair case to her top floor unit. I knocked at the door. I stood back from the window so she couldn't see it was me. I waited; she did not answer.

Maybe Lisa was in the bathroom; I knocked harder. The door swung open. It wasn't like Lisa to leave her front door unlocked. I felt suddenly uneasy, and my heart began pounding. Should I go in? What if she was sick, or had fallen? I tried to set my anger aside. If she was ill, I would have to help her. I had visions of driving her to the doctor.

"Lisa," I called. There was no answer. I said her name again, louder this time. There was silence. The kitchen light was on, breakfast was on the table. I went in to her living room. Her computer screen flickered on screensaver. "Lisa!" I called. I walked into the bedroom. There was an unpleasant odor. It took me a moment to recognize it: the smell of blood.

"Oh shit!" I said. It was dark in her room, and it took my eyes a minute to adjust. I looked at the bed in disbelief. Lisa, what was left of her, was strewn haphazardly across the sheets. I saw her jet-black hair, but she was cut and slashed violently. There was blood everywhere; the floor and even the walls were covered with it. I quickly retraced my steps.

Some detached part of me went in to overdrive, and controlled my actions, like I was a puppet, or automaton. I had probably left forensic evidence in her apartment just walking in. I went back to her kitchen, and found a paper towel. I thought I'd only touched the outside door; I pulled it closed after me, using the towel to wipe off the prints. I needed to call the police, but there was no hurry. Nothing could be done for Lisa now. I tried to block out the memory of Lisa's brutal slaying from my mind. My stomach was tied up in knots, and I felt sick, about to throw up.

I had to keep my wits about me. As horrible as the photograph of Smedley had been, the sight of Lisa would haunt me forever. Pictures don't stink of gore. I thought about the noisy footsteps I'd heard earlier. Lisa had been fighting for her life. If only I'd gone up earlier. But if I had, I would have been killed, too. The killer was close by, and I was in grave danger. If I called the cops, they would arrest me.

I'd suspected Lisa as the killer; she had told the detectives about the knife and Star of David. Now Lisa was a victim. There was nothing surgical or precise about her murder: she had been stabbed, gouged, and exsanguinated. I was gripped with cramps, and raced downstairs before finally throwing up.

I vomited outside at the bottom of the stairwell, and felt only slightly better. My hands were shaking. I walked back up to my apartment, and drank a glass of water. I washed my face, and brushed my teeth. I needed to think. I checked my phone; there was still no message on the answering machine from the rabbi. My cell phone was gone, so if Marc had called me on that line, I wouldn't know.

I was sure Lisa had defended herself valiantly. The killer probably had some bruises and cuts. He would show signs of a struggle. But who was it, and why had he murdered Lisa?   I shivered.   The murderer knew me, or at least of me;   he had been inside my apartment, and killed my upstairs neighbor.

I sat down at the foot of my bed, and tried to figure out what to do next. I needed to report Lisa's murder. I shuddered. If a police officer isn't safe, what hope was there for me? She was the second officer murdered, after the police chief. Was the killer targeting cops? But Smedley and the black-haired man weren't police. The murders made no sense, and followed no pattern that I could see. There was no connection between the four victims: Chief Herman, Smedley, the guy on the cell phone, now Lisa. The killer was moving quickly, according to some twisted purpose.

I wanted Marc to call. I could ask him to report Lisa's murder. One thing was certain: I didn't want to be home when the cops came to investigate. I'd barely escaped being charged the night before, and I doubted I'd be that lucky this time. Was the killer trying to implicate me, or had Lisa been killed for another reason? Did she know something? She had been the police chief's mistress. Maybe the killer thought she'd seen something. But if that was the reason for her death, the killer had taken a long time to get her, a full four months. My head hurt, and my stomach was in knots.

I had to get away from my apartment; that was certain. It wasn't secure there any longer. Maybe I wasn't safe anywhere, but I could try to hide. I didn't have my cell phone; at least the cops couldn't use that to trace me. I'd have to be nimble from now on, and leave no trace of my whereabouts. I took my credit card out of my billfold; I couldn't use it now. I was glad I had some cash. How long would that last me?

I grabbed a hat and sunglasses before getting my car. Maybe that would make me harder to recognize. Was the killer watching my apartment? I didn't know. I would be safest in a crowd, and wished Omaha was New York City. I thought of the shops and galleries in the Old Market district. On a Saturday, it would be busy, and the killer couldn't attack when there were people around. I drove a few short blocks. I parked fairly close to the freeway entrance, and put on my dark glasses and baseball cap. I was sick to my stomach with fear and hunger. I'd lost my breakfast, and didn't feel like eating. Still, I had to keep up strength.

I stopped in at a little café, and ordered toast and tea for lunch. I needed the caffeine; I'd slept very little. I grieved for Lisa. She'd been a troubled woman, a lost soul. Lisa didn't deserve her terrible fate. I forgot my anger at her for implicating me. I thought about the murder victims, trying to see what they had in common. There was the police chief Will Herman, Duncan Smedley, and his friend. The cops had never told me his name. I added Lisa Gans to the list. Lisa was the police chief's girlfriend, but other than that, I couldn't see anything that linked the four victims. Were the murders random, or was there a pattern that I was missing?

Maybe, I thought, munching dry toast, I was asking the wrong question. The killer was deranged, a maniac. The demons that drove him to destroy life were incomprehensible. What made sense to a murderous psychopath would not make sense to a normal person.

I had a duty to tell the police about Lisa. But I needed to think of my own safety, too. I wasn't sure if I was more afraid of the cops or the murderer. He, or she, had framed me, and been in my home. He'd planted things that belonged to me at crime scenes. Had he put something of mine in Lisa's apartment, something else that I hadn't noticed was missing? My apartment had been so ransacked by the police I didn't know what was there and what wasn't.

Something was nagging at the back of my mind. I made a list of everyone that had been in my apartment, writing their names on a napkin. Harry had been there, Lisa had visited me, and Terry had stayed in my home. I was new to Omaha, and hadn't had any parties; no friends had come over. I hadn't even found the apartment myself.

Marc, Rabbi Braun, had found the place for me. Marc hadn't been inside my home, but he knew where I lived, he'd found the place for me. Marc had given me the key. It would have been easy for him to make a duplicate. Had Marc brought me to Omaha just to frame me? It hurt to think about. I trusted Marc, I liked him. But if he was the killer, he was very clever. I'd tried to call him this morning, and he wasn't home. Maybe he'd been upstairs killing Lisa.

Whoever the killer was, he was physically strong. Marc wasn't much bigger than me. I didn't know how someone my size could overpower a police chief, and a female cop. And then there was Smedley and the other man. Murdering two people at the same time? Maybe he'd drugged them, but how? Held a gun and ordered them to drink poison? That didn't make sense.

Whoever the killer was, he'd been inside my apartment, and hadn't killed me. No, he'd done something more cruel: he had framed me. The murderer was out to destroy my reputation. I was more valuable to him alive than dead, at least for the moment. Who knew how long that would last? Did I have time to find him before the police arrested me, or before he changed his mind and killed me?

Terry told me I shouldn't be alone, that I should get someone to help. He suggested I talk to the twins. The twins. There it was, that's what had been bothering me. I'd discounted the twins' help because they were older, and didn't live in Omaha. Darrel and Earl had been to my home, on more than one occasion. They had visited separately and together. Darrel had stopped by, and then his brother came. The twins were strong, and I was sure they could handle a knife. They were older, but Darrel, at least, was in shape. You have to be strong to be a farmer. The twins admired Duncan Smedley; why would they kill him?

Could the twins, Harry's childhood friends, be murderers? It was ridiculous. But it was no crazier than suspecting the rabbi who'd gotten the job for me. I had to suspect everyone. But if it was the twins, either one or both of them, why had they done it? Why? The motive of the crimes puzzled me most. I couldn't see any connection between the victims. Sure, Lisa was Chief Herman's lover, but what did Smedley and the other guy have to do with anything?

I paid my check, and asked the server if there was a pay phone nearby.

"Not too many pay phones around anymore," she said.

"It's a local call, and it's very important," I said. I'd left a nice tip, and smiled the friendliest way I could.

"If you are quick, you can use the office phone," she said.

"Thanks. I really appreciate it," I said. The young woman would regret her kindness when the police traced my call. She showed me into a small room near the kitchen. I call 911 and spoke softly. "Officer Lisa Gans is dead in her home," I said, and hung up. I was sure the cops would respond quickly to news about one of their own.

I left the café quickly, and headed toward my car. I was going to drive to Buffalo Crossing. If the twins weren't the murderers, and it was preposterous to think they were, I would spend the weekend hiding out at their place till the police found Lisa's body. Darrel and Earl invited me to visit, and this was the time to do it.

It began to rain. There was a flash of lightning, and I heard thunder. Maybe the oppressive humidity would finally break. I turned on to the freeway, and gripped the steering wheel tightly. I tried to think. The twins were Smedley groupies. I could understand them murdering a liberal police chief; I could even imagine them butchering a young Jewish/American Indian woman, Lisa. But Smedley? The twins were old men, they were rednecks, sure, but that didn't make them killers. But if there were two killers, it would explain how they could overpower two men.

I had to be acquainted with the murderer. He had been in my home. Where was my intuition? Lisa was the only one I'd ever suspected, and now she was dead. My thoughts turned to my former students, Sam and Ahmed. Was the killer one of them? Was there a terrorist angle to the crimes that I was missing? At first, the police had suspected a recent immigrant. Had I dismissed Sam or Ahmed as the killer too quickly?

I thought about what the man with the black hair had said over the phone. He said he knew who the killer was. Had he seen the murderer? I'd had the feeling he was going to confront the killer, maybe to blackmail him. That was a good way to anger a murderer. Whoever the killer was, he'd killed before, and hadn't hesitated to do it again.

Rain poured down, punctuated with lightning and thunder. It mirrored my dark mood. The highway became so slick I had to slow my speed. I noticed a black sedan following me. How long had it been there? The road had little traffic; was I being tailed? I turned the car radio on to distract myself. I thought about what I'd tell the twins. I'd just say that I had decided to take them up on their invitation to visit. I wasn't thrilled about spending the weekend in Buffalo Crossing, but I didn't want to be accused of murders I hadn't committed.

"Tornado watch in southeast Nebraska," the radio forecaster warned. He read a list of the counties affected. He didn't mention Douglas County, where Omaha is. I had no idea where the other counties were. I drove as fast as the wet roads permitted. I was exhausted, my nerves were frayed. I looked at the dashboard clock. I'd been driving half an hour; I had another hour to go before I reached Buffalo Crossing. My stomach was unsettled. The toast and coffee hadn't helped.

I looked at my rear view mirror. A dark-colored car was still behind me, but I couldn't be sure if it was the same black sedan I'd seen earlier. I thought about Rabbi Braun. Was he the killer, and was he following me? My thoughts were scrambled; nothing added up. If the twins were murderers, how long would it take for them to get back to Buffalo Crossing? It was 3:00 in the afternoon. How long had I been in the café? I didn't know.

Detective Swenson had warned me to stay nearby in case the police wanted me for questions. I would have been an idiot to stay in my apartment. The killer had targeted me, and was planting evidence. I needed to clear my name, the police wouldn't do it. I had to find the murderer. But I'm no detective, and don't know how to find a psychopath. If the twins were involved in the slayings, I was putting myself right in their hands.

I wouldn't mention the murders unless the twins did. I'd be subtle, maybe I'd get an impression of their guilt or innocence. I doubted they were the killers, but I had to be sure. If the twins had just killed Lisa, they might still be in Omaha. If they were home, it exonerated them, didn't it?

The closer I got to Buffalo Crossing, the more ridiculous my suspicions seemed. It was crazy to think of two men in their 60's going around butchering people. They had no motive. Still, it was no more absurd than suspecting a rabbi or my troubled neighbor before she had been killed. I thought again about Sam and Ahmed; I had to suspect everyone.

The rain continued to pour, and the sky was dark. It wasn't yet evening, but the heavens were as black as midnight. It was a terrible day for driving. I turned the radio up louder. I could hardly hear it over the storm. I checked the rear view mirror again; I could still see the headlights of a car behind me. Was it the same black sedan following me all the way from Omaha? Was it the killer? If so, then I was putting Darrel and Earl in terrible jeopardy, bringing the murderer to them. It was raining so hard, I couldn't read the license plate.

The forecaster on the radio repeated the tornado warning, covering southeast Nebraska. Then the news announcer made a strange revelation: Duncan Smedley had been about to apologize to the Jewish community for his comments. I turned the radio to its loudest setting, and strained to hear the story. The reception was breaking up, and after a few minutes I could no longer get the Omaha news station. So Smedley had recanted his hate. It was too late now.

By the time I reached the turn-off to Buffalo Crossing, it stopped raining. I should have been relieved, but the hair on the back of my neck stood up. I could smell ozone, and feel the air pressure falling. The sky looked ominous, the humidity was oppressive. There was no sign of the car I'd thought was following me. I was paranoid, that was all. It had been just another driver on the road in a bad storm, and maybe he'd tailgated me to see the road better, following my headlights.

The town of Buffalo Crossing was deserted. The lights at the service station weren't on, and the elevator was closed. It was like a ghost town, the perfect place for a vicious killer to hide, I thought, and shivered. I parked my car by the twins' house, and got out. I stretched my arms and legs. I hadn't driven that long, just under a couple of hours, but I was tense and tight. What, exactly, would I say to the twins? My mission seemed ill-conceived. But what choice did I have? I couldn't stay in my apartment, waiting either for the killer to strike, or the police to arrest me.

I scanned the dark horizon. The sky was layered with black clouds, and there was a strange orange-yellow glow between the clouds. The heat was suffocating, and I longed to be cool. I thought about going back in my car just so I could run the air conditioning. I was tired, worn out. Maybe I should just let the police arrest me. Prison was at least air-conditioned, I thought grimly, and I ran no risk of being murdered there, presumably.

I walked quietly to the back door of the twins' old house. The place seemed sad and neglected. The paint wasn't peeling, the sashes weren't sagging, but it looked weary and ill, as worn-out as I felt. The back storm door was open, the screen door providing a breeze, if the air had been moving. As it was, the screen allowed me to peer in. The kitchen light was on, and Earl was sitting at the kitchen table. He sat with his face away from me; it had to be Earl because he was hunched over. If Earl was crippled with arthritis, how could he be the killer? I'd been wrong to suspect the twins. Men approaching retirement age don't take up stabbing as a hobby.

I watched and listened, half-crouching at the screen door. It began to rain again, and I longed to be indoors. I was getting drenched, as much from the humidity as from the rain. Earl didn't move, and I wondered if he had fallen asleep. I tried to see around in the kitchen; there was no sign of Darrel. Earl was too motionless, and I got a sinking feeling. No one could be stationary for that long. I opened the screen door, and quietly made my way inside. A repulsive, now familiar smell filled my nostrils. Blood, it was blood I smelled. I tiptoed toward Earl. At his feet, there was a dark brown pool. He had been incontinent, too, poor old man. That was the least of his humiliation.

Earl's eyes were open. He was tied to the chair. He had been carefully, cruelly butchered: castrated, Earl's mouth was stuffed with what had been removed. Who had done this? I was shaken to my core, and felt guilty for ever suspecting him. I wanted to run out of there as quickly as I'd run away from Lisa, but I worried about Darrel. Had the killer gotten him, too? I couldn't stand seeing another dead body, but these were Harry's childhood friends, I had to find out.

The murderer seemed to anticipate my every move. He read my mind, killing the people I suspected. I wanted to cover Earl, but I didn't dare touch him any more than I'd dared to touch Lisa. I had stomach cramps, and was about to vomit again. This was the second dead person I'd seen that day. The words of the *kaddish*, the prayer for the dead, came to my mind.

I heard steps coming towards me, and I turned around quickly. A heavy set man with a black eye limped towards me. His face was disfigured with cuts, and his bare arms were bruised. It took me a moment to recognize him.

"Darrel!" I cried out. "What happened? Are you all right? Earl is dead. Don't come any closer, you don't want to see. At least you're safe." I looked towards the bathroom door, needing to throw up, wanting to get bandages for Darrel. Had he been attacked by the killer? He was lucky to be alive.

Darrel just stood there, and a smile crept over his bruised lips. "You feel sorry for Earl? That's real sweet. You're a helluva guy, aren't you."

I didn't understand Darrel's strange words. He was in shock because of Earl's death, or else he didn't understand what I had said. "Darrel," I said, my voice shaking, my stomach gurgling, "Earl has been murdered. Someone has hurt you; who did it? We need to call the police. Do you have any ointment for your cuts, any bandages?"

Outside, lightning flashed, and thunder followed almost immediately. The rain pounded down so hard it sounded like someone was throwing rocks on the roof. The storm had returned with a vengeance. The smell of damp and ozone blew in the screen door, temporarily masking the odor of death.

"Don't bother," Darrel said, with his curious smile, "I'm going to call the police. Just as soon as I take care of you."

"Darrel, I don't..." I didn't understand, not at first. I didn't want to understand, I'd been so wrong. I fought back my nausea, feeling like someone kicked me in the guts. I didn't understand *why*, I never would--- but I realized that Darrel had mutilated his brother, he had killed Lisa and the others. Now he was going to kill me.

"Oh, my God," I croaked. "It's you, you did this. How? Why?" I couldn't catch my breath. My head began to hurt, but my stomach became suddenly calm. The thunder was deafening.

I'd been so sure I didn't know who the killer was, that I had no idea. But in that split second, convinced I was going to die, I remembered my strange nightmares about the twins. Something had been trying to warn me, speaking to me through my dreams.

Darrel just kept smiling. His face and arms were bloody, and must have hurt, but he registered no pain. He was in some other world, a place I never want to go. "Your friend put up quite a fight," he said, finally. His strange smile faded. "That whore was a real fighter, I'll give her that."

I hadn't been close to Lisa, but I didn't like her being spoken of disrespectfully. I silently cheered for the dead woman. I only wished she had been able to hurt him more. Darrel was a giant of a man; Lisa had no chance against him.

"Don't talk like that," I admonished. "It's ugly." I don't know why I bothered to chastise him. Anyone who kills people as easily as Darrel wouldn't hesitate to call them names. I wasn't dealing with a normal, rational being. I was standing close to something evil, and it chilled me. "I don't get it, Darrel. Why did you do this? And your brother? What possible reason---"

There was a loud popping sound, and the lights went out. The storm must have downed the power line. The house became very dark. I could only see shadows, the outline of the killer and his dead brother. Darrel and I each stood where we were; neither of us moved. I focused on the dark shape I'd been speaking to. I had to run away, to get to my car. Could I outrun Darrel? I weighed my options. Darrel was bigger and stronger than me, but he might not be faster, especially cut and bruised. I hoped I could find the screen door in the dark.

"You think you're so damn smart, so damn educated," Darrel spat. "You don't know shit. All that fancy learning won't help you. I'm sending you straight to hell."

My eyes were growing accustomed to the gloom; the orange glow from the sky outside occasionally shone in, casting an eerie light on Darrel's face. His features were illuminated, glowing with every lightning flash. The whites of his eyes shone with intensity, and he looked diabolic.

He held a knife in his outstretched hand; Darrel was going to kill me. I'd escaped death once; Terry had taken the bullet that was meant for me. But fate can't be forever averted. It was my time to die; it was *beshert*. Before that lunatic killed me, though, I wanted answers.

I softened my tone, and relaxed my stance. "I'm not very smart, Darrel. Why don't you explain it to me? Go slow, so I'll understand." I needed to keep Darrel talking. The longer he talked, the longer I had to think, to plan my escape. I thought I could make out the outline of the screen door, but I had to be sure. I didn't want to go running out a window by mistake.

Darrel said something, but thunder drowned his words. I'd never heard noise that loud. I wasn't sure if I was more scared of Darrel or of the terrible storm outside. The air was heavy, but the rain didn't quell the humidity. There was an odd smell, a combination of death and dampness, blood and rain.

"The coming race war," Darrel said, talking to me like I was an idiot. "Blacks, Mexicans, Jews, queers, you're trying to populate the world, you're taking over. White people have got to fight back."

Apparently Darrel didn't realize gays can't procreate. His murderous spree had something to do with racism, but he made very little sense. As frightened as I was of Darrel, something about the storm worried me more.

"John Brown, do you know who that is?" Darrel asked. He was speaking slowly, like a kindergarten teacher.

"The guy before the Civil War," I said. I didn't remember exactly, and my heart was pounding so loudly I could hardly think.

"John Brown was a guerrilla fighter. He knew the way to get the conflict started was with violence. But John Brown was a piker, an amateur. They caught up him, and killed him."

"I see," I said, even though I didn't. "So you're like John Brown. You're trying to get the race war going? You're doing quite a job," I said, my voice dripping with sarcasm. I didn't believe in the coming race war any more than I believed in Santa Claus. Darrel was insane, and that made his delusion dangerous for the rest of us.

Darrel took no notice of my tone. "Exactly. I kill one conservative, one liberal. Something for both sides to get angry about. I've been doing it for years."

Thunder rolled. I wasn't sure I'd heard him correctly. "You've been doing this for years," I repeated, in disbelief. "You've been killing people for years?" It couldn't be? He would have been caught. Darrel was a liar, as well as a murderer. He was deranged, was he caught up delusions of grandeur?

"I decided to speed things up this time," he said. He glanced downward in humility. He was proud, I realized, of what he had done. He was bragging--- pleased about being a murderer and a racist.

"You've been on quite a spree," I said. "You must be tired. You look pretty banged up. It must have been hard to kill Duncan Smedley. He was your hero." I was waiting for another bolt of lightning to illuminate the door for me. I thought I saw where it was. If only it wasn't so dark, if only the power hadn't failed. If only the storm wasn't so bad; how would I be able to drive in the flooding rain?

I looked around for something to throw at Darrel. He was bigger than me, yes, but he was older, and he was injured. Lisa had hurt him, and I silently thanked her.

"Smedley was just talk, an opportunist. Did you know he was going to apologize to the Jews? Apologize to Jews." He shook his head, like it was the most ridiculous thing, something inconceivable.

I looked around in the dark, desperately. There had to be something I could use to hit him. I wasn't going to just wait there for him to kill me. I needed to keep Darrel talking, distracted, till I threw something creating a diversion. Then I'd run.

"But your brother? Why kill Earl?" I asked. "Why kill Lisa?"

"That neighbor of yours recognized me, I'm sure. And Earl had started snooping. He was beginning to get suspicious. He started following me around."

I remembered Earl coming to my apartment, a few hours after Darrel had. He wanted to know if I'd seen his brother. Poor Earl had been trying to keep tabs on his twin. He must have suspected something. If Darrel had been killing people for years, which I didn't believe, surely Earl would have become suspicious before. And if Lisa had recognized him, she would have done something about it. She wouldn't have waited to be killed. But why the mutilation of his victims?

"I'm still confused," I said, sounding as dumb as I could. Nothing he said made sense. Maybe that was because he was crazy, or maybe his confession was a lie. "You planted the knife on me, then you took it back. Why? Why take the star of David? When did you take my dictionary?"

"You drove here with Harry, that first time, you left your car door unlocked. I put the knife in with your books. I found a dictionary, and took it out. I figured you'd get rid of the knife for me. I'd already used it. I don't like to keep evidence lying around close to me."

"You'd already killed someone with that knife. So why take it back?" I asked. "Why take the pendant that belonged to me? Why mutilate your victims?"

A kitchen window shattered, and we both started. Darrel walked toward it, and picked something off the floor. He held it in his hand. "Hail," he said. "Big stuff." He looked at the hail, then took it over to the sink. "Storm's on the way."

Storm's on the way? I thought the storm was here. How much worse could it get? The violent weather seemed like a metaphor for my predicament.

"Harry and I have been friends since we were kids. He asked me to keep an eye out for you. I felt bad giving you the knife, and when I visited, I saw you hadn't gotten rid of it. So I took it back. I keep my word," he said. "I always keep my word to my friends. If you hadn't come here snooping around, I'd have let you live. I didn't aim to kill you."

I said nothing. If Darrel thought he had integrity, he was very much mistaken. I was Harry's son, and he'd chosen to frame me. He put my dictionary near Chief Herman, and left the knife and my star of David with Smedley's corpse. There didn't seem much point in lecturing him on ethics. He was a killer and a liar.

I looked at Earl's form in the chair, and shuddered. That would be my fate, too, if I didn't escape. Darrel had killed for political reasons, but he had mutilated for his own twisted pleasure.

"You did me a favor by coming here," he said. "When you die, I'll call the police and say that I had to fight you off. They'll think it was you all along. No one will ever suspect this old farmer."

The rain and hail stopped abruptly, and the air grew calm. It was too quiet. Something was wrong. The calm was eerie, not peaceful.

"It's too still," Darrel said, no concern in his voice. "There's a twister coming."

The screen door opened with a bang. Darrel and I turned toward the noise. A tall shape wearing a cowboy hat towered in the doorway. It looked surreal. I was pretty sure it pointed a gun at Darrel. The cowboy shape pointed a flashlight at Darrel, and then at me.

"Nebraska State Highway Patrol. Hands in the air, both of you," the shape said. "Stay where you are. No one move. We're going to my police car."

Darrel laughed insanely. "I'm not going anywhere. This place is about to be blown to smithereens by a cyclone."

Those were the last words I heard him say. There was a deafening noise, like a freight train. The wind howled. The cop grabbed me and shoved me under the kitchen table. I was next to Earl's corpse.

"Hold on to the table leg," the officer said. He was crouching under the table with me. "Hold on with one hand, cover your head with the other arm. Can you do that?"

212

The policeman was talking very loudly, almost shouting, but I could barely hear him over the deafening noise of the storm. Things were happening so quickly I couldn't think. I continued crouching under the old wooden table, next to a dead man and a cop. I closed my eyes, expecting the worst. If the patrol man said anything else to me, I couldn't hear it. I was about to die, and the words of a Hebrew prayer came to mind. I don't know if I spoke them, or thought them. *"Baruch ata Adonai..."*

I don't know how long I was crouched under the table. Time slowed down, and sped up again. I heard banging, and other noises I couldn't identify. The terrible racket of the storm was made up of different sounds, whooshing, banging, tearing. There was a continuous crashing sound, and several loud thuds. I opened my eyes after what seemed like an eternity. I'd been squeezing them closed to protect them from the wind. I was soaking wet, and wondered if it was sweat or rain. I felt sorry for the officer next to me; I perspired heavily. His cowboy hat had come off, I noticed.

What I saw made no sense. Patches of dark, angry sky were showing through the ceiling. I didn't think the twins' kitchen had a skylight. And I was getting more and more wet. It was raining in the kitchen.

"Are you hurt?" the patrol man asked. He got up, and stood next to the table. "Can you walk all right?"

I nodded, and tried to stand. My legs had fallen asleep from staying crouched, and I fell over. Earl's body was gone, and so was Darrel. My head hurt, and my nausea was back. I was about to throw up. The cop was giving me orders, which was a good thing since I couldn't think.

He had a gun in his right hand, and grabbed me by the back of the pants with his left. I finally stood on my tingling, numbed legs. "This house might cave in, it's been damaged. I need you to go to the police car. I'm going to lock you inside it, and you'll be safe. I've got to look for the killer."

"I'm going to be sick," I croaked. My voice was hoarse. Somewhere on the way to the police car, I threw up. The officer turned away. Maybe I was grossing him out, maybe he was giving me privacy. It was still raining, but it seemed like the darkness was clearing. The patrol man almost pushed me to his black sedan, and I got in the back seat. The officer had been following me from Omaha, I realized. The police had been tailing me. Thank God.

I lay on the back seat, while the patrol man gave orders and directions into a hand held microphone. I felt exhausted. It must have been late at night, but I had lost all sense of time. What had happened to Darrel? I fell lightly asleep, exhausted. That wasn't wise, I thought groggily; Darrel might come back and kill me. But I couldn't keep myself awake anymore. I was tired, wet, hungry.

I woke up, and a young woman ushered me out of the car. She wore a uniform, and introduced herself as a medical technician. She was holding a flashlight.

"Are you hurt?" she asked.

I tried to talk, but my words came out funny. I coughed. "I'm fine, just sick to my stomach," I managed to say.

"OK, we're going to give you something for your stomach, and some fluids. You'll feel a poke."

I felt the needle, and fell back asleep.

When I woke up, I was in a green room with a dim light overhead. I wore a hospital gown. I didn't remember changing. I had no idea where I was, or how I had gotten there. I sat up. I was in some kind of clinic or hospital. Where was Darrel? Was I safe? I didn't know if it was morning or still night. My stomach felt better, but I was disoriented and scared.

Fear washed over me in successive waves, as I thought about my ordeal. I remembered poor Earl, and then Lisa. Had Buffalo Crossing been hit by a tornado? Who was the man who had saved my life? Where was he? I wanted to thank him. I thought about Darrel. I had so many questions. It had been a nightmare, and I hoped it was over. I wanted to call Terry and tell him everything that had happened.

I got up, wandered into a hallway, and saw a nurse's station. A plump older woman looked at me. "Are you all right, Mr. Wise?"

"Yes," I said. "Where am I?"

"You're in the clinic at St. Mary's. You were dehydrated and nauseated. The EMT worried you were in shock. Feeling better? We gave you some fluids, and something to settle your stomach. You feel like you could eat something at breakfast time?"

"I feel tired," I said.

"Just go back to your bed, and we'll have someone come in just a minute," she said. Her voice was firm. "Try to sleep a little more."

"Where are my clothes?" I asked. "What time is it?" I couldn't see any windows.

"Go back to your room, please. It's 4:00 a.m.," the nurse said. "Someone will check on you. Try to use the bathroom while you're up."

I nodded, and walked back to my little room. Where was St. Mary's, I wondered. Was I safe? I thought about Darrel. I was afraid for a moment, but that seemed like too much work. I used the toilet, and lay back down on the bed. I fell asleep.

I woke up when someone coughed. I felt more rested, but still nervous, and opened my eyes. Had Darrel found me? I sat up quickly, my heart pounding.

The tall patrol man who had helped me was sitting in the chair next to my bed. He looked tired. He was a young African American, maybe in his 30's, and a cowboy hat was on his lap. I guess he'd found it.

"You saved me," I said. "Thank you. Did you find Darrel? What's your name?"

"Officer Dwayne Bender, Nebraska State Police," he said, extending his hand. I shook it. "How do you feel?" he asked.

"I'm fine," I said, and it was mostly true. I had a lot of questions. Dwayne had been brave to come into the house by himself, no backup. If he hadn't come when he did, I would be dead. I'd cheated death for second time, and was grateful.

"How are you feeling, Dwayne?" I asked. It was probably impertinent to call him by his first name, but after what we'd been through, I couldn't be formal. Besides, he was younger than me. "It was gutsy of you to come in that house all by yourself. You didn't know what you'd find. I'm glad you did, though."

Officer Dwayne smiled. "I'd been following you from Omaha. I stood just outside the back door when you and Darrel were having your little chat. I heard everything, and didn't think I could wait any longer."

"Did Darrel really kill all those people?" I asked. "He said he'd been killing for years. That's not possible, is it?"

Dwayne shrugged his shoulders. "I'm sure he killed your neighbor, Officer Gans. He killed Smedley and Peyton Smith. No doubt he murdered the police chief. He killed his twin brother."

"Peyton Smith?" I asked.

"The man that was murdered with Duncan Smedley."

So that was the name of the man with the black hair, Peyton Smith. "Did you find Darrel?" I asked.

Dwayne looked away. "No," he said, finally, "but we're still looking. We've got bulletins out all over the state, down in Kansas, all the Midwest. They'll find him. He can't have gone far in that storm. He didn't take his car, we know that much. It's possible he was killed. We haven't located his brother's remains, either. That was some wind."

I shuddered. It wasn't wise to underestimate Darrel. He was crafty. Still, he'd been cut and bruised. How far could a man on foot get in a tornado? Was he blown into a tree, or into the river?

"Was the town destroyed by the twister?" I asked.

"There was some damage," Dwayne said. "The roof was torn off the Johnson's farm house."

I wanted to go home. My apartment was a wreck, I knew, but it was home. "And Dwayne," I said, again, addressing him by his first name, "I don't know how to thank you for saving my life." I felt tears well in my eyes, and I was ashamed. Ashamed, yes, but very grateful.

Chapter 15

Someone had driven my car to the clinic for me. I talked to Dwayne some more, but he was short on details. He said I knew as much as he did, and assured me detectives were still working on the case. Someone would keep me apprised, Dwayne told me. Darrel was still missing, and he would be found, alive, or more likely, dead. Police dogs were in the area, but the storm made things difficult for them. Dwayne was confident, but I wasn't sure. Darrel was a monster, and even in the light of the morning he seemed supernatural, a force of darkness. At least I was no longer a suspect; Dwayne had heard Darrel's confession.

Dwayne said he would be in touch. I knew there would be the inevitable paperwork, affidavits and statements that the bureaucracy requires. I signed myself out of the clinic, and drove back to Omaha. The wind of the previous day had been fierce, and all along the way I saw branches down, debris everywhere. I wanted to call Terry, but the Omaha police department had my cell phone. Although I had slept and my stomach was better, I felt exhausted and numb. I couldn't stop worrying about Darrel, wondering if he was still alive. He had managed to elude the police.

What, I wondered, had driven Darrel to commit murder? Did he really believe in some future racial wars? Or, was he a sadist who enjoyed killing, and looked for excuses? I thought about Duncan Smedley and his friend, Peyton Smith. I couldn't grieve for them, I am ashamed to say, and I even thought Smedley deserved what he got. So did Peyton Smith, especially if he had been intending to blackmail the murderer.

The mutilation troubled me almost as much as the murders, and I wondered what drove Darrel to take that twisted final step. Wasn't murder enough? Was desecration necessary, too? What deep psychological defect afflicted the man?

Back at my apartment, the mess from the police search waited for me. I felt traumatized. I had to call Marc, and I wanted to call Terry. I was too exhausted to tell either one of them what had happened. I needed a little time to process things. I was hungry, and went to the kitchen for something to eat. The kitchen had been ransacked, too, and my best knives were missing. They were doubtless being tested for blood by the Omaha police.

I ate a bagel, and decided to take another shower, though I'd already had one at the clinic. I wanted to wash off the experiences of the last few days. It was quiet, too quiet upstairs, and I thought about Lisa. I felt sad; she hadn't found peace or a direction for her life. Lisa had been a lost soul; now she was at rest. I tried to take comfort in that thought, but I was too emotionally spent to come to terms with anything. I had discovered two mutilated bodies, and come close to losing my life. It would take a while to recover.

I made the mistake of lying down before showering, and I was soon asleep. My dreams were jumbled, filled with frightening images. I dreamed about Terry, and longed to be near him. In my dream world, Terry was missing. I looked for him, but every time I thought I saw him, I was mistaken. In my nightmare world, Darrel chased me. I woke up, and drifted back into the border region between dreaming and wakefulness. I remembered that Darrel had not been found, and I wondered if he was dead or alive. Why hadn't the police been able to find him? How hard could it be to find an elderly murderer who was cut and bruised?

I thought about the grisly trail of bloody destruction Darrel had left. Why had he chosen the victims he had? Why Lisa? Did he really worry that she had seen him? Of course, if Smedley's friend, Peyton Smith, had seen Darrel, then maybe Lisa had too. It was possible that Darrel had seen Lisa when he'd killed the police chief, and it was also possible Lisa had recognized him when Darrel had visited me. Was I the link that had led to Lisa's death? I shuddered. How, I wondered, could I tell Harry that his best friend from childhood was a monster? Harry spent the night at Darrel and Earl's home. Now Earl was dead, killed by his twin brother.

I wondered about the sepia picture I'd found of Harry and the twins in the garage, and the dreams before that. Was Sister Eveline right? Were my dreams trying to warn me? If only I'd paid attention, but I didn't know what they meant at the time. It was only in retrospect I understood. That's the way with most things in life, I guess; you don't realize what you know till it's too late. Josh believed my dreams might be intuition, but I wasn't convinced.

Just thinking about Darrel made me afraid. I opened my eyes; there was so much to do. It was beginning to get dark outside, and I wondered how long I had been asleep. Nonetheless, I closed my eyes, and drifted back to sleep. My slumber was short-lived: there was a pounding at my door. My heart began to beat quickly. Who was it? Had Darrel come to kill me? What should I do? Did I dare answer the door?

I got up and slowly made my way towards the living room. There was no peephole on the door, and I couldn't see out. Whoever it was, he was persistent. I thought about not answering, but the knocker didn't go away. Was it the police again? Surely not. "Who is it?" I called.

I heard only a muffled voice from the other side, and my visitor rapped again, more insistently. It was time to meet my fate. I had cheated death twice, and now the Angel of Death had come for me. My heart pounding, my face flushed, I slowly went towards the door. Whatever happened now was *beshert*, meant to be. Hands trembling and sweaty, I unlocked the door, and opened it.

"Rico, thank God you're safe," Terry said. "I was so worried. You didn't answer your cell phone, you didn't answer your landline. Yesterday when we talked I was worried. I told my boss I needed time off to come and see you. I wondered if they put you in jail." Terry held me tight, and I squeezed him back.

Relief flooded over me, tears filled my eyes. I couldn't speak for a minute, something rare. At that moment, I knew Terry would always be there for me, the one to nurture and hold me. Terry was the one I would spend my life with, and if it was *beshert*, we would grow old together. I hoped I could be as strong for Terry as he was for me. Terry came inside the apartment, with me still holding him.

"Ric, say something," Terry said, finally, stepping back from me. "What happened? I was so worried."

I still couldn't speak. I thought about everything that had happened in the past few days, and I was overwhelmed. I said a silent prayer of gratitude. I hadn't cheated death, I realized; I had been saved two times, thanks to the actions of Terry and Dwayne. If Terry hadn't taken the bullet meant for me, if the Nebraska state trooper hadn't entered the house when he had, I would be dead. I had been spared, thanks to the intervention of others. The world is a good place.

Terry took a look at my apartment. "What the hell happened? What did you do? Must have been some party."

I laughed, a little hysterical. I didn't tell him everything at first, but sketched the outline of what I'd been through. He knew I'd been a suspect, and I explained the cops had ransacked my place.

I told him about Darrel, and the terrible storm that had taken off the roof of the old farm house at Buffalo Crossing. I told him about finding Lisa, and then Earl.

"So why didn't you just run out of the house when you found Earl's body?" Terry asked, sensibly. "Why did you stick around to confront Darrel?"

"I didn't suspect Darrel. For all I knew, he was dead," I said.

"And I was the one who told you to go and stay with them," Terry said. "Man, was I wrong. Are you mad at me?"

"Of course not," I said. I was so glad to see him, all I felt was gratitude. Finally, I told Terry that they hadn't found Darrel yet.

"What do you mean?" Terry asked. "They couldn't find an old man who was beat up and blown around by a tornado? Why the hell not? Have they been looking for him?" Terry was livid. "You're coming home to Boulder with me. I'm not letting you stay here with that lunatic on the loose."

I was touched by his concern. I was worried myself. How could they not have found Darrel? Most likely he was dead. They hadn't found Earl's corpse, either. The twister could have transported their bodies far away, or completely destroyed them.

Terry wanted to go out to eat, but before we left, someone else knocked on the door. It was my new friend Officer Dwayne. He was accompanied by the detective I'd already met, Detective Swenson, the one who questioned me at the police department.

"Dwayne!" I said, shaking his hand, once again calling him by his first name. I introduced him to Terry, and the two men shook hands. I nodded to Detective Swenson. I wasn't kindly disposed to Swenson, even though he had just been doing his job.

"I'm sorry, I didn't know you were busy, we wanted to check on you and give you an update," Dwayne said.

"Come in. Please, you can speak freely in front of Terry. I've just told him the whole story. We were about to go out and get a sandwich."

"We wanted to fill you in on some information," Dwayne said. "There are things you have a right to know; you were involved in all this."

"Have they found Darrel?" Terry asked. "Please tell me they have." He paused. "And look at this apartment. Did you guys really have to tear Rico's place apart?"

Detective Swenson shook his head sadly. "I wish I could tell you we found Darrel," he said, not addressing Terry. "He's surely dead. If not…"

"If not? You think he isn't dead?" I asked. I didn't want to hear that.

"There is a network, a patchwork of anti-government, racist groups, like the Coming Race War people here in Omaha. We don't even have the names of everyone who's involved. The Feds investigate that kind of thing. We've told them to be on the lookout for Darrel. It's possible he might be in some kind of safe house, run by these nut jobs."

"That is, if he's even alive," Dwayne interrupted. "I was in that tornado, and I very much doubt he lived through it. Hell, Rico and I barely did," he added, smiling.

"So Darrel will heal his wounds, and be back at it," I said. "If he's out there, he'll come and kill me." I thought for a minute. "Lisa, that is, Officer Gans, beat him up."

"Good for her," Detective Swenson said, echoing my thoughts. "Look, Mr. Wise, Darrel Johnson's an older man. Besides, his secret's out. He doesn't need to kill you to keep your silence, he can't frame you. Everyone knows what he's done."

"I don't know," Terry said. "The guy is clearly crazy. Darrel could come back to his house after a few months, and pretend like all this has never happened. Rico says no one lives in his town anymore."

"Darrel Johnson's a wanted man," Dwayne said. "He'd be real stupid to go back to Buffalo Crossing. We'll be on the lookout. And the people Darrel's staying with, if he's alive, understand he's a liability. Look, I wish I could tell you we've found him, but I think you will be all right."

I wanted Darrel brought to justice, even though I knew that wouldn't bring back Lisa, the chief of police, or Earl. I didn't want Smedley resurrected; his kind are too easily replaced by other *schmendriks*. Detective Swenson's words about a secret network of anti-government bigots chilled me.

Detective Swenson and Dwayne said goodbye, and Terry and I went to Goldman's deli. It was so good seeing Terry. I felt happy, at peace in spite of everything that happened. With Terry there, it all felt like a bad dream. Terry stayed through the next morning; he had to be back at work, and I felt safer. We said goodbye; I would be going back home to Boulder at the end of the semester, just a couple of weeks away. I was lucky to have Terry's love and concern.

The next day, Monday, after work, I drove to the main campus and told Marc all that had happened. He was supportive.

"I wish I could tell you to take some days off, but the semester's almost over. Can you hang in there?" Marc asked.

"Of course," I told him, "I'm fine. I thought you needed to know."

"Omaha has not been good to you," Marc said. "You must wonder why this happened. You're barely over last year."

I thought about his words that evening at home. I wondered about Sister Eveline, and recalled her words. She had said that evil, once it has a taste of you, sometimes comes back for more. Would the evil come back to finish me off? Had my luck run out finally, and would Darrel, or some new lunatic, come and kill me? I hoped Eveline was out of the hospital, and decided to phone her.

Her granddaughter, Melissa, answered the phone, and we spoke briefly. She assured me her grandmother had recovered, and the stroke had not done any permanent damage.

"Hello, sugar," Sister Eveline said, before I had even identified myself. "I knew you'd be calling. I was terrible worried."

For a split second, I wondered how she knew I'd been through an ordeal. Maybe she figured I wouldn't call otherwise; maybe she did have special insight. Who am I to question? There is much that is inexplicable in this life.

"I'm sorry you've been ill," I said. "I'm glad you're better."

"Not my time, honey, not my time yet," she said. "And it's not your time yet, either."

"No, I was saved at the last minute," I said. I didn't feel the need to burden Sister Eveline with the details. She probably knew, anyway.

"You were close to the darkness again, weren't you?" Sister Eveline mused. "They need to search the river. That's where he is."

"Excuse me?" I said. I was confused. I remembered that Darrel and Earl's farmhouse was near the Blue River. Did Sister Eveline somehow know that Darrel's body was in the water? I waited for her to explain her words, but she didn't.

"Rico," Sister Eveline began tentatively, "you're not a married man?"

I had never discussed my sexuality with Sister Eveline. "It's complicated," I began. Was I married to Terry? I couldn't say.

She waited for me to elaborate, but I chose not to. "You see," she said, "I got this picture in my mind's eye of you holding a baby. You're going to have children."

"Really?" I asked, amused. "I think that's pretty unlikely." We spoke a few minutes longer, and then I rang off. "Children," I repeated to myself, later that night, giggling at the thought. Terry would be surprised by that medical miracle.

My students seemed antsy, and everyone was ready for the semester to be over. The weather was nice, and they longed to spend time outdoors, with their families. I couldn't blame them. Marc hadn't told me anything about summer school, or even the fall semester. My future was uncertain. I didn't mind; I longed to be back in Boulder with Terry. Being apart had been very difficult for both of us. At least I'd have a couple of weeks at home after finals.

I told Harry and my mother what happened. I skipped the most gruesome details. Harry was dumbfounded to find out that his childhood friend was a killer. He hadn't kept in touch with the twins over the years, and felt sure something terrible must have happened to Darrel to make him do what he did. Darrel was emotionally and spiritually tainted, a truly evil man. Harry couldn't explain Darrel's actions, and knew of nothing in his childhood that caused him to become a monster.

"If I hadn't introduced you, you never would have been on that freak's radar," Harry said. "I had no idea."

"It's not your fault," I assured him.

"I feel terrible," Harry said. "I don't know what to say."

223

"Don't feel guilty," I said. "There was no way you could possibly have known."

"We were childhood friends," Harry said. "What made him into a monster?"

"We'll never know, I guess," I said. I reconciled myself to not understanding, and was glad I couldn't see inside Darrel's psychopathic mind. I had no idea what had drawn Darrel to the darkness anymore than I understood the source of my dreams, or Sister Eveline's intuition.

I thought about calling Detective Johnson or Dwayne and asking them to search the Blue River. There was the possibility that Sister Eveline was right, and his remains were floating down the river. She'd been right about a lot of other things.

The newspaper ran numerous articles about the murder, under the headline: "Police Chief's Murder Solved by Local Detectives." It wasn't exactly true, but at least the accounts left my name out of the ordeal. Marc had contacts, and the center had a lawyer who saw to it that I wasn't mentioned. I was grateful; I didn't want or need notoriety. It was fine to let the local cops take all the credit, though I knew the real hero was my friend State Highway Patrol Officer Dwayne Bender.

Finally, it was the end of the semester. Three days before my last class, I greeted LeVon as usual. He was a genuinely nice guy, and for whatever reason, he liked me.

"Something's wrong this morning," he said, as he waved me through the metal detector. "Hardly anyone here."

"Really?" I asked. I didn't give his statement much thought until I walked into my classroom. My first section was for the Latino students who worked at Katzenheim brother's meatpacking plant. None of my students were there. Instead, there were half a dozen children. The children should have been in school, although some of them were probably too young.

"Where are your parents?" I asked the oldest child, in Spanish.

"La policia," she answered, explaining to me that the police had come for them.

That made no sense. Their parents weren't criminals. The youngest children looked bewildered, and the two little twins, Juan and Joselito, began to cry. That wouldn't do. I gave the kids paper and pencils, and told them to draw pictures. There were not toys in my classroom. I wasn't sure what to do. Little Susana's tale about the police coming was bewildering. I needed to find Marc. Maybe he would know what was going on. Still, I couldn't leave the children alone unsupervised. How, why, had the children come to my classroom without their parents?

Marc strode into the classroom. By the grim set of his face, I knew that there was bad news. He was rarely on my campus. Something was wrong.

"I.C.E.," Marc said.

"Ice? I don't understand. It's 75 degrees today."

"Immigrations and Customs Enforcement," he said, softly, obviously not wanting to upset the children.

"I don't get it," I said, completely perplexed. "Everyone who worked at Katzenheim had their green card, or was a citizen. The Katzenheim brothers aren't stupid."

"Morris Katzenheim isn't returning calls this morning. According to one of the managers, the meatpacking plant was raided very early. Mr. Katzenheim took a vacation, no one knows where. Things weren't quite what they seemed at one of Omaha's most prosperous businesses."

I felt a sinking in my stomach, and my face grew red. "No," I said, with the dawning realization. Was that what Susana meant when she said the police came for her parents?

"Katzenheim was crooked?" I asked, realizing the implications for not only the workers, but for the Jewish center, as well as my job.

"If their paperwork wasn't in order, the workers will be held in immigration custody, a virtual prison, till they are deported," Marc continued, not answering my question about Katzenheim.

"But what about the children?" I asked. "If the children were born here…"

"Yes," Marc sighed. "This is a real mess. If the children were born here, they are citizens, and will stay, even if their parents are deported. I guess that's why most of these little ones weren't taken. Can you imagine tearing their parents from them?" He was incredulous. "What kind of country is this, Rico?"

"That's monstrous," I said, keeping my voice low. I glanced behind me. There were seven children in the room. Three of them belonged to Marisa: her daughter, Maria, and the twins, Joselito and Juan. Then there was the oldest girl, Susana, who was about 10, and three other children whose names I couldn't remember. I wondered how they had found their way to my classroom. "What should we do?" I asked.

"We can't send these children away, they're our responsibility. They have nowhere to go. The kids might have relatives in this country, it will take time to find out. I've arranged for them to spend the day in our childcare center. After that," Marc paused. "I guess they're going home with families from the center." He sighed. "There's children's protective services, maybe they'll be put in foster care."

"You can't possibly manage seven children," I said. "I'll take care of those three," I whispered, pointing at Marisa's children. It wouldn't have been right to separate the siblings. I had a tug of paternal feeling. I wanted to take all of them, but that wasn't right.

"In your place?" Marc asked. "Do you have room?"

"The sofa makes a bed," I said.

"All right. It's not part of your job description, you know. Thanks. I'll keep you posted on what I find out."

I couldn't explain why I wanted Marisa's children so badly. Looking at them, I ached. Marc took four of the kids over to the day care center; we decided not to take any of them to school that day. For one thing, we weren't even sure where they attended. After the trauma of seeing immigration officers taking away their parents, we wanted them close, and we wanted them pampered--- at least I did. Marc was an old softie, too, though I didn't tell him that.

I realized that if the Katzenheim brothers were in trouble, the ramifications were far-reaching. Two of my three classes, after all, were for Katzenheim employees. I still had my refugees, but that was just one section, and I doubted the center would keep me around for just one class. They could easily find a part-time teacher for that. And what would happen to the center? The Katzenheim brothers were their principal benefactors.

That afternoon, I took Maria, little Juan and Joselito home with me. The little twins were four; Maria was six, grown-up and somber. Her English was fairly good, but the little ones spoke only Spanish. I buckled all three children in the backseat: Marc had called around and found some children's car seats for me. I was new to parenting, and when I was back at my apartment, I called Terry.

"Terry," I said, "have a cigar. We're fathers."

Terry choked or coughed; I'd caught him at work. "Ric," he said softly, "you've been through a terrible ordeal. Maybe you need to lie down, you're not making sense."

I explained the happy news. As I did, I thought about Sister Eveline. Once again, she was right.

Terry groaned, but I think he was secretly delighted. I knew he would fall in love with the kids when he met them. My job in Omaha, it was true, was over, but I had work as a new father. I looked forward to seeing Terry, and spending some time as a stay at home dad--- that is, till Marisa's family was reunited.

If I learned anything from my experience in Nebraska, it was to try and trust my dreams, even though I didn't understand them. I had respect for Sister Eveline and her visions. I resolved to accept the mystery, and come to terms with it.

In addition, I had a renewed respect for my religious tradition, and decided to follow my grandmother's advice. I had once again come in contact with the things religion held taboo: blood and death. I asked Marc to arrange the ritual for me. There was only one ritual bath in Nebraska, and it was located in Omaha. A woman from the center watched the children, and I went. I put on the loose-fitting robe, feeling part of a tradition. I assumed a fetal position, and, after prayers were said, bathed in the cold spring water. Maybe the healing was psychological, it doesn't matter. I felt cleansed both physically and spiritually. I was better prepared to return to Boulder, and assume my responsibilities as a loving partner to Terry, and father to the children.

Driving back across the state of Nebraska, with three children in the backseat, I felt happy and at peace. I was going to be reunited with Terry. He knew about kids, having raised a daughter himself. Maria, Juan and Joselito were well-behaved, gentle children, and a pleasure to have around. My eyes were wide open, and I knew life wasn't going to be domestic bliss, all sunny days. I knew the children belonged with their parents, and my time with them would be brief.

Postscript

Miles from Omaha, along the banks of a river, someone had built a small fire. A man emerged from a one-man tent, where he'd slept in a down-filled sleeping back. He made coffee in a metal carafe, and took food out of plastic trunk. The man was older; thin, almost emaciated. Still, he looked strong for his age. His hair was gray, and he walked with a slight limp. His beard was full, and his face was scarred; a black eye looked almost healed.

The man took a crescent-shaped knife from his pocket, and opened his food packet savagely. He had a healthy appetite, and when he was finished, he took a cell phone from his pocket.

"I'm better," the man said into the phone.

The wind blew across the green prairie, down to the banks of the wide river where the man camped. The day was warm and summerlike; a hawk flew overhead.